Rules and Processes

995

Rules and Processes

John L. Comaroff · Simon Roberts

The Cultural Logic of Dispute in an African Context

The University of Chicago · Chicago and London

The University of Chicago Press, Chicago 60637
The University of Chicago Press, Ltd., London

Paperback edition 1986
Printed in the United States of America
96 95 94 93 92 91 90 89 88 87   6 5 4 3 2

Library of Congress Cataloging in Publication Data

Comaroff, John L   1945–
    Rules and processes.

    Bibliography: p.
    Includes index.
    1. Law, Tswana.   2. Domestic relations (Tswana law).
3. Law and anthropology.   4. Tswana (Bantu tribe)—
Social life and customs.   I. Roberts, Simon, joint
author.   II. Title.
Law   349.68'089963   80-26640
ISBN 0-226-11424-4 (cloth); 0-226-11425-2 (paper)

Contents

List of Cases

Preface

Despite a long history of converging scholarly concerns, there has, with the notable exception of Llewellyn and Hoebel, been little direct collaboration between anthropologists and lawyers. As Twining (1973) has shown, there are several reasons why cooperation between these disciplines is never easy. Our present study represents an attempt to examine what may be gained by overcoming such difficulties.

Our collaboration was not planned in advance. Though each of us set out from the London School of Economics at about the same time to work among Tswana, we first met in the field, more or less by chance, and there discovered a similarity of interests. Roberts was then acting as Adviser on Customary Law to the Botswana Government, and Comaroff was undertaking his doctoral research among the Tshidi-Rolong of the South Africa–Botswana borderland. While our early theoretical concerns were not identical, they rapidly converged when it became apparent to both of us that dispute processes—and the ideas that Tswana have about them—provide a unique and privileged insight into the intricacies of everyday life and the sociocultural order of which it is a part. As we explored this further, we found ourselves compelled to reconsider many of the arguments that pervade the literature of legal anthropology and to confront the influence that jurisprudence has had on the development of anthropological theory at large. While it is firmly grounded in Tswana ethnography, our present study is addressed to these issues of theory.

This study has its basis in extensive field research and the collection and analysis of a large number of case records.

Roberts first worked in the Kgatleng, in eastern Botswana, from November 1968 until May 1969; he returned on several occasions over the next twelve months, between visits to other parts of the country, and spent the (English) summer of 1971 and February–March 1973 there. His work began with an analysis of the records kept by the Kgatla chief's *kgotla*. These records, which have been described elsewhere (Schapera 1943a; Roberts 1971, 1972a, 1972b), are more or less complete from 1954. They consist of an index of disputes brought to the *kgotla* and vernacular accounts of the cases that were eventually heard there. Such accounts vary in depth, from terse summaries of what was said and decided in *kgotla*, to verbatim statements laboriously taken down as the dispute proceeded. Once the records had been translated by James Mpotokwane, they were used as a basis for discussions about family and property matters with the immediate parties and other persons involved. Subsequently, Kgatla "rules" (see chap. 3) were discussed with a panel of informants. Finally, further disputes were directly observed in the chief's *kgotla* and in dispute-settlement agencies lower in the hierarchy (see chap. 4).

Comaroff worked in Mafikeng, the Tshidi-Rolong capital, and Mareetsane, a provincial village, for nineteen months during 1969–70 and in Good Hope, among the Botswana Rolong, for fourteen months in 1974–75. Most of his time was devoted to documenting political and economic processes and to making a general study of the sociocultural order of the Tshidi. At the same time, however, he examined the available case records at both Mafikeng and Good Hope—which are less rich in detail than those of the Kgatla—and, where possible, discussed the relevant disputes with those involved. He also made full studies of contemporary cases. These studies were based on verbatim recordings of *kgotla* hearings and informants' commentaries on them, as well as the observation of relevant events prior to, during, and after formal dispute procedures. These techniques were again complemented by lengthy discussions and by collecting texts about the nature of rules and processes.

We should like to acknowledge the generous aid that many people have given us. First, we must thank those Tshidi and Kgatla who devoted time and thought to discussing disputes with us and who tolerantly introduced us to the complexities of Tswana life. Second, we are grateful to James Mpoto-kwane for his translations of the Kgatla records that we use here in verbatim form. Back in London, Professor Isaac Schapera was a source of endless help and advice and kindly read the manuscript of this book, making invaluable criticisms and suggestions. Professor Jean La Fontaine was also a perceptive and constructive critic of our work in its various stages. The writing-up of Comaroff's early fieldwork (1969–70) was aided by a grant from the Esperanza Trust, and his later research in southern Botswana (1974–75) was funded by the Social Science Research Council. Roberts's work during 1968–70 and again during 1971 was carried out under the auspices of the United Kingdom Government's Special Commonwealth African Assistance Plan. The assistance given by all these bodies is gratefully acknowledged. Marian Roberts and Jean Comaroff, lawyer and anthropologist, respectively, have lived with our preoccupations both in and out of the field. For their patience and critical support, we dedicate this volume to them.

For Jean and Marian

Rules and Processes

Introduction

1

This is a study of dispute processes, based on ethnography drawn primarily from two Tswana chiefdoms. Our major concern is to comprehend the logic of these processes and, in particular, their location within the sociocultural orders in which they occur. But this ethnography also provides an opportunity to reappraise the established theoretical paradigms in terms of which the anthropology of law has developed; more generally, it speaks to the fundamental question of the relationship between the constitution of sociocultural systems and the nature of everyday life, of which dispute is merely a part. Our analysis leads us to conclude, paradoxically, that, while the area usually labeled "legal anthropology" may yield insights of the greatest theoretical importance to the discipline at large, it is doubtful whether it should exist at all as a generic field of study.

The development of legal anthropology[1] has been marked by two conspicuous tendencies, both of which are relevant to this analysis. The first, noted by Twining (1964:34–35; see also Moore 1970:270), is the "enormous diversity of purpose, method and emphasis of different writers." Comparing six major African ethnographies, he goes on to state:

> It is not much of an exaggeration to say that if these books had been written about the same tribe, each would still have contributed a good deal in its own right; certainly if you set out to do a comparative study of the Tiv, the Barotse, the Sukuma and the Tswana relying solely on these books, it would soon become apparent to you that it is virtually impossible to find a real basis for comparison from the information provided.

And this is in spite of the fact that many influential writers (e.g., Gluckman 1955a, 1965; Pospisil 1971; Hamnett 1975, 1977) appear to believe that the phenomena covered by such basic terms as "judicial system," "law," and "legal institutions" are clearly circumscribed and readily comparable across cultural boundaries.

The second tendency, although more diffuse, is related to the first. It shows itself in the periodic emergence of disputes, often arid and unproductive, over the proper object of study of legal anthropology. Such debates have occurred at widely varying levels of abstraction. At their most specific, they have raised the problem of whether, for instance, it is rules or processes that demand prior analytical attention; on a more general plane, they have addressed such issues as whether all societies have law; at their most rarefied, they have sought to establish the nature of social order itself. At first glance these debates appear to constitute a series of disparate and largely unconnected controversies of variable significance, but they are in fact closely related. Indeed, we would suggest that they are different facets of one central underlying question, which dates back to the genesis of the discipline, namely, whether Western legal arrangements may validly provide a baseline for cross-cultural analytical purposes—and, by implication, to what extent the concepts of English or American law should delimit the content and scope of comparative legal theory. This question, of course, has echoes elsewhere in the social sciences (the "substantivist-formalist" argument in economic anthropology represents an obvious analogue), and its epistemological implications are recognized and complex.[2]

These broad tendencies, though often noted, have never been adequately explicated. We believe that they are a corollary of the emergence of two opposed approaches in legal anthropology, which may be typified as the "rule-centered" and "processual" paradigms. Despite the fact that they are predicated on obviously contrasting theoretical assumptions, the paradigmatic opposition between them has not always been fully recognized.[3] In order to locate our own discussion in this context and to identify some of the themes with which we shall be concerned, we begin by considering briefly the competing positions.

Conceptual Foundations

The opposition in legal anthropology between the rule-centered and processual paradigms and the assumptions underlying them has echoes in the cleavage between the "normative" and "interpretive" approaches in sociology at large. Indeed, some scholars (e.g., Dahrendorf 1959; Giddens 1979) have suggested that a similar opposition is evident across the entire compass of Western social theory. At its most fundamental, the rule-centered paradigm is grounded in a conception of social life as rule-governed and of normal behavior as the product of compliance with established normative precepts. Consequently, dispute acquires a pathological character; it signals a deviance, a malfunction, that the control institutions of a society are essentially designed to put right. Associated with this view of order is the contingent assumption, which goes a long way back in political theory,[4] that societies do not cohere effectively in the absence of centralized authorities, which formulate rules and ensure conformity with them. The opposed standpoint, of course, envisages man as a self-seeking being, whose willing cooperation with his fellows is an expression of enlightened self-interest. Where rules cannot be utilized to achieve such interest, they are disregarded as far as possible, the implication being that individual enterprise is constrained primarily by the actions of others who are located within shared networks of relations and reciprocities. The analytical corollary of this is to seek the dynamics of order in the social process itself and to focus less on institutions than on the interactions of living men in everyday contexts. It follows, too, that the processual paradigm envisions dispute as normal and inevitable rather than pathological or dysfunctional.

The Rule-centered Paradigm

Within the anthropology of law, as in the general theory of the discipline, the genesis of the contrasting positions is usually associated with the writings of Radcliffe-Brown and Malinowski, respectively. But scholarly research in the tradition of the rule-centered paradigm can be traced back at least as far as Maine's *Ancient Law* (1861). Maine was himself a lawyer whose major interest lay in the origins of the English legal system, about which a considerable body of theory had already emerged. Influenced by contemporary evolutionary ideas, he sought insights from exotic cultures, which seemed then to represent earlier developmental stages. His intellectual predilections were thus unequivocally "law-centered," and they were addressed specifically to understanding the legal institutions of his own society.

This early link with jurisprudence has been maintained by later scholars working within the rule-centered paradigm, and it has influenced them in important ways. First, when other cultures came to be studied in their own right rather than as a mere adjunct to the analysis of Western legal history, social theorists did not hesitate to view "law" as a natural category of phenomena and as one of the fields of inquiry into which their subject should properly be divided;[5] Radcliffe-Brown (1952:195, 198–99), for example, treated law as a discrete and privileged element in his proposed "social physiology." Second, the manner in which some anthropologists saw law as a matter of sovereignty, rules, courts, and enforcement agencies closely reflects the predominantly imperative and positivist orientation of Anglo-American legal theory at that time. This influence is also evident in both the working definitions of law that were formulated and the nature of the empirical research that was undertaken. Thus Radcliffe-Brown (1933:202) explicitly followed Roscoe Pound, the American jurist, in stipulating law as "social control through the systematic application of the force of politically organised society." Similarly, Evans-Pritchard (1940:162) identified it with a situation in which there is some "authority with power to adjudicate" and to "enforce a verdict" (cf. also Fallers 1969:13–17). Both conceded that such formulations could be of little relevance in a number of ethnographic contexts and that, if law were to be defined in this fashion, certain societies could not be considered to have any (Radcliffe-Brown 1952:212; Evans-Pritchard 1940). But other writers were less ready to accept this, and there developed a substantial literature in pursuit of universal definitions.

No purpose would be served by examining this literature

in any detail; two examples will suffice to reveal some of the fundamental assumptions on which the rule-centered paradigm is based and to illuminate its dependence on the concepts of jurisprudence. One example is provided by Pospisil (1971:39–96), who argues that law should be seen as "principles extracted from legal decisions" and suggests that any such decision requires four attributes in order to be considered "legal": authority, intention of universal application, *obligatio*, and sanction. The other example comes from Hoebel (1954:28), who asserts that,

> for working purposes, law may be defined in these terms: *A social norm is legal if its neglect or infraction is regularly met, in threat or in fact, by the application of physical force by an individual or group possessing the socially recognized priviledge of so acting.*

Both of these definitions, being derivations of Western legal theory, relate law directly to authoritative social control, and it would be difficult to accommodate them to the diverse societies—with and without centralized governmental arrangements—that anthropologists regularly study. Moreover, they entail a number of tacit presuppositions that frequently appear in ethnographic accounts presented by scholars working within this paradigm. Schapera's classic *A Handbook of Tswana Law and Custom* (1938), for example, contains richly detailed inventories of recorded rules, organized and presented in categories corresponding closely to those found in Western systems; it is implied throughout that these normative statements have the same characteristics as legal rules in that they constitute a code employed by judicial agencies to determine the outcome of disputes.[6] In the same vein, Pospisil (1958a) represents "Kapauku law" as a catalogue of rules, although he orders them according to indigenous categories. However, in defining law as "principles extracted from judicial decisions," Pospisil is insistent that these rules operate in a manner similar to that contemplated in the more formalistic accounts of the English legal system. To sustain this characterization, Kapauku "big men" who intervene in disputes are made to conform to a rather rigid judicial mold.[7]

It would be wrong, however, to portray writers working within the rule-centered paradigm as invariably seeking to do no more than fit non-Western systems of social control into a conceptual framework provided by Western legal theory. In Gluckman's *The Judicial Process among the Barotse* (1955) and Fallers's *Law without Precedent* (1969), for example, sophisticated attempts are made to *compare* Lozi and Soga judicial institutions with those of common-law and civil-law systems and to establish both the similarities and differences between the various systems concerned. Furthermore, neither of these authors assumes a mechanical relationship between rule and outcome of the kind that pervades the older accounts. Gluckman, particularly, stresses the flexible quality of Lozi rules and shows how their various levels of generality provide judges with considerable leeway in decision-making (1955a:chap. 6), although in the final instance he does accord the indigenous normative order considerable significance in the determination of disputes. However, both he and Fallers consistently assert that legal rules can be distinguished from other kinds of norms in the societies they studied and that "law" must be regarded as no less than an irreducible phenomenal category (cf. Hamnett 1975; 1977:7–8).

Work within the rule-centered paradigm[8] has been criticized from a number of standpoints. Of these, the best known, possibly as a result of the "Gluckman-Bohannan debate,"[9] concerns the derivation of analytical models. Several writers (e.g., Bohannan 1957; van Velsen 1969) have sought to demonstrate why it is inadvisable to assume that the linguistic, conceptual, and institutional categories of Anglo-American law may be used to account for those found in other systems. First, there may simply be no analogues of those categories in another culture, and, even if there are, their sociological significance in that context may be quite different. In any case, their applicability always requires empirical demonstration, so that they cannot logically be elevated, a priori, to the status of comparative analytical tools. Second, as van Velsen (1969:137) has pointed out, the concepts that rule-centered comparativists have used have often been based on "an imperfect understanding of their own legal system." It certainly seems true that much of the earlier work within this paradigm relied heavily on naive accounts of Anglo-American arrangements, which postulated an unproblematic relationship between rule and decision in settlement processes. However, this criticism hardly applies to all later research; Fallers, for instance, had access to sophisticated jurisprudential sources in Levi (1949) and Hart (1961) and made skillful use of them in his interpretation of Soga judicial reasoning. Third, it has nonetheless been asserted that the Western models typically employed by legal anthropologists have been *folk* rather than *analytical* ones and that the essentially arbitrary organization of ethnographic description in terms of such folk categories involves serious pragmatic dangers. Not only may it lead to the elimination of potentially important subject matter (cf. Gulliver 1969b:17); it also tends to generate distorting questions and mistranslated answers (Nader and Yngvesson 1973:886, 896–97). It might well have been precisely this that persuaded Evans-Pritchard (1940)—once he had defined law in formal English terms and had concluded that, strictly speaking, the Nuer had none—to forsake a legalistic frame of reference and seek the logic of order in Nuer society in terms of the segmentary lineage model.

Similar criticisms have been addressed to the more specific issue of the way in which normative propositions are conceived within the paradigm. Elsewhere (Comaroff and Roberts 1977a) we have shown that the specificity and value attributed to stated rules typically vary widely within a system; on empirical grounds alone, they cannot be treated equally as homogeneous "rules of law."[10] Even in societies in which people themselves speak easily about such matters and ostensibly have rough terminological counterparts for the term "law,"[11] there is rarely (if ever) a separate class of *legal* norms, functionally and conceptually distinguished from other types of precept or "especially organized for jural purposes" (Bohannan 1957:58). The case of the Tswana—often portrayed, along with the Barotse, as a prime example of a small-scale legal system markedly similar to our own in its conceptual foundations—is instructive in this respect. The stated rules found in Tswana communities, known collectively as *mekgwa le melao ya Setswana,* constitute an undifferentiated repertoire, ranging from standards of polite behavior to rules whose breach is taken extremely seriously. We shall examine this repertoire in chapter 3; here it is sufficient to note that the norms that are relevant to the dispute-settlement process are never distinguished or segregated. *Mekgwa le melao* thus do not constitute a specialized *corpus juris,* such as Gluckman claims is found among the Barotse, who use broadly the same terms to describe their normative repertoire.[12] But even if it could be established that such repertoires do bear analogy to legal codes, it is a matter of debate whether the rule-centered paradigm has as yet offered a convincing answer to its most fundamental problem in this respect, namely, that of explicating the systematic relationship between rules of various kinds and the determination of dispute processes. Indeed, Gluckman (1955a:95; see also Krige 1939:114–15), speaking of Barotseland, admits that it would have been difficult for "a White to adjudicate in any complicated issue between Lozi, even with the help of assessors." Whatever the present measure of our understanding of the nature of rules and reasoning, of legal principles or their relationship to judicial decisions, it appears that the cultural and practical logic of Lozi normative precepts—not to mention those in societies that have been less thoroughly and perceptively described—still remains somewhat impenetrable at this level.

There have, finally, been a number of other contingent criticisms of the paradigm. Thus, for example, it has been pointed out (Beattie 1957; Gulliver 1969a:26; Roberts 1976:666) that specialized judicial institutions, even in societies that have them, do not always enjoy the exclusive preeminence in dispute settlement that English courts ostensibly enjoy; that, in some systems, the ability of third parties to effect a particular decision may rest on a legitimacy that varies over time and depends on political factors rather than a nonnegotiable jural authority (J. L. Comaroff 1973, 1975; Gulliver 1969a:34); that, more generally, it may be dangerous to impute a judicial character a priori to third-party intervention (see above p. 8); and that the analysis of dispute settlement as an essentially legal activity may, in some contexts, obscure its political nature (see, e.g., Gulliver 1963). Nevertheless, the rule-centered approach has had a considerable influence both within and outside legal anthropology. Nader and Yngvesson (1973:884 ff.) and Roberts (1976:668) observe that its influence appears to be declining, although Moore (1970:260) states the opposite. Certainly, none would disagree that many contemporary scholars persist in using it (e.g., Goldschmidt 1967; Myburgh 1974; Hamnett 1975). In fact, Hamnett (1977), in his capacity as convenor of the recent conference of the Association of Social Anthropologists (U.K.), sought to justify the paradigm in its orthodox form, despite the contrary view of many of the participants.

The Processual Paradigm

The processual paradigm, by contrast, owes little or nothing of its genesis or elaboration to legal theory. By general agreement its origins are traceable to *Crime and Custom in Savage Society* (1926), in which Malinowski sought to account for the mechanisms through which order was maintained in the Trobriand Islands, a society lacking "courts and constables." Malinowski's position has been discussed frequently (e.g., by Schapera 1957a); it derives from his view (1934:lxiii) that

> In such primitive communities I personally believe that law ought to be defined by function and not by form, that is we ought to see what are the arrangements, the sociological realities, the cultural mechanisms which act for the enforcement of law.

Although Malinowski uses the term "law," here as elsewhere, it seems clear that he usually intended it to embrace all modes of social control. His methodological charter, therefore, was quite explicit: while our legal institutions have no direct counterparts in some societies, their functions in maintaining order and managing conflict must nevertheless be performed in all of them, and the range of mechanisms by which they are performed—irrespective of their institutional nature—should thus define the universe of research. This assumption, in turn, underlay Malinowski's belief in the need to look beyond Western legal concepts for purposes of comparative explanation, and, of course, it also located the problem of law and order, analytically as well as definitionally, firmly in the broader context of the study of social control. Moore (1970:258) has suggested that

> the conception of law that Malinowski propounded was so broad that it was virtually indistinguishable from a study of the

obligatory aspect of all social relationships. It could almost be said that by its very breadth and blurriness of conception Malinowski's view made it difficult to separate out or define law as any special province of study. Law was not distinguished from social control in general.

For Malinowski's critics, particularly those of the rule-centered persuasion, this was a serious shortcoming. For others it was one of the major virtues of his position, and several scholars have derived their insights directly from his original premises or from their implications. Of these, perhaps the most significant was the notion that behavior is constrained primarily by the intrinsic properties of social relations—obligations, expectations, and reciprocities—and by the exigencies of interaction. It is therefore in social processes, not institutions, that the analysis of order is ultimately to be grounded. At the same time, Malinowski's own insistence, throughout his writings, on the proclivity of men to manipulate and exploit established rules, institutionalized social arrangements, and everyday social circumstance has added yet another problematic element; for how, if this is true, are we to comprehend the relationship between individual action and social form?

Although it was some time before many of these issues were taken up, a number of studies, most of them published after 1950, have now securely established what may be referred to as the "processual" paradigm. We use this label purposely to stress that, with the parallel shift of emphasis in political anthropology from structure and institutions to process and interaction (see, e.g., Swartz et al. 1966; Cohen 1975), there has been a convergence of methodological orientation between like-minded scholars in each of these subdisciplines. Indeed, for those of this persuasion, the phenomenal boundary between politics and law has proved largely chimerical. Again, it seems pointless for us to open debate here on the advisability of political anthropology and legal anthropology remaining discrete fields of inquiry—except to say that the convergence will be seen to have substantive implications for our own ethnography. More immediately, however, this convergence makes sense of the fact that, among writers who have contributed to the development of the processual paradigm, several are not recognized primarily as legal anthropologists.

We have already outlined the theoretical foundations of the processual paradigm, but two well-known ethnographic studies are often taken to exemplify its underlying assumptions. Thus Colson (1953) has demonstrated how, among the Plateau Tonga, disputes are constrained by a prevailing structure of relations. Moreover, in exploring the potential of the sociology of conflict for understanding social integration, she also illuminates the way in which parties seek to exploit social arrangements in the course of such dispute processes. Similarly, Turner's analysis of conflict and competition among the Ndembu (1957) posits a dialectical relationship between the strategic activity of individuals and the structural context in which they are contained. He argues that the form disputes take is largely a function of the operation of contradictory principles of social integration; hence, the activities, successes, and failures of the protagonists, in both the short and the long term, are to be explained by reference to these principles.[13] At times, though, Turner does accord considerable significance to the affirmation of the normative order and the determination of processual outcomes by structural exigency; in fact, he suggests, in the Preface to the second edition of his *Schism and Continuity*, that this analysis was "transitional" between the older tradition of structural functionalism and the newer processual approach. Nonetheless, it does mark a significant shift of focus from institution to interaction. Like Colson, Turner does not address the question of "law" directly. Indeed, Nader and Yngvesson (1973:890) see his study as a confirmation of the view that the dichotomy between "law process and social process is nonexistent," and they list the work of, inter alia, Bailey (1960) and Gulliver (1963) as other examples.[14]

These familiar studies share a number of features that together constitute the remaining elements of the paradigm. First, as we have noted, conflict is treated as an endemic feature of social life. This implies, second, that the sociological meaning of such conflict is revealed only by a methodology that analyzes it in the context of extended social processes. An adequate account of a dispute therefore requires a description of its total social context—its genesis, successive efforts to manage it, and the subsequent history of the relationship between the parties. Even greater temporal depth is necessary if more embracing patterns (or cycles) of conflict are to be abstracted, as Turner (1957) has tried to show. Once disputes are no longer seen as discrete and bounded pathological events, they may not be neatly excised from the ongoing flow of community life, even for heuristic purposes.

It follows, third, that this relatively wider definition of scope also involves a shift in focus *away* from judge- (and judgment-) oriented accounts of the character and function of dispute settlement. Hence, the so-called litigant's perspective has increasingly been stressed in descriptive analysis. The justification for this is clear enough: since rivalry and dispute represent merely one phase in the intersecting biographies of the parties concerned, it is their respective circumstances, goals, strategies, and actions that determine the nature of the interaction between them. The decision whether, or in what manner, to precipitate a public confrontation is often predicated on these factors. If the form and content of dispute-settlement processes are to be explained, attention must therefore be given to the disputants' ostensible motives in pursuing a quarrel, how they recruit support, their strategic efforts to influence the procedural course of events, and so on.

Fourth, it will be apparent from the other paradigmatic elements that indigenous rules are not seen a priori as "laws" that have the capacity to determine the outcome of disputes in a straightforward fashion. It is recognized, rather, that the rules may themselves be the object of negotiation and may sometimes be a resource to be managed advantageously (J. L. Comaroff 1978). This fact in turn reiterates the self-evident need to regard the cultural logic of such rules and precepts, in whatever manner they happen to be expressed, as problematic. It also underlines the advisability of reconsidering the nature of third-party intervention. Thus, efforts have been made to account for the manifest range of possible third-party roles, and such figures as go-betweens and mediators are being subjected to ever greater scrutiny (e.g., in Gulliver 1977).

In terms of the processual paradigm, then, the dispute-settlement process is viewed largely as a conceptual and organizational framework for competitive bargaining, transaction, and compromise. Where specialized legal institutions exist, their operation has typically been analyzed as one element of this framework. Of course, the precise ways in which such activities have been described and comprehended by different writers—whether by recourse to, say, game theory, symbolic interactionism, or transactional analysis—reflect broader methodological allegiances within the context of a shared commitment to the heuristic value of processual models, a commitment that has gained increasing adherence in the social sciences at large over the past twenty years (cf. Gulliver 1979).

The paradigm has drawn criticisms on two major fronts. Predictably, most have come from advocates of the rule-centered approach, for a commitment to the latter in itself implies the rejection of many of the fundamental tenets of the processual approach, and vice versa; if this were not the case, the two methodologies could not be said to constitute opposing paradigms.[15] One general objection has been that the broader perspective lacks rigor, since it places no explicit conceptual or definitional limits around the phenomena to be studied (see Moore, pp. 11–12 above); taken to its final conclusion, the subdiscipline of legal anthropology would no longer enjoy analytical hegemony over *any* demarcated field of social action. By contrast, the rule-centered paradigm, founded on the notion of the irreducibility of law, offers comforting boundaries, and some effort has been made to assert their value on empirical and logical grounds. Thus Hamnett (1975:107), invoking Fallers's view (1969), remarks that, on the basis of the African evidence,

> A continuous scale of "legalism" . . . could be constructed, and empirical legal systems placed along it. . . . For Fallers, in fact, law is a discrete variable of which there can be "more" or "less." In this he has made a major contribution to legal anthropology, by reinstating law as a specific mode of social action and showing the way back from the theoretical desert of "social control". . . .

In order to avoid the alleged amorphousness of the processual paradigm, then, Hamnett advocates the solution of treating law as a variable yet specific mode of social action. This, however, does not, in our view, provide a convincing route out of the "theoretical desert." It merely reasserts, by implication, the familiar assumptions of the rule-centered paradigm and reiterates the uncontentious point that other systems differ in the extent to which they bear manifest resemblances to our own. Beyond that, it affords no ready analytical prescriptions with which to answer the paradigmatic criticisms rehearsed above. Nor does it "reinstate" law as a specific mode of social action or demonstrate why it would be valuable to do so.

A second level of criticism addressed to the processual paradigm is, in our view, much more serious. It involves the allegation that a pervasive concern with strategic negotiations leads to a simplistic conception of man, reminiscent of the Malinowskian view that

> Man was self-seeking, and he co-operated only as a form of enlightened self-interest. . . . Where rules inhibited the realisation of satisfactions they were broken where possible, or convenient. [Kuper 1973:40]

While this conception emphatically rejects the idea that behavior can be adequately comprehended by reference to obedience to customary norms, it has its own difficulties. As Hamnett (1975:7) puts it, writing of Malinowski's ethnographic characterization,

> The Trobriander, from being an automaton enslaved by custom, becomes at a stroke a utilitarian positivist endowed with a nice sense of individual costs and benefits. This second stereotype is scarcely less implausible than the first.

In this way, the argument proceeds, human motivation is now attributed to the crude monocausal principle of maximization, and social control is viewed as an epiphenomenon of strategic interaction. This conception, in turn, has the effect of misconstruing and underplaying the undeniable normative element in the social order: if rules do not constrain and determine behavior, there remains the question of why they exist at all and sometimes constitute elaborate repertoires. Moreover, men clearly do *not* always act strategically, so that the a priori denial of any compelling force to accepted norms and precepts leaves a wide range of behavior inexplicable.

The same point may be taken an important step further. Once process is linked with utility—whether utility be conceived in terms of the universalist maximization of interest or the pursuit of indigenous values—it is a short step to treating the sociocultural context as "given" and its relationship to dispute as unproblematic. Any utilitarian conception of man that does this, whether it is clothed in substantivist or formalist analytical terms, leaves the same issues unresolved: wherein lies the systematic relationship between rule and process? And how are individual actions and social experiences articulated with the context in which they occur? These questions are crucial if the logic of dispute is to be finally understood, and they cannot be answered as long as processes and procedures are excised from the total context that imparts meaning to them. Just as the rule-centered paradigm has sometimes emphasized structure and institution at the expense of process, so processual studies that have given inadequate attention to the sociocultural order have erred in the opposite direction.

It would be a caricature to pretend that these strictures are intended against all the work conducted within the processual paradigm. Even those who entertain a strong sympathy for the Malinowskian notion of the "manipulating man" would not deny the normative element of social life; equally, few of their critics would still sustain a rigid jural determinist approach or view life solely in terms of compliance with rules. Moreover, some anthropologists have sought, in a variety of ways, to integrate the major concerns of the two positions (see Moore 1978). The criticisms, in this sense, are to be understood as paradigmatic, i.e., as the evaluation of one coherent methodological approach in terms of the premises of another. Nonetheless, the paradigms remain, and they retain their integrity; both their insights and their limitations serve to clarify the problem to which our own analysis is addressed.

Toward a Definition of the Problem

Tswana institutions of social control have been extensively documented by Schapera, most notably in *A Handbook of*

Tswana Law and Custom (1938). Schapera found that, unlike members of some small-scale societies, Tswana do acknowledge explicit rules of behavior, which they talk about frequently, invoke in the context of disputes, and will discuss freely with interested outsiders. We have already noted that the *Handbook* exemplifies the rule-centered paradigm; it is deliberately restricted to a recording of the "rules"—a compendium drawn from informant interviews, the examination of vernacular texts, and the analysis of case histories—and does not discuss dispute processes or the actions and motivations of living men. But Schapera's manner of presenting these rules implies certain assumptions about their relationship to the social order and the human activity within it. They are depicted as an internally coherent set in accordance with which Tswana are seen to pursue daily life and resolve any conflicts that may arise to disturb its course. The suggested causal connection between rule and outcome is thus closely similar to that envisaged in the more conservative accounts of Western legal systems.

Our own fieldwork, however, forced us to the conclusion that these assumptions are impossible to sustain, for it became clear, in the parallel contexts in which we studied them, that the rules consisted of a loosely constructed repertoire rather than an internally consistent code, that Tswana were not unduly concerned if these rules sometimes contradicted one another, and that almost any conduct or relationship was potentially susceptible to competing normative constructions. Moreover, although they were invoked in argument and decision-making, it proved extremely difficult to predict outcomes by applying them deductively to the facts of any particular case. In other words, we found that Tswana dispute processes simply cannot be reduced to, or explained by, formalistic models or derivative legal logic. This is significant in the light of the fact that the Tswana should, in terms of Fallers's continuum (see above, p. 15), fall near to the "legalistic" pole and ought therefore to be especially well suited to law-centered analysis. The fact that this turns out *not* to be true must enter an uncompromising empirical question mark against the paradigm as a whole. Thus, quite apart from the theoretical and logical criticisms raised earlier, a rule-centered approach does violence to our ethnographic data.

At the same time, Schapera rightly emphasized an important point. Tswana do share the view that their normative repertoire governs the regularity of everyday life, just as it provides the framework, a conceptual context, within which social interaction occurs. Yet, in apparent contradiction to this, they also perceive their social universe as inherently enigmatic, intensely competitive, and highly individualistic. Behavior is frequently explained as motivated by personal interest, and rules, rank, and relationships are held to be readily negotiable in the cause of pragmatic advantage. While these facts underscore the importance of examining disputes in their processual dimension, the censure of the processual paradigm for its sometimes ingenuous image of *homo politicus* is also warranted: the Tswana may entertain an emphatically Malinowskian view of individual enterprise in their own society, but it would be mistaken to reduce all their social processes to a mechanical series of profit-motivated transactions (see chap. 2). While rules may be negotiable, and are indeed negotiated, it is simply untrue that, among the Tswana, behavior is never rule-governed. Nor may it be denied that the normative repertoire plays a significant part in the arguments and decisions that occur in the dispute process. We are thus left with a series of related questions concerning the relationship between rules, processes, and the determination of social action:

—What accounts for the contradiction in Tswana ideology, according to which the social universe is typified as at once rule-governed yet highly negotiable, ordered yet ambiguous, constrained yet competitive?

—Why is it that the dispute process is associated by Tswana with social control and yet is simultaneously regarded as the appropriate context for confrontation, a context in which pragmatically motivated individuals may manipulate the rules in order to subordinate their rivals?

—What determines the course of disputes and motivates or constrains the actions of those involved in them?

—Wherein lies the processual *form* of these disputes and the meaningful structure of the normative order to which they refer?

—Finally, how may we arrive at an understanding of the relationship between rules and processes that depends upon neither crude transactionalism nor simple jural determinism?

These questions compel us to look beyond the orthodox boundaries of legal anthropology, for, to answer them, it is not enough to analyze the form and content of Tswana disputes, important through this might initially be. It becomes necessary to account for the nature of Tswana ideology itself; for it is the latter that imparts meaning to the manner in which Tswana experience, and seek to contrive, their lived-in social universe and, a fortiori, the dispute process. There has been a recent tendency in political anthropology (see, e.g., Cohen 1975; Cohen and Comaroff 1976) to make a broadly similar point by demonstrating that political interaction consists primarily in the construction and management of meaning and value with reference to culturally inscribed categories.[16] Although in relation to different analytical concerns, Barkun (1968:92) has argued that law, too, ought to be seen as a "system of manipulable symbols." At one level, the same thing may be said of Tswana dispute processes. Most of them involve confrontation either over the rival construal of facts in relation to agreed norms or over the normative evaluation of agreed facts; but, whichever it is, value and meaning are negotiated, and this negotiation is predicated on shared symbolic categories and ideological assumptions. As we shall show, however, the latter themselves become analytically comprehensible only by virtue of their relationship to the constitution of the sociocultural order at large. If it is to be adequately explained, therefore, the dispute process requires finally to be located within the logic of this encompassing order. That, then, defines our present objective. We do *not* seek to offer a description of "the Tswana legal system" in the sense of a comprehensive ethnography. Indeed, we consider that there is no such thing as the "Tswana legal system" if that implies the institutional boundedness, functional specificity, or semantic closure of a dimension of Tswana life that bears analogy to the categories subsumed in the Anglo-American term "law."

We begin, in the concluding section of this chapter, with a brief description of the ethnographic context. In chapter 2 the essential features of the sociocultural order are analyzed, and an effort is made to explain the dialectical relationship between its constitutive principles and its lived-in forms. In chapter 3 we consider the nature of the indigenous normative repertoire and the logic of its invocation in the rhetoric of argument and decision and in chapter 4 examine the procedural and institutional characteristics of dispute processes, seeking to account for systematic variations in the relationship between their form and content. Against this background, we deal in the next two chapters with two substantive examples of such processes: those arising out of marriage and the negotiation of conjugal status (chap. 5) and property devolution and the definition of kinship linkages (chap. 6). In chapters 7 and 8 we draw together the various strands of the analysis, paying particular attention to the relationship between rule and outcome and, more generally, to that between the logic of dispute processes and the sociocultural order itself. The Conclusion is devoted to a summary discussion of theoretical implications.

The Ethnographic Context

There has been a growing recognition that the familiar label *"the* Tswana" may be sociologically misleading—that the established tendency to treat this diverse cluster of chiefdoms and communities as a uniform or undifferentiated analytical universe may obscure significant social, political, and economic variations. The point is well taken. It should be understood at the outset, then, that while we draw most of our data from two similarly constituted groupings, our descriptive analysis is not intended as an essay in ethnographic generalization per se. Thus, when we use the collective term "Tswana," we do so, unless otherwise specified, to refer strictly to the Kgatla and Barolong boo Ratshidi.

The Kgatla constitute a chiefdom that occupies 7,960 square kilometers in east-central Botswana. Its population, according to the 1971 census, is 35,752. Some 13,000 of these people have permanent homes in the capital, Mochudi; the remainder live in the smaller villages outside or in isolated hamlets near their agricultural holdings. The area has been inhabited by them since about 1870, when they migrated westward from the Transvaal. Ever since Mochudi was established in 1871, there has been a continuous Christian presence there, and, even before then, the Kgatla had had extensive contact with missionaries, traders, and settlers. In 1932 the capital village became a district center, and, when Botswana gained independence in 1966, it became the administrative headquarters of the Kgatleng District Council. Most Kgatla have also traveled outside their territory; the great majority of males have spent periods of employment abroad, and increasing numbers of females now leave to seek work. Latterly, too, individuals of both sexes have been moving away in pursuit of education.

The Kgatla are, in the main, mixed farmers; they like to see themselves primarily as cattle-keepers, but they also depend on dryland grain production for their subsistence needs. Their territory falls within a marginal rainfall area—the long-term seasonal norm is 480 mm.[17]—but, compared to the overall national distribution, it is well-watered. In most years the pasture is better than average, and a good crop of sorghum and maize is expected once every three years. As in some of the other Tswana chiefdoms, many families maintain a homestead within a village as well as a more rudimentary dwelling alongside their fields outside, where some (or all) members remain for the duration of the agricultural season. The majority also keep cattle-posts elsewhere. These posts typically consist of one or more enclosures for the cattle and temporary dwelling shelters for the herders, although families sometimes establish more permanent residences alongside the cattle pens. This latter practice is proscribed in some chiefdoms, and the usual pattern is for the posts to be manned by youths, employees, or dependent kinsmen. In recent years government policy for rural development has been to stimulate the growth of successful cash cropping by introducing improved techniques and the wherewithal to increase production; nevertheless, the Kgatla continue to depend, in considerable measure, on working as migrant laborers to supplement their income.[18]

Until recently the Barolong boo Ratshidi also constituted a single chiefdom, with its capital at Mafikeng in South Africa and its territory on both sides of the Botswana–South Africa border. In 1970, however, in response to an initiative taken by their government, the segment in Botswana formed a separate chiefdom and installed its first officeholder. Known simply as "Barolong,"[19] it falls into the Southern District, is

1,120 square kilometers in extent, and has a population of almost 11,000. Although there are a few small settlements and, at Good Hope, an administrative center, most of the domestic units are situated permanently on scattered "farms." In this the Botswana Rolong differ from the pattern typically associated with Tswana groupings, that of moving seasonally between the centralized village and the land.

Although they keep stock in small quantities, this population enjoys a wide reputation for successful grain farming. Their average outputs and per capita incomes far exceed those of any other indigenous rural aggregates in the country; indeed, Barolong is often referred to as "the granary of Botswana."[20] The recent success of this community in the sphere of commercial agriculture has its roots in a complex process of structural transformation and the emergence of a class of large farmers (J. L. Comaroff 1981). In addition, it is favored by a slightly higher annual rainfall than anywhere else (500 mm.), by its proximity to agricultural service centers across the border, and by its easy access to local markets. As a result, the present rate of labor migration is somewhat lower here than in neighboring chiefdoms. In fact, there has been something of a return to the land in recent years as the productive reputation of the area has spread. Nonetheless, Barolong has a rudimentary communal infrastructure; relative to, say, the Kgatleng, its community services, communications, and transport facilities are poorly developed.

The large parent chiefdom of the Tshidi-Rolong (or, simply, Tshidi) in South Africa[21] resembles that of the Kgatla in structure more than it does that of the Botswana Rolong. It has a densely populated capital, of approximately 25,000 residents,[22] and five provinces, each with a main village of at least 1,000 members and smaller satellite settlements. Its total area of some 2,500 square kilometers falls today into two blocs within the "homeland" of Bophuthatswana; its overall population is about 58,000.

The Tshidi have lived in roughly their present territory, apart from periods of defensive migration in the early and mid-nineteenth century, at least since the fragmentation of the united Rolong "nation" around the year 1760 (Molema 1966). Boer land encroachments during the nineteenth century reduced the extent of this territory, and it was in the course of the intermittent hostilities between these two groupings that the present (internal) administrative and residential arrangements took their particular shape.[23] The Tshidi also have a long history of contact with missionaries, traders, colonial officials, settlers, and adventurers. Not only were they located on the major trade, travel, and evangelical route to the north (the nearby "white" town of Mafeking has been a railway junction since before 1900), but the proximity of the headquarters of British Bechuanaland, the Bechuanaland Protectorate, and, more recently, Bophuthatswana[24] has long made them familiar with various forms of official presence. Like the Kgatla, they are a comparatively mobile population, given the statutory limits imposed on blacks in this respect by South African law; most men and women have spent periods away as urban laborers, a large number work seasonally on white-owned farms, and many find other reasons to travel from time to time.

The Tshidi terrain is much the same as that across the border, except that the arable soil and the pasture are of lower quality, and there is marked erosion in places. It is good ranching country; but, for purposes of sustained dryland production of crops, the rainfall is unreliable and the earth lacks natural fertility. As grain farmers the Tshidi are thus less successful than their counterparts in Botswana, and a far greater proportion do not cultivate at all; and, although almost every family would like to keep stock, the per capita cattle population was less than one in 1969–70, and its distribution is very uneven. As this suggests, there are conspicuous differences in wealth, with some domestic units barely able to feed themselves. Although some local employment is available, the rate of labor migration is high. By 1970, 84 percent of men and 56 percent of women above the age of twenty-five in the capital had been away for more than nine consecutive months at least once in their lives.

The politicoadministrative arrangements typically associated with Tswana chiefdoms are thoroughly familiar from the writings of Schapera (e.g., 1938, 1940a, 1956), and those that are relevant here are detailed briefly, where appropriate, in later chapters. Nevertheless, in order to set the ethnographic scene, a few basic features need to be outlined. Of these, perhaps the most important is the conceptual centrality of the chief*ship* (*bogosi;* chief = *kgosi*) in political and legal processes at the local level. The office devolves within a ruling agnatic descent group, ostensibly according to clearly defined genealogical principles; in many cases, however, it has long been the object of intense ongoing rivalries between royals and their respective supporters (see Schapera 1963a; J. L. Comaroff 1978). The ruling descent group is differentiated internally not in terms of the operation of segmentary lineage principles but by relative genealogical distance from its senior living member, the chief (Kuper 1975a:70; chap. 2, below). Many headmen of administrative units within the chiefdom (wards, sections; see below) are members of this grouping, their offices having been created for them in the past by chiefs who in this way rewarded or recruited loyal followers among their kin. The exact proportion of royal, as opposed to commoner, headmen varies between chiefdoms; in Mochudi about half of the forty-eight wards are held by men with some genealogical connection to the Kgatla chief, while in Mafikeng only 20 percent claim any royal links. The proportion depends largely on whether former chiefs placed immigrant groupings under their own agnates or retained the indigenous leadership.[25]

While they accord great respect and ceremonial precedence to the chiefship, Tswana distinguish clearly between the office and its incumbent. In formal terms, the latter is in full control of the legislative, administrative, and executive processes of (internal) government; but as a human being he is regarded as fallible, and informants regularly point out the differences in power and legitimacy enjoyed by past and present holders of the office. Moreover, their performance is often debated, evaluated, and criticized in public; indeed, there is a demonstrable link between such public debate and variations in the authority and influence wielded by incumbents at different times in their careers (J. L. Comaroff 1975). The importance attributed to the ideal of good government is repeatedly stressed; to the Tswana this involves, among other things, the enactment of just legislation, the achievement of material improvements and developments, and the efficient and fair working of the dispute-settlement agencies. But, above all, it implies a commitment to rule by consultation and consent.

Public consultation and decision-making, whether concerned with new legislation, administration, or chiefly performance, occur within three spheres. First, the chief has advisers (*bagakolodi*), drawn by him from among his close agnates, his senior matrilateral kin, and any others who hold special positions of trust and influence. His relationship to these men is a personal and informal one, although incumbents differ in the extent to which they meet with their advisers as a council or merely consult with them on an ad hoc basis. Most everyday decisions are taken within this arena; they are then transmitted to the ward headmen, who pass them on in turn. More serious matters also tend to be aired here before being taken further. Second, all advisers and headmen together constitute the *lekgotla* (council), a body which should meet periodically to consider affairs of policy and administration. Finally, there is the largest forum, the public assembly (*pitso, phuthego*), to which all adult males are summoned. Any major issue affecting the chiefdom must be discussed at such a gathering. In both the *lekgotla* and *pitso* the procedure tends to be quite flexible; the chief makes opening and closing statements, and others speak in between, without any rigid order of precedence. Ideally, free speech is encouraged, and the chiefly decisions, announced at the end, are expected to reflect the weight of manifest opinion. In theory all such decisions are binding (it is said that "a chief's word is law"—*lentswe la kgosi ke molao*); but an incumbent would find it almost impossible to execute a blatantly unpopular one, and he would soon lose his legitimacy, and possibly his office as well, were he constantly to make unilateral pronouncements. In the past, age-regiments (*mephato*) carried out whatever decisions required large-scale action.[26] These regiments are no longer formed among the Tshidi; coercive (and, more generally, public) action today depends either on informal recruitment at the chief's *kgotla* (court) or, in formal situations, on support from state agencies, such as the local or national police.

The Tswana conceive of their political community as a hierarchy of progressively more inclusive coresidential and administrative groupings: households, local agnatic segments (or, in some places, family groups), wards, and sections.[27] Units at each level have agnatic cores—as well as other kin and unrelated members—and well-defined authority roles predicated on agnatic ranking principles. Of these, the ward is unquestionably the most conspicuous and significant unit of organization. Within the capital and in other large villages, it typically occupies a contiguous residential area, often forming an arc around the central meeting place (*kgotla*) and cattle enclosure (*lesaka*), and it has a recognized dispute-settlement agency, which operates along similar lines to the chief's *kgotla*. Indeed, the ward is described indigenously as a lower-order homologue of the chiefdom as a whole, and its headmanship is regarded as a microcosm of the apical office. For administrative and legal purposes, wards are treated as the effective constituencies of the state.

As we shall show in chapter 4, the politicoadministrative hierarchy also contains within it all the various dispute-settlement agencies.[28] In fact, many Tswana see this as its defining feature, which is consistent with what is often described by observers as their thoroughgoing—even obses-sive—interest in dispute processes, reflected in their large vocabulary of relevant concepts, their elaborate repertoire of "legal maxims" (Schapera 1966), and their propensity to conduct lengthy postmortems on disputes. Considerable intellectual energy is devoted to evaluating speeches and arguments, questions and judgments, for their cogency, persuasiveness, aesthetic quality, and effect on particular outcomes. Moreover, individual prestige is achieved (or lost) by performance in *kgotla,* and nicknames are sometimes allocated on this basis; for example, in Mafikeng there are men known by such titles as "Advocate," "Judge," and even "Nonsense." The reputations of chiefs and headmen are also held by Tswana to be closely linked to their display of rhetorical and judgmental acumen. In assessing officeholders, evidence of wisdom and fairness is always given first priority. Such qualities are not only valued in themselves but are taken as symptomatic of the overall quality of the incumbents and regimes concerned.

The interest of Tswana in dispute processes is not confined to the evaluation of personal performance or the aesthetics of verbal confrontations. It also extends to the repertoire of norms they see as regulating their everyday lives. (It should be noted, in light of the endless terminological debates, that we use "norm" throughout to connote *a statement of rule that is indigenously regarded as relevant to the regulation of social conduct;* see chap. 3). As we have already noted, this repertoire is known in the vernacular as *mekgwa le melao ya Setswana* (cf. the Barotse *mikwa* and *milao*), a phrase that has been loosely translated as "Tswana law and custom."[29] The norms that compose it are seen also to provide criteria and standards that may be invoked in dispute settlement, but they do not constitute a segregated set, distinguished for jural purposes from other kinds of norm and corresponding to "rules of law" in the sense understood in Western jurisprudence (see p. 9 above).[30] *Mekgwa le melao,* to reiterate, cover a wide range of undifferentiated norms, breaches of which are regarded with greatly variable degrees of seriousness. Thus, the norms governing proper behavior on a visit to someone else's homestead will be described as falling within the repertoire just as clearly as those that prescribe what is to be done when one man's cattle destroy another man's corn. Everyone, even the chief, is expected to recognize these rules: "The law is blind, it eats even its owner" (*Molao sefofu, obile otle oje mong waone*). At the same time, Tswana are perfectly aware that norms can be adduced in such a way as to conflict with each other, since they do not form a coherent set. As we shall demonstrate, the essence of many confrontations lies in the litigants' efforts to impose contrasting normative definitions on the dispute between them.

As this suggests, the Tswana speak freely and often with relish about *mekgwa le melao.* Indeed, it is possible to elicit from most informants a considerable inventory of substantive statements[31] and lengthy exegeses on the nature of the repertoire itself. There is no sense in which the latter is regarded as esoteric, the special preserve of a particular category of persons. Moreover, the norms are held to inform *all* aspects of everyday life and are perceived to have an existence beyond, and largely autonomous of, the dispute-settlement process. This is reflected, to some degree, in the manner and context in which they are invoked. Norms need not be expressed in *kgotla* except under specific conditions, which relate to the logic of strategic argument (see chap. 3). In fact, they are viewed as self-evident correlates of the social order, implicit in the fabric of Tswana society itself. People are assumed to know them, and the mere claim that "Molefe's son has impregnated my daughter" or that "Lesoka's cattle have trampled my corn" is sufficient to invoke, by implication, the norms associated with the impregnation of unmarried women or the damage to crops by cattle. The origin of the norms is diverse. Most are held to derive from long-established patterns of approved behavior; some arise out of decisions made by a chief in handling disputes (see Comaroff and Roberts 1977b) and others out of announcements made formally in *kgotla* in what we would see as statutory form. New legislation of this kind usually follows public deliberations in a *pitso*, but Tswana recognize that additions to, and changes in, the normative repertoire can occur simply as the result of transformations in social patterns as these become expressed in the context of dispute.

The dispute process, then, represents the main forum in which Tswana converse daily among themselves about the organization of their society, the nature and content of their normative repertoire, and the attributes of their culture. Indeed, if we are to follow Bloch's recent call (1977) to revivify Malinowski's "long-conversation" approach to social understanding, this process would appear, at least among the Tswana, to be the logical starting point. For there the "conversation" proceeds in its most explicit and revealing form, unsolicited by the observer, as Tswana negotiate their own models of the lived-in universe. No discourse, however, is comprehensible without regard to its systemic context, for it is this context that establishes its social and semantic referents, the ideologies and values that it reflects, and the goals and exigencies to which it is addressed. Before we turn to the dispute process itself, then, we must first outline the main features of the sociocultural order, and, thereafter, its normative representation in *mekgwa le melao ya Setswana*.

The Sociocultural Order

2

Radcliffe-Brown once observed (1950:69) that certain features of their social arrangements made the Tswana "decidedly exceptional in Africa," so that they might "almost be regarded as an anomaly." Whether this is true or not, there have certainly been difficulties in typifying the structure of these sociocultural systems. Kuper (1975a:71), who has recently discussed some of the confusions bedeviling the literature on the subject,[1] identifies one source of the problem (p. 72):

> On the one hand, then, the administrative structure is clearly defined from above. On the other hand, all the administrative units, indeed all residential agglomerations, are formed around an agnatic core and may be talked about in an agnatic idiom. Writers on the Sotho-[Tswana] often ask (in effect) what is primary, the "lineage" or the administrative unit.

We consider this question to be of secondary analytical significance, however, for the structural complexity of Tswana society derives primarily from the marriage system and its relationship to other organizational principles.[2] The Tswana express a preference for, and practice, all forms of cousin union, including the FBD type. Now so-called endogamous systems of this particular kind, as is well recognized today, are not merely difficult to describe. They

This chapter is based on a series of lectures, entitled "Three Studies in the Political Culture of an African Chiefdom," delivered by Comaroff as a visitor to the University of Chicago in May 1978. We should like to thank Marshall Sahlins, Nancy Munn, and Terence Turner for their constructive criticism.

also present a formidable theoretical challenge to the dominant modes of structural analysis. Several writers have argued that they controvert the fundamental assumptions of both descent theory and alliance theory (Barth 1973; Bourdieu 1977). It is not necessary here to enter the methodological discussion that has surrounded this question; the issues involved have been well rehearsed—especially with respect to Middle-Eastern ethnography—and our account, in any case, represents a substantive and constructive effort to confront them. Nevertheless, one introductory point ought to be made.

For reasons that will become evident, systems in which there are both an agnatic-descent ideology and preferred FBD marriage are typically marked by a conspicuous stress on individualism and pragmatic interest in the construction of social aggregations and relations. The social field tends to be highly fluid, its definition often being complicated by overlapping and ambiguous linkages, which actors seek to negotiate and contrive to their own advantage. Under these conditions the relationship between the structural principles that underlie the sociocultural order on the one hand, and the experienced negotiability of everyday life on the other, becomes extremely difficult to grasp in analytical terms. Not that this difficulty is confined to such "endogamous" systems; Firth's early effort (1951) to typify and contrast "social structure" and "social organization" is merely one of many attempts to confront the generic problem at a theoretical level (cf. Murphy 1971). However, in endogamous systems, it presents itself in an especially obvious and intractable fashion to the ethnographer. It is therefore not coincidental that methodological individualism in general—and transactionalism in particular—has appeared as a convenient analytical approach in such contexts (Barth 1959, 1966). For by postulating, as Barth does, that culture and structure are the product of strategic interaction, this approach promises a superficially convincing means of relating the pragmatics of everyday interactional processes to patterns of social regularity and their normative dimension. This view has been subjected to criticism from several perspectives (see, e.g., Kapferer [ed.] 1976; Asad 1972), but its appeal is sustained by the seeming appropriateness of treating what appear to be patently individualistic social orders from a methodological individualist standpoint. Hence it is worth stressing at the outset why utilitarian models of this kind fail to comprehend the logic of these sociocultural systems and the processes that occur within them.

Methodological individualist approaches usually have it that an integrated order of values—for Barth (1966:12), "culture"—is the *outcome* of transactions entered into for the purpose of maximizing material or social profit. But as Sahlins (1965) has effectively argued, different modes of exchange (including "negative reciprocity," the analogue of interest-motivated transaction) are themselves elements in culturally constituted value systems, as are the ideologies that impart symbolic form to them. In other words, far from being the product of transaction, any order of values—of which "maximization" itself may be part—must have a prior existence in culture before transactional processes can be rendered socially meaningful. This is not to deny that members of some societies *do* perceive their universe as individualistic and competitive and the actions of their compatriots as motivated by pragmatic interest. Nor is it untrue that particular kinds of value may be contrived and modified in the course of everyday interactional processes. But these processes cannot be assumed to generate sociocultural forms. Quite the reverse: the analytical problem in any ethnographic context is to demonstrate the relationship between the principles that constitute a sociocultural system, the ideological forms that are inscribed in them, and the modes of transaction and exchange that they potentiate. We reiterate, then, that pragmatic individualism, precisely because it *may* be a critical element in some ideologies, cannot account for the logic of structure or culture. No indigenous ideology or the activities that occur in its name can ever explain the system of which they are a feature.

Essentially the same point can be made about the contention that social regularity and structural patterns are the emergent product of strategic interaction. As our account will show, this view confuses the surface forms manifest in a social universe at a particular historical moment with the structural principles that give rise to them. It is quite true, again, that transactional processes may *realize* particular social forms and relations; but they do not generate them, for their ontogeny lies in the systemic character of the sociocultural principles themselves. In short, transactionalism misplaces the essential project of sociocultural analysis by deriving an explanatory principle from precisely what requires to be explained, namely, the location of utilitarian ideologies and transactional processes within the logic of a total system. This is crucial; the manner in which we comprehend everyday social activity and patterns of relationship depends upon it.

The Lived-in Universe

In describing their own lived-in social universe, Tswana typically give primacy to the hierarchy of coresidential administrative units that compose any chiefdom. Its component levels have already been mentioned; briefly, at its base is the polygynous household,[3] which is generally depicted as the major property-holding group, although in fact it is usually divided into houses whose material and political interests are kept separate. In theory, and often in practice, adjacent households with agnatically related heads form a local agnatic segment under the leadership of an elder, who should be the genealogically senior member. Domestic groups with matrilateral and affinal links to such a unit may also come to live alongside it and be incorporated in its affairs.[4] Internally, the segment is ranked according to a series of ascriptive rules (to be discussed below), according to which nonagnates are always junior to core members and derive their relative positions with reference to the order of their incorporation.

In general, two or more segments constitute a ward, the most significant administrative grouping in Tswana society. Typically, again, a ward occupies a defined residential site and contains a core segment (or agnatically related segments), within which the headmanship devolves by the same ascriptive rules as apply to lower-order units. Finally, wards are grouped into sections, along similar organizational lines; that is, each includes a number of ranked core wards whose heads are agnatically related, the genealogically senior among them holding the headship. Sections vary in size and should also be territorially contiguous; together they make up the chiefdom. In ideal terms they are held to function as wards writ large,

but today some have become moribund as politicoadministrative units (J. L. Comaroff 1976).

Four related features of this hierarchy must be stressed.
First, units at the different levels are homologous, replicating
the form of the chiefdom as a whole. The principles associated with their internal composition apply throughout, as
do the rules according to which rank is internally reckoned
and in terms of which positions of authority devolve.[5] Consequently, succession to *any* office or status ultimately involves the assumption of seniority within a particular household, the establishment of the primacy of that unit within a
given segment, and so on. Thus, while the administrative
structure is not coterminous with a segmentary lineage system (see below), the patterns of aggregation and authority
relations that occur within it are broadly similar at the various
levels. This, as we shall see, is important, because the articulation of political process and social formation is repeated at
all but the lowest stratum of the hierarchy.

Second, Tswana link the elaboration of this hierarchy with
the working-out of agnatic relationships. They associate the
fragmentation of the household with the ubiquitous tendency
of its component houses to compete—or, at the very least, to
resist cooperation—over property and status after the death
of the father (see chap. 6). This process of fragmentation in
turn is held to generate a cycle in which the establishment of
independent units leads inevitably to the emergence of a
local agnatic segment, provided that the fragmenting units
continue to live contiguously, which is strongly (if not always
successfully) encouraged by significant outsiders. Similarly,
as segments proliferate, hostilities and rivalries between their
members may end in fission, although the new groupings that
result are, again, often contained within the boundaries of the
higher-order grouping. The process of fragmentation may
also be repeated at the ward or section level as the result of
conflict at the agnatic core.

Third, as the foregoing suggests, even though agnation and
politicoterritorial arrangements do not correspond neatly,
the relationship between them is socially significant. Most individuals living in a Tswana chiefdom belong to a descent
grouping whose span usually stretches beyond the bounds of
the ward or section. (Conversely, of course, the latter are not

recruited exclusively with reference to the ideology of descent.) These descent groupings, however, are *not* segmentary lineages, for these reasons: they are internally ordered only in terms of relative genealogical distance from the senior member; the creation and definition of segments depends primarily on coresidence, incorporation into the administrative hierarchy, and, possibly, short-term political alliance against outsiders;[6] these segments are not generated by a principle of structural opposition or by an enduring unity of corporate interest; descent groupings never meet or engage in common action, with the partial and rare exception of the one that controls the chiefship, and they also do not constitute the major universe of effective kinship for their members. The descent grouping represents primarily a *category* of people, that is, all those to whom the rules of agnatic ranking, if reckoned to their logical limits, may extend. Its boundaries, however, seldom require to be defined and in practice are not sharply drawn. Moreover, in everyday terms, agnatic links that cut across coresidential units—and are not overlain by other kinds of relationship, cooperative enterprise, or political alliance—tend gradually to lapse. Remote kinship is regarded by Tswana with detached neutrality. As a result, significant agnatic bonds, those viewed as "close," are usually clustered within local units, except for the few external ties that may be activated in the cause of mutual interests. This coincides with the fact that agnation, as an ideology, is most relevant *within* such local groupings; for it is there that it orders rank and authority, and, because it does so, it is of direct consequence only to those members of a descent grouping who happen to live in the same politicoadministrative units. Agnation, then, may provide a ground for alliance outside these units, but so may other kin ties, as may common membership in an association, the contiguity of agricultural holdings outside the village, and so on; indeed, these linkages are often found to be much more compelling.

Fourth, and closely related to this, the administrative hierarchy provides the structure in which are located the material and political values to which Tswana themselves attribute major significance. Thus, for example, the distribution of land was, until recently,[7] vested in ward headmen, who received allocations from the chief and had a virtually free hand in parceling out holdings. Similarly, the management of disputes, control over public arenas, councils, and communications, liaison with higher-order units and the devolution of rank within lower-order ones, the right to represent the group and, sometimes, to ratify guardianships over persons and property—all these fall within the (potential) jurisdiction of positions of authority at the various levels. Clearly, the more inclusive the unit concerned, the greater the jurisdiction and the resources and power to which the relevant status may give access. Furthermore, precisely because these statuses and values are firmly situated within the hierarchy, it is this hierarchy that defines the fields in which competition over their acquisition and control generally takes place. Competitive processes of this type, as we have already suggested, are ordered in terms of the ideology of agnation. From the Tswana perspective, however, the converse is also true: the administrative structure represents the politicosocial context in which agnatic relations and rivalries are negotiated. There is little perceived value in genealogical seniority if it does not entail a status, or a set of authority relations, in the encompassing hierarchy.

The ideology of descent and the rules of rank, with reference to which social relations and groupings are constructed within the administrative hierarchy, are expressed in the Tswana theory of ascription and achievement. This theory, as will become evident, also illuminates the link between everyday social and political processes and the constitutive order that underpins them.

Tswana share a uniform repertoire of ranking rules associated with the devolution and incumbency of statuses throughout the hierarchy, from the household to the chiefship. In fact, if these rules are taken literally, the Tswana would seem to have a thoroughgoing ascriptive sociopolitical system, and they have usually been portrayed as such.[8] However—and quite apart from the logical problems involved in conceiving of any political system in these terms,[9]—the incidence of "anomalies" in the transmission of rank appears to be remarkably high. Thus, for example, the Tshidi royal genealogy, as it is presently formulated, suggests that 80 percent of all instances of chiefly succession fall into this category, and the rate is not significantly less for lower-order statuses. Now there has been a tendency in the past, in accounting for any deviations of this kind from ascriptive principles, to rely on functionalist teleology (Gluckman, e.g., 1955b:44 f.; Goody 1966); but this results in failure to comprehend the cultural logic of ascription among the Tswana, which is explicable only in terms of its dialectical coexistence with an ideology of achievement.

The apparent contradiction between ascription and achievement, which is manifest in many societies, is expressed with great clarity by Tswana. Expressions of it take various forms. Most directly, explicit public statements often assert that, while status is *always* determined by birth, and authority is *always* contingent upon status, legitimate power *always* depends upon personal acumen and achievement, which cannot be inherited. The implicit paradox is compounded by the fact that a person "born" to any position may be displaced only in highly exceptional circumstances, yet "good government"—a generalized metaphor for access to and the proper incumbency of statuses at all levels by able individuals—is perhaps the dominant ideal in everyday Tswana life. The contradiction is, in part, reproduced in indigenous conceptions of authority. Tswana regard their hierarchy of statuses, with the chiefship at its apex, as giving form to the chiefdom, yet they distinguish sharply between these statuses and their holders. The former are highly valued; their existence, ascriptive devolution, and investment with particular properties are considered nonnegotiable. The latter, in contrast, are viewed in an acutely critical fashion; they are fallible humans who may grow more or less powerful from one moment to the next, depending on their performance.

The resolution of these contradictions, in the lived-in world of the Tswana, lies in the nature of the prescriptive rules themselves and, in particular, in their relationship to the norms that govern incumbency. The primary prescriptions begin with a straightforward formulation of the principle of primogeniture, relative seniority and access to any status being reckoned by age within ranked houses. Lineal transmission always takes precedence; a man's sons are genealogically senior to their father's junior brothers, and, when they predecease their father, their rights pass to their own successors. Moreover, the rightful occupant of a position cannot be removed, except in extreme circumstances.[10] There are, in addition, secondary rules, which serve ostensibly to ensure that every house will be perpetuated, that there will be heirs to every status, and that doubts concerning these heirs' identity will be obviated. The first of these rules refers to the ranking of unions and cowives, upon which the standing of a house ultimately depends; although in the past it was not so (see Comaroff and Roberts 1977b), today the order of marriage is accepted as the norm in this regard. The remaining secondary prescriptions concern surrogate parentage. For example, if a man dies without sons, a leviratic arrangement ought to be made on his behalf; formerly, if the deceased had not married at all, or had not married his principal wife (Tshidi), a house had to be duly established for him. Although the levirate is rarely found today, it remains an important element in the negotiation of rank, which proceeds invariably with reference to previous generations and genealogical linkages within them. Further, some Tswana— and especially the Tshidi—persist in speaking of this rule as a prescription. When instances of its nonfulfillment are pointed out, the typical response is that there has never been a time limit and that, when convenient, the appropriate arrangements will be made. It should be added that, given the ambiguities surrounding conjugal status, some unions continue to be construed after the fact in leviratic terms, whether or not this had been the intention behind their establishment in the first place. The same applies broadly to the accompanying sororatic rule, which, as the data in chapter 6 will indicate, is still invoked in the negotiation and definition of relationships. Finally, there are tertiary rules, which regulate guardianship and regency (see, again, chap. 6) on behalf of minors. These roles usually devolve upon a close older agnate; where an office is involved, the regent should be the one next in order of seniority who is also sufficiently mature. He enjoys all the rights and privileges of the position but must hand it over to the heir once the relevant assembly (*pitso*) so decides. If a guardian or regent exceeds his authority, mismanages affairs, or refuses to withdraw when necessary, he may be removed.

While the primary rules would appear to define access to status and position with sharp clarity, the set *as a whole* affords considerable room for the manipulation and negotiation of rank and seniority. Indeed, in spite of formal statements to the contrary, it *is* possible to remove incumbents and to redefine genealogical relations without violating either the ascriptive ideology or its underlying logic. Moreover, this rule set is not invoked merely to justify competing status claims; it also constitutes a code in terms of which meaning may be imposed on the flow of everyday politicosocial actions and events. The following example, taken from a campaign to appropriate an office, demonstrates this and illuminates some of its implications:[11]

H aspired to an office occupied by D, whom he thus wished to remove. How was this to be legitimized? The solution chosen by H was as follows:

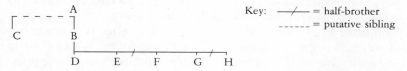

Key: ——/—— = half-brother
        ------ = putative sibling

He argued that B, the previous incumbent, had had a senior brother (C), who had died in infancy. By virtue of his seniority, C had been the heir of A; therefore, a son raised in his name would actually be entitled to the office. Because C had died before marrying or having children, B, as the next in seniority, had assumed the position as a regent. But, claimed H, B had recognized his duty to father a son for C. He had thus married H's mother in C's name. As her eldest son, H was the heir of her (jural) husband and was hence in the direct line of descent from A. The genealogy should therefore be altered accordingly:

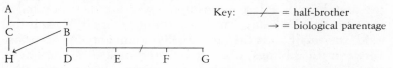

Key: ——/—— = half-brother
        → = biological parentage

Now, according to the rule of primogeniture, H should, if his claim is accepted, succeed to office.

When he first entered this campaign, H began by secretly organizing a support group, whose members sought subtly and systematically to discredit D. In fact, they enjoyed some success, which was what persuaded H to precipitate an open confrontation when he did. But this failed, for he misjudged the division of support. Nevertheless, he made another attempt two years later, and on this occasion he succeeded. Significantly, by this time D's standing had decreased noticeably, and some of the men who had argued for his genealogical seniority earlier now rejected it. It should also be noted that, in this case, as in every one where status is renegotiated, the "official" genealogy of the unit concerned changed to reflect the outcome.

Although this is a relatively straightforward example, it illuminates the way in which Tswana experience the practical logic of their ascriptive rules. Most conspicuously, it indicates how these rules are employed in the strategic negotiation of rank and status. Thus H invoked the leviratic prescription in justifying his claim and then argued for the removal of D in terms of the norms of guardianship and regency. The effect of this campaign, which eventually succeeded, was to establish his own seniority and rights in terms of the primogeniture principle and to demote a man who, two years before, had been recognized as heir to the office. Clearly, what had altered in the interim was the distribution of support. That many people who initially rejected H's claim could later accept it merely confirms what Tswana take for granted: ascriptive status may be a function of personal achievement, and not the reverse. While this case involved high office, similar ones occur within lower-order segments, a fact to which our later evidence will attest. Indeed, as we have stressed, processes like these are recognized as a pervasive feature of community life.

Three further properties of the rule set are significant. First, it defines a competitive field composed essentially of the members of a descent grouping who are incorporated in the unit to which any particular status refers.[12] Within that field, the *only* bonds that are usually nonnegotiable are those between full siblings, who are ordered by age.[13] The house, therefore, becomes the irreducible atom of aggregation and rank; any configuration of genealogical linkages and statuses is, in effect, an arrangement of interhouse relationships at a specific historical moment. Second, while genealogical reckoning provides the idiom of strategic argument, it patently cannot determine the outcome. And third, although the removal of a person from his rightful status is prescriptively debarred, competition for that status is rarely precluded, and such competition is not confined to moments when the status lacks an occupant. But the fact that this is so implies the existence of a mechanism, alluded to earlier, that permits the replacement of incumbents without contravening the ascriptive principle. Now, as the example indicates, the tertiary rules allow a regent or guardian to be ousted. The corollary is that anyone may be relieved of a position if it can be established that he holds it only on behalf of someone else. This is exactly what H sought to do in respect of D; it is the typical way of justifying the appropriation of any status. Moreover, in making such claims, a pretender *must* assert his jural preeminence over his rival. When he is successful and the relevant genealogy is altered accordingly, the defeated rival will be recognized publicly as the junior of the two men. In terms of prescriptive logic—according to which the rules must be applied, or reality be treated as if they have been or will be—this means that he *must* have been a guardian/regent and should hand over the position. In other words, the tertiary rules admit the possibility that those who occupy a status ineptly or unpopularly can be replaced without violating the ideology of ascription. It also follows that they expedite the transformation of genealogies in such a manner as to legitimize and reflect contemporary relations.[14]

The primary rules, then, embody the ascriptive basis of the system, while the secondary ones order the negotiation of rank and power relations. The tertiary arrangements, in turn, ensure that most statuses represent an achievable goal and, simultaneously, provide ascriptive justification for strategic activity. Thus the total set constitutes the systemic basis of, and imparts form to, the politicosocial process, and, in doing so, it underlies the resolution of the ascription-achievement paradox. Successful politicosocial management, the exercise of control over the construction of reality in the pursuit of interests and values, necessarily involves an "achievement." But its ascriptive coding is entailed in this: the triumphant aspirant to any position becomes its rightful heir, and his mother's status as a principal wife is affirmed as a result. Consequently, Tswana appear *to themselves* to sustain a performance-oriented ideology within the context of an ascriptively ordered society. The classical analytical dichotomy between ascription and achievement as principles of political determination may no longer be defensible (J. L. Comaroff

1978), but a dialectical relationship between these "principles" lies at the heart of the politicosocial process.

There is, however, another and more complex dimension to these rules. It flows from the fact that, while any pretender to a status *must* offer an ascriptive justification, the nature of the set is such that there is virtually always a multiplicity of ways in which this justification may be formulated. As a result, he is *compelled* to choose between these alternatives. In some instances the choice is straightforward: an individual may merely assert that he is the jural heir of his genitor—his decision to do so depending, perhaps, on the latter's recognized rank—and thereby lay claim to the devolution of that man's status in terms of a preexisting and established genealogical configuration. However, this alternative is not always taken, for there may be complicated strategic problems at issue, and their resolution may have significant social implications. This is well demonstrated by the case of Lotlamoreng, who acceded to the Tshidi chiefship on the basis of an intricate argument.

It was widely accepted that Lotlamoreng had been fathered by Chief Montshiwa. However, in asserting his right to the chiefship, Lotlamoreng and his supporters offered a convoluted justification. This had it that his jural father was Kebalepile, who, they declared, had been Montshiwa's senior son. Kebalepile had predeceased Montshiwa and had also died two years before the birth of Lotlamoreng; but the latter claimed to be his son, nevertheless, on the basis that Kebalepile's house had been entered according to the leviratic arrangements. This argument was complicated by the fact that Kebalepile's widows had no children. But, to account for this, it was insisted that Lotlamoreng's mother had actually been a surrogate for Kebalepile's senior wife. In other words, *both* Lotlamoreng's genitors were construed as having been substitutes for his jural parents. Of course, the fact that Montshiwa was Lotlamoreng's natural father meant that this claim transformed biological paternity into social grandfatherhood. (It may be added that some informants aver that Lotlamoreng's jural parents never actually met.) But why did Lotlamoreng go to all this trouble?

The simplest legitimization for him would have been that his mother had actually been Montshiwa's (rather than Kebalepile's) principal wife—or the *seantlo* (substitute) for her childless elder sister, who had also been married to Montshiwa. This straightforward argument would certainly have been tenable. But Lotla-

LOTLAMORENG'S GENEALOGY

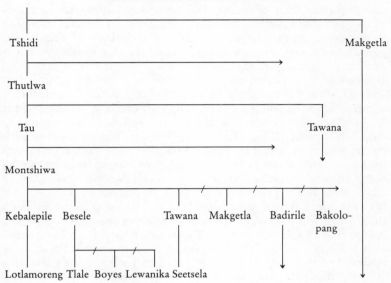

Key: ——/— = half-brother
        → = unlisted siblings
        ↓ = unlisted descendants

moreng's assertion of descent from Kebalepile had two perceived advantages. First, had he claimed to be descended directly from Montshiwa by a separate house, he would have excluded himself from the segment that had raised Besele and Tawana (see genealogy), each of whom had adolescent sons. While this segment promised no short-term support, it could later become a powerful unit. Had it been relegated to a position of juniority (the implication of a justification by Lotlamoreng through Montshiwa), its members might later respond by claiming the chiefship in terms of their relationship to Besele.[15] On the other hand, by declaring himself its senior member, Lotlamoreng might not have *guaranteed* the elimination of subsequent opposition from this quarter, but it did make the interests of this grouping converge with his own. For any further *external* campaign against him would threaten the status of the segment as a whole and thus encourage it to support him. In contrast, direct descent from Montshiwa would have made him vulnerable as the only member of his house. Also, affiliation to Kebalepile's house allowed him to influence the marriages of the late Besele's children; as their older FBS, he could also claim guardianship over their property. The second advantage lay in Lotlamoreng's relationship to the boo Makgetla, a powerful grouping drawn from among the descendants of a brother of Tshidi (see genealogy), who had been wife-givers to the chiefly line over several generations. Although his mother came from this grouping, Besele had also married a woman from it, who had borne his eldest son, Tlale. If Lotlamoreng had claimed affiliation to a different segment from Besele, he risked losing Makgetla support later, for he and Tlale shared matrilateral kinsmen, and there was nothing to stop them from backing Tlale against himself. The outcome of such rivalry would not affect the senior Makgetla men; their relationship to the incumbent would be the same. However, by arguing that he was Kebalepile's son, and hence descended from the same house as Tlale, Lotlamoreng ensured that Makgetla interests coincided with his own; for, if it were ever suggested that Kebalepile had *not* been the heir of Montshiwa (and Lotlamoreng not the chief), it would follow that Besele, his younger full brother, could not have been, either. Thus it would have been difficult for them to support Tlale against Lotlamoreng. In fact, according to Lotlamoreng's son, this strategy did yield the advantages it had promised, for the descendants of both Besele and the boo Makgetla later proved faithful and powerful allies when Lotlamoreng faced campaigns against his incumbency.

Apart from indicating the resource potential of the rules, and why it is that the ability to manipulate them skillfully is so admired, this case illuminates the relationship between sociopolitical processes and social forms. We have already noted that, given the logic of the set, the appropriation of any status involves either the affirmation of an existing genealogy or its transformation. Which it will be depends on context and the construction of particular claims. For example, transmissions of rank that occur during uncontested devolutionary cycles tend to leave extant patterns unchanged, while successful efforts to wrest a position from its incumbent entail their alteration; either way, there is a direct connection between the reckoning of genealogical linkages and the negotiation of seniority and status. As the case of Lotlamoreng demonstrates, moreover, such reckonings are not merely abstract classificatory exercises. Rather, they provide the idiom in terms of which relations and alliances within the relevant areas of a descent grouping are *pragmati-*

cally constituted. Thus Lotlamoreng's attempt to create a set of ties around himself by reformulating the genealogy was intended to have a material effect on the field of kin concerned. But even where there is no apparent strategic motive behind activities that configure genealogical links, the very fact of their configuration may have a similar outcome. For instance, as we shall see in case 25, one of the disputants, Lesoka, had appropriated a bridewealth payment some years before the relevant dispute. In doing so, he had not specifically intended to manipulate a network of bonds. Nevertheless, his act *implied* the assumption of a status, and this, in turn, contrived a wide range of linkages and groupings in a manner that had dire, if unforeseen, results. Only when these became obvious to him did Lesoka seek explicitly to redefine the social relations involved. But he was ultimately trapped when the consequences of his maneuvers took their inexorable course. In short, then, social aggregation and alliance— that is, the *manifest* segmentary composition of descent groupings and the patterning of relations within them—are dialectically entailed in sociopolitical processes by virtue of the logic of the prescriptive rules.[16]

To put it in more general terms, it seems clear that the rule set embodies, in synchronic form, the transformational elements that generate descent formations and the social aggregations within them. These elements are realized in the course of sociopolitical processes, in which the negotiation of rank and status configure relations within the context of the hierarchy of territorial units. It follows from this, too, that, while the ascriptive rules are phrased in terms of *descent,* the social groupings that they constitute are, in effect, *ascent* groups.[17] That is, their segmentary form flows upward and outward from particular reference points as members of a generation define relationships among themselves. Again Lotlamoreng's claim illustrates this aptly: the acceptance of his version of the genealogy radically altered the internal alignment of the royal grouping over three generations (see also note 15), and it did so by a series of steps that followed upon his construction of a set of statuses immediately surrounding himself. These properties of the rules, then, go some way in explaining why the Tswana descent system, while it allows for the ready rearrangement of segmentary units and permits the realignment of houses as atoms of structure, may yet be perceived from within as having a constancy of form. The latter—the perception of constancy—is entailed in the synchrony of the set; the former—the negotiability of relations between units—in the pragmatic logic of its application in everyday life.

Thus far we have decontextualized our analysis by not referring it to the constitutive values that motivate the system or to the elements of structure that generate its surface patterns. The indigenous theory encompassing the principles of ascription and achievement might provide the crucial analytical key to this structure, but it cannot, of itself, account either for the negotiability of the experienced universe or for its underlying semantic form. In order to confront these problems, it is necessary to explore further, and look behind, the construction of Tswana sociopolitical theory and the ideology of descent.

The Constitutive Order

In our discussion of conjugal and property relations in chapters 5 and 6 it will become clear that Tswana distinguish sharply between the normative content of agnation and matrilaterality. The opposition between them is expressed, in a variety of forms, as one between the values of rivalry-conflict and support-alliance—between material and political antagonism on the one hand and moral and social protagonism on the other. The essentially hostile agnatic universe, beyond the confines of the house, is the scene of individual management, competitive activity, and the negotiation of power relations. In contrast, the matrilateral domain is characterized by a nonnegotiable moral unity that is constantly affirmed in ritual, symbolic, and structural terms. "A man and his mother's brother *never* fight," the Tswana say; nor do they engage in mystical action against each other.

At the same time, only a limited proportion of social bonds actually fall into one or the other of the categories of agnation and matrilaterality. The preference for kin marriages of all types, and the frequency of those between members of the same agnatic descent grouping in particular, preclude their doing so. Moreover, Tswana appear even to deny that kinship relations *ought* to be unambiguous and single-stranded; for, as they conceive it, the effective unit of kinship, the *losika,* is a bilateral stock, whose indigenous definition assumes that *all* unions take place between cousins. Clearly they do not, but it is significant that the confusion of categorical relations is culturally inscribed in this manner. In other words, the opposition between agnation and matrilaterality might embody the fundamental social values—and value contradictions—in Tswana culture, but the marriage system ensures that few existing relations can, or ought to, fall exclusively within either universe in its social aspect. The opposition between the domains of "support" and "hostility," whatever substantive form it may take in a particular society (often some transformation of the "we-them" dichotomy), is of course a very general one.

Indeed, its universality has often been assumed or asserted, albeit in a number of different theoretical guises. In the Tswana context, however, its *cultural* expression appears not to be reflected neatly or obviously in *social* terms, at least not in the organization of enduring groups or the unambiguous assignment of persons to categories. Nevertheless, we would suggest that this very fact provides an important insight into the constitutive order underlying the Tswana sociocultural system.

The House as Cultural Paradigm

In order to illuminate this, it is necessary to examine briefly the conceptual and semantic significance of the *house* among the Tswana, for this unit, as we have indicated earlier, appears to represent an "atom of structure" in that its irreducibility is fundamental to the sociopolitical process and to the construction and transformation of relations entailed in it. It will be remembered that the ascriptive rules associated with access to status, like those governing inheritance, preclude the negotiation of relative rank per se within these groupings; that the leviratic and sororatic prescriptions exist ostensibly to ensure their perpetuation; and that the ordering of genealogies specifically involves their arrangement, as undifferentiated entities, in relation to one another. The house, furthermore, is the basic property-holding group, and its internal unity is stressed for the duration of the devolutionary cycle (see chap. 6). This unity is also marked terminologically; in classificatory terms of address and reference, a sibling is not distinguished from a half-sibling or a patrilateral parallel cousin of the same sex or relative seniority, but there is a distinct label for "all children of one house." This term, *setsalo,* is derived from *tsala,* which is commonly translated as "friend" (Brown 1931:325) or "ally." Finally, despite minor variations between the chiefdoms with which we are concerned, the only persons an individual is invariably prevented from marrying are the members of his or her own house and of the houses of their children, their siblings' children, and their parents.[18] Among the Tshidi a father's widow and half-sibling were, traditionally, permitted to be partners. The exogamic range, then, includes little more than an ego's natal unit and the units that gave rise to it and to which it will give rise. In his own generation, moreover, his or her house is the elemental wife-giving and wife-taking group, a point whose importance will become clear as the discussion proceeds.

During the later phases of the developmental cycle, however, the house is eventually going to fragment. Indeed, if it is an "atom of structure," it *must* be both reproduced and elaborated into higher-order units. Again, the process by means of which this occurs is culturally recognized at one level: when brothers become adults and have children, they are expected to separate as the devolutionary cycle draws to a close and their interests diverge. That the natal house breaks up as its (male) members create their own households is conventional wisdom. Significantly, this is held to be the source of agnatic conflict and, more generally, of the internal differentiation of the politicoterritorial hierarchy.[19] At the same time, and in direct opposition, the brother-sister bond transcends, and is external to, the dissolution of the original grouping and the generation of new ones in endemically rivalrous relationships with one another. Now it is an established and valued cultural tradition that fathers should "cattle-link" their children into brother-sister pairs, a linkage that is sustained for life. The brother, who is obliged to represent his sister and look after her well-being, receives her bridewealth and should employ it to give her succor when necessary. It is also said that he may use it to secure a union of his own; in fact this is very rarely done, but the statement itself is a symbolic expression of the merging of their interests and of their social and moral complementarity. In ideal terms, moreover, this man becomes a "special" mother's brother to his sister's children: he will protect them against their agnates and will participate in any deliberations concerning their affairs, to which he is an intimate party. In short, the close brother-sister and mother-child bonds are fused and perpetuated in the mother's brother–sister's child relationship.

In other words, the Tswana conception of the house embodies both a set of primary social values and elementary structural forms, along with the principles of their reproduction and elaboration. With respect to the primary social values, the hostile agnatic domain has its origin in the relationship between brothers, which begins in social and material unity and is transformed, as the reproductive process unfolds, when they found discrete and opposed units. It is then transmitted across the generations through the potentially ambivalent father-son bond[20] to the linkages classically associated with divergences of interest, antagonism, and competition: those between half-brothers, father's brothers and their brothers' sons, and patrilateral parallel cousins. This is the domain in which the great majority of disputes, accusations of sorcery, and personal confrontations are held to, and do, occur (see Schapera 1963a). One of the terms used collectively for agnates, although not the most frequent, is *kgotla*. Its other referents are "ward" (or, more precisely, "politicoterritorial unit above the level of the household and below that of the chiefdom") and "central meeting place" —i.e., the primary contexts of competitive political activity and dispute processes. In contrast, the supportive matrilateral universe is notably free of such hostility and confrontation. Its genesis in the complementary brother-sister tie is refracted through the maternal relationship to that linking mother's brothers and their sisters' children, and it extends, finally, to matrilateral cross-cousins. The difference between the two domains is again expressed terminologically: for a man, male agnates are addressed and referred to as either senior or junior to himself, which implies not merely relative rank but also the ultimate negotiability of the bond.

Conversely, sisters, mother's brothers, and cross-cousins are labeled as equal and unranked.[21] Furthermore, as we shall demonstrate, the sociocultural conception of marriage into the respective domains echoes this value opposition: MBD unions connote the perpetuation of alliance; FBD ones, the attempt to transform agnation by relegating a (real or potential) rival into a supportive client.

It is not surprising, then, that the separation of the opposed domains is marked symbolically in other contexts as well. For example, the agnatic universe is associated with public space, i.e., with the open front yard of the homestead (*lolwapa*) and the common ground of the politicoterritorial unit beyond; by contrast, the inviolable back yard (*segotlo*) belonging to a linked sister, mother, or mother's brother denotes privacy, sanctuary, and support.[22] The former represents the (male) arena of political competition and mystical threat; the latter, the (female-articulated) one of mutual protection and moral unity. Moreover, the danger of categorical confusion is carefully avoided. Thus, to take a further example, it will be seen in chapter 5 that a mother's brother is rarely eager to lay claim to his sister's children if bridewealth has not been transferred in respect of a union that is under threat of dissolution, for to do so could transform the brother-sister tie into one akin to a conjugal bond when her offspring took their place alongside his own, and the sister, as would be expected of her in her capacity as a mother, sought to protect the interests of her own children against the interests of his. Under these conditions it is not the *pragmatic* confounding of the mother's brother–sister's child bond with a quasi-agnatic one that is the problem, since there exist culturally established modes of mediating this. In symbolic terms, however, the violation of the linked sibling relationship, and hence the violation of the value order itself, is a more fundamental and serious matter.

The sociocultural logic of the house and of its reproduction has further aspects. In order to examine them, it is helpful to represent in diagrammatic form what we have just been describing.[23]

First, it will be clear from the diagram that the bonds between a child and his matrilateral and agnatic kin are founded

THE PARADIGM OF THE HOUSE

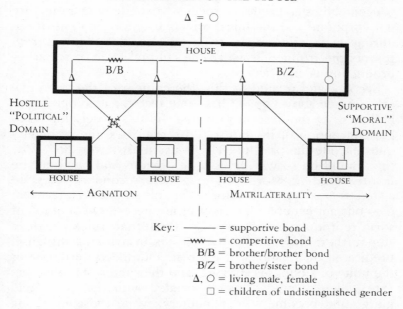

Key: ———— = supportive bond
        —ww— = competitive bond
        B/B = brother/brother bond
        B/Z = brother/sister bond
        Δ, O = living male, female
        □ = children of undistinguished gender

on those between M/MB (Z = B) and between F/FB
(B = B), respectively—that is, on intrahouse linkages in the
ascendant generation. It will also be clear that *descent* transforms these intrahouse relationships into the opposed domains. In other words, the theory of descent, which here
implies the transmission of values associated with these basic
relationships, is a principle simultaneously of structural constitution and of value reproduction. This has one significant
corollary: since descent transmits value, and the latter is ordered as an opposition between the domains, descent must
necessarily reproduce both domains and their properties at
the same time. This is precisely what it does: it generates a
bilateral universe. As we have already noted, the *losika,* the
effective network of kin, is just such a bilateral universe; its
transformation into a stock occurs when marriage is introduced into the equation. We shall elaborate upon this
shortly. At the present juncture, the points to be stressed are
that descent (*a*) generates the opposed domains from the
internal structure of the house, (*b*) links houses across generations, and (*c*) formally constitutes a bilateral universe.

Perhaps this begins to explain why the ideology of descent is conceptually significant in a society where descent groups are not corporate and the lineal principle is not the basis of enduring aggregation; apart from all else, this ideology represents the manner in which the cultural logic of social reproduction is experienced.

Second, and related to this, the content of the ascriptive rule set (see above, pp. 37 ff.)—in effect, the ideological embodiment of the descent principle—is also closely linked to the conception of the house. Of these rules, the secondary ones encode the precept "The house must never die." Why this should be so will by now be obvious and need not be labored further. Moreover, that these secondary rules are stated as *prescriptions* is critical, for this stresses the fact that the constant generation of houses is a necessary condition of social reproduction in this system. The tertiary rules take this a step further. The reproductive cycle is, in an important sense, predicated on relations of interest. During its early phases the unity of siblings is stressed, and their interests converge. Later, they diverge: those associated with the B/Z bond merge and become complementary, while those involving brothers eventually become opposed. This process is entailed in the rules of guardianship. Until the house reaches the point at which it is ready to fragment, its social and material interests are fused and vested in the *role* of the (external) guardian. But when this critical point is reached, its occupant must relinquish the position or be removed, whereupon the reproductive cycle may take its course.[24] Finally, the primary prescriptions order the domains that are generated from the bonds within the house. As we have stressed, the matrilateral domain is internally undifferentiated, being characterized by moral unity and complementarity of interest. In contrast, the agnatic universe is differentiated; it is here that most sociopolitical and material resources are located and distributed with reference to rank. The primary rules give form to this opposition. On the one hand, they leave the matrilateral realm solidary and *un*ranked. Within it, relations are thus perceived as similar in quality; they are privileged and non-negotiable. On the other hand, these rules are the basis of agnatic differentiation, for they stratify the linkages that derive from the B/B and F/S relationships. By extension, they also embody the principles according to which houses are integrated into higher-order aggregations—principles that, as demonstrated earlier, are given practical expression in the course of political processes.

The analysis is not yet complete, however. There are other societies, for example, in which houses are basic structural units, sharing a similar pattern of interests and relations, and yet are contained within embracing corporate groups. Furthermore, their inclusion in such groups need not preclude the negotiability of rank between agnates or the attribution of moral unity to the matrilateral domain. The distinctive character of the Tswana sociocultural order, therefore, is not to be found solely in the conception of the house. We suggest that it lies rather in the relationship between this conception and the particularities of the marriage system. It is to the substantive nature of this relationship that we now turn.

The Marriage System

Among the Tswana, it will be recalled, the basic range of exogamic proscriptions includes only ego's house and those of his parents, his children, and his siblings' children, i.e., those involved directly in the reproductive cycle.[25] The establishment of unions beyond this range necessarily occurs within a field of categorical relations associated with the values and expectations implied in the conception of the house. To reiterate: agnation = rivalry/hostility; matrilaterality = support/privilege; remote kinship (bonds outside the two domains) = neutrality (see chap. 5). Affinity itself also implies a valuation: it is characterized by easy cooperativeness: " 'Wife-givers' and 'wife-takers' are equal" (Kuper 1975a:73). The reason for this will become evident; for now, it is enough to stress that, in formal terms, conjugal exchange must be situated within a domain of hostile relations, or one of existing alliance, or the neutral world beyond.

According to Schapera (1950, 1957b, 1963b), all Tswana state the same order of marriage preferences: MBD → FBD → FZD → MZD, an order actually followed by commoners. Senior royals, on the other hand, who are more likely to marry close kin of *all* categories, appear to select their FBDs more frequently than their MBDs. Schapera explains this by suggesting that unions between patrilateral parallel cousins transform rivalrous agnatic ties into egalitarian affinal ones and thus neutralize them; in contrast, unions with matrilateral cross-cousins provide less-powerful males with a route to positions of influence. An explanation in these terms, however, assumes that the values associated with affinity are realized once the relevant bond is established. But this raises three problems. First, in FBD unions, the agnatic component of the relationships with the WF and WB—and the divergence of interest it implies—does not simply disappear when overlaid by an affinal link. How, then, can marriage actually alter the *content* of the existing ties? Second, because the prior occurrence of FBD unions ensures that persons within the *losika* are related agnatically and matrilaterally in the first place, any particular "agnatic" union must take place within a field of persons *already* connected by precisely the kinds of relations this union is ostensibly intended to create. And, third, Tswana often insist that individuals do not necessarily behave in accordance with normative expectations. Yet Schapera's observation is essentially correct. The resolution of the paradox implied in all this begins, we suggest, in the structure of choice.[26]

Although ethnographic accounts tend to order marriage preferences in terms of cousinship, and informants will respond readily in these terms to questioning, spontaneous exegeses suggest that this calculus of kin relationship does not configure choice; rather, it renders it meaningful after the event. In the everyday world of the Tswana, it is often impossible actually to select a spouse on the basis of cousinship alone, for, as is well known (see pp. 31 ff.), the most conspicuous implication of intradescent-group marriage is its generation of multiple ties; in such systems few people can ever isolate a single-stranded linkage with a close kinsman, and in fact, as the established conception of the *losika* suggests, Tswana do not believe that they ought necessarily to be able to do so (we have already stressed that the confusion of relational categories is culturally inscribed). This leaves the conundrum, to which we shall return, of why Tswana recognize cousinship as a meaningful mode of rationalizing preference at all.

The structure of choice, as it presents itself to Tswana,

involves three major categories, each corresponding to an established set of values. An individual may decide to seek a spouse from among (a) those recognized as agnates, (b) those classified as matrilateral kin, or (c) those who are distantly related or unrelated. To make clear the implications of this pattern of choice, it is necessary to describe briefly the way in which Tswana themselves perceive the alternatives that confront them.

Broadly speaking, the three categories of choice are conceptualized in terms of the potential risks and returns inhering in the affinal relations they may generate. Unions with unrelated persons and distant kin are seen as relatively uncomplicated in this respect; that is, they are thought to involve the prospect of neither great risk nor great return. They may yield the expected benefits normatively associated with affinity: a mutually advantageous partnership of equals between a man and his wife's immediate kin. If they do not, they can either be dissolved at no substantial cost to anyone, or they may be perpetuated if the parties cease their efforts to pursue their interests in the sphere of conjugality and affinity (see below).[27]

When a man enters a union with a woman to whom he is only affinally or matrilaterally linked, thereby taking a partner from the supportive domain, he reinforces an existing set of bonds. In this case, no value contradiction arises, since the new linkage reinforces established ones of the same content. In fact, this is usually the stated motivation behind such choices: the existing alliance is already tried and tested and is known, therefore, to be worth perpetuating in the next generation. But there is held to be a degree of risk involved, for an unsuccessful union may *introduce* tension, violate the moral unity of the domain, and damage privileged relations. A corollary of this is that an individual who seeks a spouse from this source is constrained not to withdraw later. This type of union may thus narrow the room for subsequent maneuver; nevertheless, its advantages are anticipated to be relatively secure.

Marriage to a partner linked by a multiple bond—to one who is drawn, that is, from the hostile agnatic universe but is also a matrilateral kinswoman—entails a fundamental contradiction.[28] As informants are wont to acknowledge, a union of this kind involves much greater complexity and considerable skill in social management. The major risks and the potential returns associated with it derive from the fact that such unions articulate the rival (agnatic) careers of wife-giver and wife-taker, who may well be engaged in efforts to "eat" one another, each seeking to reduce the other to clientage. While the creation of a conjugal link does not, of itself, resolve the issue either way, men are here brought into the sort of relationship that gives access to their affines' affairs. In this, the participation of the wife and her children may be crucial, for they may be strategically recruited by either party to influence the actions of the other. In short, relations between agnatically linked, rivalrous in-laws are frequently characterized by subtle and long-term attempts to establish social and material indebtedness. Success in this respect is thought to represent a substantial return, but the dangers involved are concomitantly large. Other things aside, unions of this category often prove the most difficult to withdraw from without heavy cost. From the analytical perspective, however, there is the further complication of the value contradiction itself.

The contradiction implicit in a multiple bond is held to be impossible to sustain in the behavioral context (see chap. 5), for a person who is not a neutral outsider must be either an ally or a potential rival. In categorical terms, as we might expect, the boundaries of the domains are not confused. However, because social linkages *are* labeled—as they must be, following the logic of the system—there has to be some extrinsic criterion according to which ambiguities and contradictions are pragmatically managed. It is a matter of empirical observation, moreover, that, even when the term for affine is used reciprocally (see below), kin terms will *also* be employed in address and reference, especially in public contexts. How, then, are multiple bonds reduced and labeled? The most obvious rule would lie in the proximity of relationship, but this is demonstrably not applied (see Cohen and Comaroff 1976); indeed, it is difficult to see how it could be in such a fluid social universe. The answer lies, rather, in the content of the relations obtaining between wife-givers and wife-takers and the manner in which that content is coded. Thus, when a wife-taker enjoys a position of *clear* sociopolitical subordination *or* superordination—that is, where the state of the relationship is sufficiently unequal to mitigate rivalry—the wife-giver will be regarded as MB, his daughter as MBD, and her brother as MBS; for in this situation the bond is one of complementarity rather than competitiveness. Conversely, when the parties are more equal and more competitively arrayed, the patrilateral component will take precedence. Finally, in contexts in which the actors, wishing to avoid imposing any construction whatsoever, assert (usually temporary) equivalence or else sustain ambiguity, the affinal linkage will be terminologically stressed.[29]

The relational definitions surrounding marriage and affinity are not, then, assigned by "objective" genealogical criteria. This would, in fact, be impossible with respect to most agnatic unions in a so-called endogamous system of this type. The labels employed represent, rather, a set of constant markers—their points of reference deriving from an order of constitutive values—in terms of which potentially ambiguous everyday political relations can be meaningfully construed. At the same time, this code provides a medium through which the management of these relations may proceed. Thus, for example, when a party to a bond wishes to assert his superordination or to acknowledge his subordination or wishes merely to denote the supportive complementarity of the bond, he will tend to emphasize that his affines are his *bomalome* (MBs). If power relations are clearly unequal and/or noncompetitive and a complementary relationship is mutually recognized, this designation may be accepted by all concerned. For a partner who does so, it may legitimize access to a measure of influence through a prominent in-law; for one seeking to express his seniority, the assertion that the wife-giver is a matrilateral kinsman implies that the latter is no longer a member of the inner circle of his senior agnates and is thus ineligible to compete with them for status. Of course, wife-givers may strive to resist such a construction by stressing the agnatic connection and, therefore, their relative equality and involvement within that circle. In fact, sociopolitical processes are often marked by rival efforts to construe linkages in this way, and Tswana tend to be highly sensitive to, and interested in, the nuances of labeling.

All this, in turn, illuminates the way in which Tswana

marriage preferences have been documented elsewhere. We concentrate again on MBD and FBD unions, since the other forms are largely residual.[30] It will be remembered that both royals and commoners are reported to express a greater preference for the MBD type but to differ in the incidence of choice (see p. 53). We suggest, as Schapera (1957b, 1963b) himself implies, that the critical analytical distinction to be made is not so much between royals and commoners as between the politically prominent and nonprominent, that is, between (a) those whose households and/or segments either hold an office or are in a position to seek one and (b) those for whom effective access to authority is remote. Though members of these two categories may state the same preferential order in response to inquiry, they in fact differ in the way they rationalize their choices. The politically nonprominent see unions within the domain of support and alliance, with partners already recognized as nonagnatic kin, as a genuinely attractive prospect. The returns are reasonably assured and, where wife-givers are powerful, offer the possibility of relatively influential clientage. But—and this is just as significant and is perhaps more frequently the case—when such persons do enter conjugal bonds with multiply related women, it is the matrilateral component that will most often be stressed, for wife-takers coming from the less-prominent sector of the population *are* often in positions of unequivocal inferiority or noncompetitive complementarity. This makes it clear why the politically nonprominent—the category into which the majority of commoners happen to fall—prefer MBD marriages. This preference expresses power relations as much as it expresses "objective" patterns of choice.

In contrast, the politically prominent do more often elect to marry those defined as agnates, for it is the politically ambitious and powerful who show themselves most prepared to take the high-risk option and choose partners linked to them by multiple ties. This implies that they are willing to make the effort to neutralize rivalries, alter the construction of relationships, and assert the noncompetitiveness of affines by stressing the matrilateral component of the bond. The strategy, in its baldest form, is to marry a FBD and seek to transform her into a MBD by "eating" her father and/or brothers.[31] The reported preference of the politically powerful for MBD marriage, then, refers less to abstract issues of selection than to the ideal embodied in the successful management of affinity. Nor is it surprising that FBD unions are noted actually to occur more frequently among the influential, for it is these individuals who engage in agnatic rivalries with high stakes and whose relationships do not, despite their strategic efforts, resolve lightly into ones of complementarity, of clear subordination or superordination. That most of their conjugal and affinal bonds are denoted in agnatic terms reflects the pervasive ambiguities surrounding power relations. It is, quite simply, not easy to "eat" a prominent wife-giver and relocate him in the matrilateral domain, although it sometimes happens.

The two categories—the politically prominent and the politically nonprominent—of course represent ideal types; individuals in fact may move, or be moved, from one to the other; moreover, from the actor's perspective it is through a successful marital career, among other things, that he may strive to increase his prominence (see chap. 5).

The paradox noted earlier now stands resolved, as does the problem of the connection between cousinship and the rationalization of marriage choice. It is not the fact of marriage per se that generates alliances or transforms relationships. Rather, unions create the context within which affinity may be negotiated and careers articulated. They occur, that is, in the course of sociopolitical processes that are characterized, in the indigenous perception, by the pursuit of individual interests—processes in which the assigning of relational labels is the medium for construing the "state of play." In this respect the Tswana observation makes patent sense: behavior is *not* motivated by the uncomplicated desire to conform with normative expectation. Nevertheless, there *is* a manifest correspondence between normative expectations and the content of existing bonds. The reason for this will be evident. These normative expectations—which are, in fact, an ordered set of values represented metonymically in categorical kin terms—represent the means by which interactional processes are meaningfully constituted as they unfold. The correspondence between norm and the substance of relations is, in other words, indexical and dialectical, not motivational. When Tswana state that a MB and his ZS never fight, they are passing neither a metaphysical nor a statistical judgment; they are merely implying that, when the content of interaction conforms to the values associated with the matrilateral domain, it is indexed and encoded by the appropriate label.[32] That cousinship is a construction after—or, more precisely, of —the fact is equally clear and requires no further explanation.

Let us return to the implications of this marriage pattern for the sociocultural system at large. As we have seen, the significant categories of choice are constituted by the agnatic and matrilateral domains and the neutral world beyond them. In terms of the logic of this "endogamous" system, however, the *coexistence*—or, more precisely, the conflation—of the preferred agnatic and matrilateral forms is particularly important because each has different social corollaries. Were it to occur alone, matrilateral cross-cousin marriage in this context would imply aggregation and hierarchy, for it would entail the emergence of wife-giving groups, defined by descent, in complementary relationships to wife-taking ones (see Fox 1967:208–12). Patrilateral parallel cousin marriage, in contrast, blurs group boundaries because it generates categorical linkages of all types between close kin, and, in doing so, it potentiates competitive and individualistic relations between (relative) equals.[33] This fact, in turn, suggests the presence of two contradictory tendencies in Tswana society: between hierarchy and equality, on the one hand, and collectivism and individualism on the other.

The phenomenology of marriage processes now becomes relevant once again. The point of agnatic unions, as it is indigenously conceived, lies in the transformation of rivalrous relations into complementary matrilateral ones. This transformation may be experienced, in sociopolitical terms, as a strategic effort to subordinate others or to accept subordination and its rewards. But it also connotes the replacement of an exchange between relative equals by an alliance between unequals. When this alliance is perpetuated across generations, it implies the emergence of a *group* of classificatory *bomalome* (MBs), whose point of agnatic connection to the wifetakers is then viewed as remote. One example of this, among the Tshidi, is provided by the boo Makgetla, a line founded by a man who, despite having been the first officeholder, is now regarded as having been the junior brother of the eponymous founder of the chiefdom. The descendants of Makgetla and Tshidi exchanged women over several generations. In the course of extended sociopolitical processes, however, the former became subordinated to their chiefly (agnatic) affines, who consistently appear to have made them out to be *bomalome*. Gradually they came to be identified as a collectivity enjoying the complementary role of king-makers and chiefly allies, a position they continue to hold today. But this tendency toward collectivization and hierarchization is simultaneously counterbalanced by the incidence of agnatic marriage, which fragments groups and categories and redefines linkages between precisely those who might otherwise solidify into alliance units.

Apart from the singular example of the boo Makgetla, the generation of hierarchy and enduring aggregation is therefore countered in the very process of its development. At the ideological level, this fact illuminates the indigenous view that affinity implies equality, even though relations between some affines may be distinctly unequal; because the elaboration of stratified alliance units is constantly broken down, the social field is perceived to consist of an assemblage of individuals and impermanent aggregations regularly confronting each other in an essentially fluid universe. At the systemic level, this means that the fundamental value opposition, and its expression in the two domains of agnation and matrilaterality, can never be finally eliminated, at least while "endogamous" marriage persists in its present form. This opposition may be resolved in particular instances (some people may succeed in transforming their agnates into matrilaterals in the course of the conjugal process), and, when this occurs, it reaffirms the *manifest* political value expressed in the structure of choice. But, as a contradiction in the system, the coexistence of the two marriage patterns remains to reproduce basic structures and social values and thereby to motivate and give meaning to interaction.

This contradiction—its inevitable reproduction at the systemic level but the possibility of its pragmatic resolution in the everyday world—does not merely explain the relevance of marriage in the sociocultural order of the Tswana; it also

provides an essential link between that order and the emphasis on individualism and pragmatism that pervades community life.

Culture, Ideology, and Social Management

Our analysis of the marriage system and the systemic and
experiential contradictions it entails serves to reintroduce
a theme that we have stressed throughout. From the individual perspective the primary characteristic of the multiple
bonds produced by close-kin marriage is the confusion
of social and cultural categories that they entail; they are
generically ambiguous and contradictory and do not fall
neatly into one or the other domain of value. While it may be
theoretically possible to sustain such relations, in practice it is
not, for sociopolitical processes involve the intersecting biographies of actors, and this requires coding if it is to have any
social or political currency. But the principles of coding,
which themselves derive from the semantics of the value
order, are embodied in a set of metonymic labels whose application entails the *reduction* of contradiction in all but exceptional circumstances. There is no established everyday
usage for "multiply linked relative"; both within and beyond
the *losika,* a person must be construed as *some*thing.
Moreover, within the agnatic domain, which is ordered in
terms of the ascriptive rules, the constant and inevitable
negotiation of rank and status (and therefore of power relations) depends for its meaning on the precise differentiation of kinsmen; indeed, as will now be evident, such
differentiation is an essential feature of sociopolitical activity
among the Tswana.

Social interaction, then, implies that significant relationships must be meaningfully construed even if the act of construal connotes merely the perpetuation of existing definitions
(see below). The corollary is that an individual has no choice
but to contrive his universe, and particularly the bonds within
his or her *losika,* where a large proportion of the important
ones are clustered. If he does not do so actively, his universe
will be contrived for him, for inactivity or repetitive conduct
in this area is seen as no less consequential, no less a
contrivance. It is impossible to avoid appearing to be a

manager, either by intent or default, for almost all behavior is assumed by others to be strategically motivated and interest-seeking. This makes it easy to understand why community life is seen to be redolent with secretive intrigue, why mystical evil is considered a ubiquitous, if lamentable, human pursuit, and why social aggregation, the surface patterns of which undergo regular transformation (see pp. 44–46), is viewed as a function of temporarily coincident interest. These perceptions express an ideology of pragmatic individualism in the context of a system whose constitution ensures that reality is both fluid and enigmatical. It will be clear, moreover, that the negotiation of marriage and affinity, status, and property relations represent the primary substantive elements in the continuing process of its construction.

Vansina (1964) has told of three highly independent Bushong thinkers, one of whom had concluded that there is no reality and that all experience is shifting. For the Tswana, the latter observation describes an endemic characteristic of their sociocultural order. However, this order at the same time generates the manifest values and ideals to which individuals may aspire in everyday terms. Specifically, the fact that some agnates may be transformed into matrilateral kin and others relegated to subordinate rank, with all that this entails, gives point to managerial enterprise and renders it comprehensible. In other words, these values provide the terms in which the Tswana sociopolitical world may be purposively navigated. Its fundamental contradictions may be reproduced at the systemic level, but, if they were experientially unresolvable, social life would have no meaning or coherence and the ideology of pragmatic individualism would make little sense.

We have come some of the way toward answering the conundrum with which we began the present chapter, for we have shown how the essential ambiguity of the lived-in universe and the concomitant emphasis on individualism and social management are the products of contradictions in the constitutive order that motivates the system at large. But we have not yet accounted satisfactorily for the perception of constraint, a problem that is particularly important for comprehending the relationship between rules and processes.

Career, Constraint, and Structural Reproduction

In chapters 5 and 6 we shall demonstrate that the Tswana life-cycle is marked by a gradual increase of constraint upon individuals in the management of their careers. Despite the fact that a person begins adulthood by being located in a set of linkages previously negotiated by others, the very nature of social existence is such that he *must* act upon them, whether or not he does so actively and deliberately. For, as soon as he is drawn into the marriage process and the devolution of property and status, ambiguities are *introduced* into his network of relationships, and he thereby becomes involved in their construction and definition. The data we shall present later indicate that such ambiguity, which is an endemic feature of conjugal-type unions and the transmission of rank, allows Tswana room for maneuver in sociopolitical interaction; moreover, some seek to sustain it for as long as possible. We shall also see, however, that it is easy for men to lose the initiative in this respect and to become cumulatively and inexorably trapped by the consequences of their managerial activities—as do, for example, Molefe (cases 8 and 9) and Lesoka (case 25). Indeed, the progressive manipulation of relations and resources and hence the effort to control the social field have the effect of locating the actor himself ever more tightly within that field and, consequently, of removing its internal ambiguities and reducing its negotiability, at least as far as his own position is concerned. By attempting to build a set of linkages around himself, he may also be contriving linkages between other people and may, as a result, initiate processes over which he may easily lose control. Lesoka's predicament (case 25) exemplifies this: the corollary of his actions was to draw together a complex set of relations, thereby consolidating a previously fragmented segment against himself. As a result, the lack of definitional clarity, upon which his managerial activities had earlier depended, was eliminated. Although Lesoka himself did not become aware of his loss of initiative until late in the day, many Tswana appear to envisage the life-cycle as being characterized by a gradually diminishing potentiality for social management of this kind. Thus, for example, there is a tendency among career-minded Tshidi, in the course of their marital biographies, to seek early alliances with unrelated partners and later ones with kin; it is a pattern that reflects both an increasing preparedness to take risks and an acknowledgment that unions with agnates, being progressively more difficult to redefine without great cost, typically involve the growth of pragmatic constraints on the strategic manipulation of ambiguity.

The subtle equation involved in sustaining and eliminating ambiguity is one that most Tswana face at some point, although there is wide variation in the degree to which such subtleties are apprehended and successfully negotiated. As we showed above, the politicoresidential hierarchy represents the context of all strategic activity, for within it are located the manifest political values to which this activity is addressed. As a consequence, much of the purpose of social management, from the standpoint of any person, lies in situating himself somewhere in the hierarchy. And, while the avoidance of status definition—in all its aspects—may facilitate the achievement of an advantageous position, it follows that ambiguity must be removed once such a position has been achieved and/or no further effort is to be made to improve it. This does not mean that it is impossible thereafter to renegotiate the relevant relations, but it does become ever more difficult; this is why some ambitious men bide their time before laying claim to a position.[34] Just as failure may imply entanglement in an unfortunate predicament, achievement is ultimately to be expressed by defining one's relative location in the sociopolitical field; both are characterized by the reduction of options. Career cycles therefore move with varying rapidity toward this denouement. Individuals differ in their decisions as to when to close their options finally—if, that is, they still retain sufficient initiative to make such decisions—since circumstantial factors usually play an important part. In general, however, it seems that they are believed to do so, where possible, when they perceive their conjugal and property relations to have run their full course as social investments. This point may be reached because they have failed to negotiate successful alliances and have become resigned to the fact, or they have been "eaten" by others, or they have contrived such a strong position that they have no reason to doubt the value of existing linkages. Whatever the particular motivation, this point is often marked by two symbolic acts: the transfer of bridewealth and the final distribution of estates.

Even if a man could sustain ambiguity until his death, then, there is an evident tendency to remove it once and for all in his later years. This tendency reveals something of the systemic limits upon the negotiation of the social universe. As one Tshidi informant, Rre-S, suggested, in reflecting on his career,

I am a man of the world, and I had three women [*basadi*]. I just left the first [a previously unrelated partner], and she took the daughter. I paid *mokwele*,[35] and we lived together. But there was no *bogadi* [bridewealth]. When her father took me to the *kgotla,* I said we were not married; she was just a concubine. Her father said we were married; but the chief listened to me, and I only got a fine for seduction. The second woman [a remote agnate] died after we had a son, also before I paid *bogadi.* And the third woman [a multiply linked partner] is still with me. But the time has come for me to pay *bogadi* for both. All my children are becoming men of the world too. I have had a career [a life]. I can rest, and they must know where they come from, where they belong. It's the turn of the next generation. So I must pay *bogadi.* Then there will be a feast, and I will kill a beast. Everyone will know my two houses and that I am a respected old man whose children come from this ward.[36]

The same informant added, on another occasion: "If children cannot know where they are from, everything is finished; there will be no nation [*morafe*]."

These statements allude to a conception of the relationship between individual career cycles and the reproduction of structural forms. Above all, they indicate that the final definition of the status of parents is seen as a prerequisite for the initiation of the independent careers of their progeny. This does not mean that children may not in retrospect attempt to redefine status relations in the ascendant generations; on the contrary, they may later do so actively, as may others. Nonetheless, the Tswana view has it that, in order to engage in the negotiation of rank and relations, "they must know where they come from." The status and structural location of their houses—and, therefore, both the unions that produced them and the property relations in which they are involved—provide a necessary baseline, a point of departure in the social field. An individual cannot, as Tswana see matters, begin to define alliances and oppositions or compete for position unless a set of ordered linkages exists to start with. Indeed, the genealogical mode of negotiating the social universe would lack a frame of reference otherwise; it is impossible to transform something that is not there in the first place. As the text states, "If children cannot know where they are from, everything is finished; there will be no nation."

The processual character of marriage and the devolution of property and status, then, are closely linked to the articulation of career and structure. This is illuminated by the nature of bridewealth arrangements among the Tswana. *Bogadi,* whose transfer is typically delayed until late in the developmental cycle, is a dominant metaphor for a series of critical connections in the social universe (see chap. 5). For, as we shall demonstrate, the definition of everyday unions is intrinsically ambiguous and negotiable for much of their duration, and this tendency is inscribed in the logic of their formation and the semantics of their classification. A union, if it lasts, ultimately *becomes* a marriage when, with the removal of ambiguity, its sociopolitical content is determined. At this juncture, with the passage of bridewealth, it is reduced to structure. The transfer of the marriage prestation, therefore, marks the anchoring of a union within the social field, locating it in a set of formal relationships and statuses that may subsequently be renegotiated by its offspring. It also signals the moment at which the sociopolitical processes involving members of one generation are reckoned and the initiative for social management is transmitted to the next. For the individual, then, a career may begin with the transfer of bridewealth for a mother and draw to an end with the presentation of bridewealth for a wife. This is reflected in the fact that children among the Tshidi may present *bogadi* to their mother's agnates if, for some reason, their father (or guardian) has failed to do this by the time they reach middle age. Demographic factors sometimes, of course, intervene to affect the precise timing of these events, but the general pattern appears clear.

The cyclical pattern of bridewealth transfers corresponds with the devolutionary process, which effectively starts when a man enters his first union and should conclude at, or soon before, his death.[37] Moreover, in terms of structural regularity, these two cycles are intimately connected with the reproduction of the house; for, as they reach their end, the fragmentation of the unit is about to occur. It is at this stage that the B/Z bond is released from the natal grouping to become the point of origin for a new set of matrilateral ties, while the B/B one is gradually elaborated into a field of agnatic rivalries. This is also the moment at which the siblings begin to contrive their own conjugal careers and initiate the devolutionary process yet again. The reproduction of houses and the management of careers are therefore mutually interdependent, since each makes possible, and places final limits on, the other. In this respect, the constitutive order and the lived-in social universe exist in a dialectical relationship, motivated and given form by the same contradictions, which lie at the heart of the system.

The sociocultural order of the Tswana, then, encompasses two analytically distinguishable levels.

The first level, *the constitutive order,* is contained in a set of value oppositions and structural elements. These have their point of origin in the conception of the house and its internal relations. We have sought to show how marriage and descent are integral to this order and to do so in such a way as to reveal the fundamental contradictions in the system, its semantic foundations, and the principles of its reproduction.

The second level, which we have described as *the lived-in (experienced) universe,* is marked by great fluidity in social and political ties. It is a shifting, enigmatic, and managerial world in which persons repeatedly negotiate their relations in terms of a set of constant referents encoded in categorical labels. As such, it is a world seen from within to be pervaded by an ideology of pragmatic individualism. The character of the lived-in universe, however, is shaped by the constitutive order, in that the latter establishes the manifest sociopolitical values to which this ideology and the activities conducted in its name are addressed. It also gives form to the logic in terms of which competitive processes—and their corollary, social aggregation—are ordered and rationalized.

As this formulation suggests, surface social arrangements —and they may assume a wide range of forms—represent the historical realization of the constitutive order at any point in time. The relationship between the two component levels of the system is, however, a dialectical one, for processes in the lived-in universe may, under certain conditions, transform the constitutive order and the values subsumed within it. It is beyond the scope of this study to explore further such processes of transformation or to consider the wider theoretical implications of this approach (see the Conclusion). The analysis of the sociocultural order presented in this chapter is intended primarily as a basis for understanding the logic of dispute processes. We turn now to the normative repertoire that in the Tswana view gives form to everyday social life.

The Normative Repertoire

3

In chapter 1 we introduced *mekgwa le melao ya Setswana,* the body of norms that Tswana perceive as ordering their everyday lives and providing the terms of discourse in the event of a quarrel. We now discuss the nature of these norms and the logic of their invocation in dispute processes.

Descriptive Features
General Characteristics

Two features of *mekgwa le melao* are immediately striking. The first is the color and quality of the language by means of which these rules are expressed. As Schapera has repeatedly shown (especially 1966), Tswana thoroughly enjoy talking about their rules and often do so in speech that is rich in proverb and metaphor. The second lies in the fact that, rather than constituting a coherent and internally consistent set, *mekgwa le melao* comprise a loosely ordered and undifferentiated repertoire of norms, the substantive content of which varies widely in its nature, value, and specificity. This is reflected in indigenous ideas concerning the semantics of the phrase itself. The terms *mekgwa* and *melao* have drawn the attention of a number of writers, some of whom have suggested that they are clearly distinguished by the Tswana themselves. Thus Casalis (1861:228) and Ellenberger[1] have stated that *melao* refers specifically to laws enacted by a chief in his *kgotla,* while *mekgwa* are traditional usages. At the level of purely formal statement, this would appear to be true. Informants will sometimes observe that a chief can declare only a *molao,* not a *mokgwa,* and, conversely, that a custom not

70

associated with chiefly legislation is always a *mokgwa,* never a *molao.* The Rolong, in fact, tend to emphasize the temporal dimension implicit in the distinction: *mekgwa* have their origins in antiquity, while *melao* seem to have acquired recognition and social approval within human memory. But as Schapera (1938:36; 1943a:4) suggests and our data confirm:

> the two terms are really not sharply discriminated in ordinary Tswana usage: the same rule of conduct may be spoken of on one occasion as *molao,* and on another as *mokgwa.*

Schapera goes on to note that, if pressed, a Motswana may suggest that a person can be punished in court for transgressing a *molao* but not for infringements of *mekgwa.* It should be stressed, however, that this observation was never spontaneously offered by an informant. It was only when confronted with a fieldworker's initial search for precise definitions that the two categories were (often tentatively) differentiated. Moreover, in accounting for examples that did not sustain the distinction, Tswana either agreed that the latter did not hold up in practice or they simply reclassified the transgressed norm. In any case, no one seemed to think the question especially important, and a few informants stated expressly that it derived from a Western misperception. Furthermore, indigenous dispute-settlement agencies never operate on the assumption, implicit or explicit, that the discrimination between *mekgwa* and *melao* has any pragmatic significance.

The undifferentiated nature of the normative repertoire is also inscribed in the way Tswana speak of the concepts that would be expected to make up its constituent categories. Schapera (1938:35) lists these as:

> *popego* or *maitseo* (manners, etiquette, polite usages), *letso* or *moetlo* (custom, traditional usage), *tlwaelo* (habitual practice), *moila* (taboo), and *tshwanno* or *tshwanelo* (duty, obligation).

These categories are not exclusive or bounded, and Tswana rarely attempt to classify substantive norms in terms of them. Furthermore, they are not clearly established as a *set,* which informants will commonly identify when asked about the component elements of *mekgwa le melao.* The list is, quite simply, an observer's inventory of vernacular terms, not the expression of an articulated taxonomy. In short, the classification of norms by their content, origin, or any other criterion holds little interest for most Tswana; it is regarded as largely irrelevant in the day-to-day life that the repertoire is held to regulate. As a Rolong informant suggested:

Mekgwa le melao are different. They come from many things. Some are just our tradition, they come from long, long ago. We do not know much about that. Some just become *mekgwa* because people are doing a certain thing all the time, and we expect that they should go on doing these things. Some come from the *kgotla;* they are given by the chief. Some are just from the way we live: where our places are, who we inherit from, how we marry or grow our crops, our duties to others. But it does not matter where they come from. They are all just *mekgwa le melao* today.

This statement also underlines another general feature of the repertoire, the fact that from the Tswana perspective it embraces both a set of ideal patterns and expectations derived from the regularities of everyday behavior.

Substantive Features

Being perceived as a somewhat amorphous repertoire, *mekgwa le melao* embody a range of norms widely varying in their specificity and in the value attributed to them. This is true even of the norms most frequently invoked in the course of disputes. Thus *mekgwa le melao* include precise substantive prescriptions (e.g., the youngest son should inherit his mother's homestead), precepts of a more general character (e.g., *lentswe la moswi ga le tlolwe,* "the voice of a dead man is not transgressed"), and ideal principles of a broad, abstract variety (e.g., agnates should live in harmony with one another). But such levels of specificity are not expressly demarcated by the Tswana themselves. There are no vernacular labels by means of which norms can be arranged according to this criterion; whatever its location on the implied continuum, a particular norm is expressed simply as one item in an internally undifferentiated repertoire.

Gluckman (1955a) and Moore (1969), among others, have noted this characteristic in the normative orders of other African societies. Indeed, Gluckman has argued that it is the presence of different levels of specificity in Barotse legal precepts that facilitates the precision with which their judges may apply them in actual cases. As case 1 indicates, the Tswana may also, under certain circumstances, abstract precise substantive norms by a process of reduction from more general precepts.

CASE 1: THE HEADMAN'S "TRIBUTE"

In a case heard at the Rolong chief's *kgotla* at Mafikeng in 1969, the chief fined a headman for soliciting a gift in return for a land allocation. Previously there had been no specific or explicit rule governing such an action on the part of an officeholder. But the headman's behavior, which departed conspicuously from common practice, could be comprehended and evaluated in terms of two quite separate normative expectations: (*a*) that powerful headmen often received tribute from members of their politicoadministrative units and might legitimately expect to do so and (*b*) that every citizen had the right to be allocated sufficient residential, agricultural, and pastoral land for his needs. The parties involved in the dispute did not differ over the facts of the case; rather, the issue between them revolved around the question of whether headmen could properly assert the expectation of tribute in the context of land allocation. No stated proscription barred it; but neither did precedent suggest that it was accepted practice. In short, the repertoire simply did not include a substantive norm to cover this contingency. The defendant argued that he had acted within his rights, since this followed from the more general precept that allowed headmen to receive tribute. The complainant, on the other hand, disclaimed this by reduction from the broader *mokgwa* of the entitlement of citizens to free land allocations. He argued that the headman had in fact been trying to *sell,* rather than allocate, the land to him. In his judgment, the chief also construed the headman's behavior by means of a reduction from broad precept to substantive normative statement. He invoked the abstract notion that chiefs and headmen "should not sell [*rekisa*] the land like this, because it does not serve the Rolong." The precise injunction follows logically from the more general one.

The coexistence within the repertoire of norms of varying specificity clearly affords Tswana dispute-settlement agencies a degree of room for maneuver in the handling of cases, although the reduction from general precept to substantive rule is less of an omnipresent principle in Tswana processes than Gluckman (1955a) seems to suggest for the Barotse.

But equally important is the fact that the undifferentiated nature of the repertoire is also perceived to create a strategic resource for disputants, for different *mekgwa le melao,* as we have already implied, may be adduced in such a way as to contradict one another and hence to legitimize competing constructions of reality. Such normative conflict may reside at two levels: the situational and the logical.

Situational conflict occurs when two norms or sets of norms, not necessarily logically discontinuous or incompatible, are invoked in such a way as to impose rival constructions on an agreed set of facts.[2] Although it is possible for a debate of this kind to involve a dispute over the validity of a particular normative precept stated by one party, this is not the usual pattern. More generally, litigants assume the theoretical validity of the norms invoked—or at least do not deny it—but attempt to assert the *situational precedence* of one norm over another. Typically, too, the competing norms at issue in this type of confrontation are located at different levels of specificity. This may be illustrated by the following example:

As noted in chapter 2, the Tswana perceive the relationship between a FB and his BS as an endemically rivalrous and disharmonious one, a fact that is reflected in court records. This endemic rivalry is expressed in the competition between close agnates over control of property and position (see also chap. 6); and it tends to become particularly acute when a FB assumes guardianship over his BS. The FB has the right and obligation to supervise the property and affairs of his brother's children if they are minors when their father dies. But, as our account will indicate, Tswana believe that guardians frequently manage such property to their own advantage and, hence, to the disadvantage of their brother's children. Typically, as the eldest BS grows to adulthood, he begins to agitate for control over the estate, arguing his right to do so as heir to his father's status as household head. Often his FB resists by claiming that the heir is not yet old enough. In doing so, he exploits the lack of precision in the norms governing the transition from immaturity to jural majority. The Tswana do not discriminate sharply between these two statuses: traditionally, initiation was only part of the transition; nor does the establishment of a marriage-type relationship define a critical point at which an individual clearly becomes an (adult) man/husband (*monna*). There is thus a period during which a man's status as an adult is subject to competing interpretations. A guardian may, and often does, employ this ambiguity to resist the efforts of his BS to exercise control over family property. While the heir asserts his rights, as embodied in the substantive norms governing the transfer of assets, his FB invokes the more general ones associated with maturity; and both strive to impose the situational priority of their normative arguments.

Situational conflict, then, derives from the politics of everyday life, not from the intrinsic content of the particular norms involved. The latter are neither inherently contradictory nor compellingly complementary; they are merely contained side by side within *mekgwa le melao*. Thus, the norms associated with guardianship, jural maturity, and the transfer of property are brought into conflict only by virtue of the strategic and pragmatic contingencies that arise in the course of dispute processes. As a result, the Tswana see no need to explain their coexistence in the repertoire, but they do see the potentiality for situational conflict as having to do with the fact that the substantive precepts embodied in *mekgwa le melao* vary so widely in their generality/specificity. This is not believed by them to represent a weakness in their judicial logic or to warrant abstract speculation, however. It is merely a taken-for-granted feature of the sociocultural order.

Logical contradiction, on the other hand, implies an intrinsic incompatibility in the content of different norms, so that the substance of one would appear to negate the validity of the others. It is to be stressed that Tswana informants, when they recite inventories of such precepts in response to questioning, rarely attempt to offer exegetical explanations for the coexistence of contradictory ones, nor do they ever state the internal logic of *mekgwa le melao* as a series of abstract propositions. Nevertheless, at the level of application—i.e., in the context of dispute processes—the means of resolving substantive discontinuities are revealed (cf. Geertz 1973:24 ff.). In order to demonstrate this, we consider a normative paradox, associated with property relations, that will become directly relevant to the discussion of devolution in chapter 6.

The Kgatla state the norm that most of a man's property should be distributed while he is alive, ostensibly to reduce conflict among his descendants when he dies. Yet they also hold that the eldest son must inherit a major portion of the unallocated residue (*boswa*) that remains at the death of the father so that he may look after the surviving members of the agnatic segment. Now, if the first norm is applied, the cattle involved in the "major portion" of *boswa* will be few—perhaps only two or three—and certainly not enough to fulfill the stated duty of extending succor to the segment.

However, the view that the eldest son should receive a major portion of *boswa* "so that he may look after the members of his agnatic segment" is not a simple exegesis on communal resource management. Dispute-settlement processes, and commentaries on them, indicate that this normative statement encodes an elaborate set of ideas about the nature of inheritance, the transmission of property, and the structure of Kgatla society (Roberts and Comaroff 1979). Briefly, the only phase in the devolution process at which the preeminence of the eldest son is insisted upon—i.e., the moment of his father's death—is also the point at which he succeeds to the headship of the emergent agnatic segment. His major portion of *boswa* is the token of legitimacy by which this transition is publicly recognized.

Moreover, it is to be reiterated that, according to indigenous theory, Kgatla society is organized into a hierarchy of progressively more inclusive politicoadministrative (coresidential) groupings founded upon agnatic cores. The growth and elaboration of lower-order units create, and give form to, higher-order ones. The Kgatla suggest that, in order to sustain this structure, it is crucial that the agnatic segment remain united after the death of its founder. If its component households scattered, the agnatic basis of higher-order units would disappear. This, in the indigenous view, would threaten chaos, because the fundamental principle of structural form (i.e., the articulation of agnation and residence) would be vitiated.

However, the unity of the segment is most fragile when its founder dies. Common interest in the ownership and management of the family estate no longer binds it, and the overarching control of the ascendant generation is absent, a consideration often expressed in the desire of junior siblings to shed the authority of their senior brother. This second factor is particularly crucial, since the Kgatla believe that the continuity of the segment, as well as its location in the structural hierarchy, is defined in terms of allegiance to the position of segment head.

As a token of legitimacy, then, *boswa* is associated with public concern for smooth intergenerational transitions, which facilitate the continuity of the segment and, hence, the viability of the social order. It is to be stressed that the heir's extra portion is not an unencumbered private asset like the rest of his inheritance. It has communal properties, since the cattle concerned are expressly to be used for the purposes of members of the unit. The animals, however, cannot realistically support the material needs of the grouping. In fact, they do not even represent a concrete reality, for the extra share allocated to the heir is never physically isolated and the cattle are not actually identified; they are simply integral to the inherited herd. Yet the Kgatla see these cattle in specific terms: it is *these* unspecified beasts of the extra share, not the total inheritance of the eldest son, that are supposed to be employed for the well-being of the segment. In other words, the common interest of the grouping lies not in a herd of real cattle but in the idea that it exists as a heritage. This "symbolic herd" is the only shared asset in which the interests of the segment converge, and it is emphasized at precisely the point in the structural cycle at which the threat of fragmentation is most compelling. Thus we may begin to explain the coexistence of two apparently contradictory norms concerning devolution at death. The Kgatla stress that *boswa,* the residue devolving at death, should be as small as possible in order that disputes be kept to a minimum during the segment's most vulnerable phase. Moreover, they insist that the heir must be given preeminence in such a way as to assert the segment's solidarity in this phase. In these terms, the norms are perfectly consistent; but their consistency derives from the fact that the Kgatla are not being literal about their expectation that the heir must use his greater portion to "look after" the segment. "Look after" does not necessarily connote material support; rather, it implies that he is invested with the duty to protect the unity of the segment and perpetuate its common interest. Having had the authority conferred upon him, he becomes the *modisa* ("herdsman") of the unit. The Tswana usage emphasizes the analogy between the management of cattle and the management of people.

Three important points emerge from this example. First, when stated as substantive prescriptions, the norms appear logically incompatible since, at face value, the literal application of one precludes the literal fulfillment of the other. Moreover, no explicit attention is paid in the abstract to such logical discontinuities; they are not explained, or even noted, by informants. Second, contradictions are resolved by the tacit elevation of one of the two norms from the literal to the symbolic. Thus, "looking after" (in material terms) becomes "protection of the unity of the segment." This semantic transformation of the one norm permits the other, previously discontinuous, one to be accommodated, for it now refers to another level of reality. In other words, the resolution of normative contradiction may be achieved by relocating one of a set of incompatible norms of like order at a different level of generality and value by a process of transforming a substantive statement into a metaphorical or symbolic one. Third, this transformation does not occur in the context of abstract exegesis. It is expressed only in the context of action, when norms are adduced in argument or when actual disputes are being discussed and evaluated.

The undifferentiated nature of the repertoire—its lack of internal elaboration, organization, and necessary consistency —is fundamental to the way in which Tswana comprehend and utilize *mekgwa le melao,* for this property provides the basis for (*a*) the legitimization of competing constructions of reality, in terms of which situational conflict is expressed; (*b*) the imposition of order on the passage of everyday events, of which disputes are just one category; and (*c*) the process of transforming a substantive statement into a symbolic one, by means of which the logical consistency of norms can be mediated. Of course, the undifferentiated character of the repertoire itself depends both on the inclusion of norms of widely ranging specificity and on the (emic) assumption that the values attributed to them are not, and cannot be, immutably predetermined.

Mekgwa le melao include rules of etiquette and good manners; ideal prescriptions, which may enjoy token approval but are seldom achieved or even aspired to in practice; norms that enjoy wide social acceptance, are typically complied with, and are generally regarded as obligatory; and legislative directives that the chief and his councillors may take great pains to enforce (Schapera 1943a, 1970). The indigenous value of a given norm is difficult to assess in vacuo except in the most general of terms. Because such values are rarely universal within the population and fluctuate over time, they are usually seen to be open to negotiation; indeed, dispute processes are sometimes primarily devoted to debate over precisely this question of competing norms.

The Tswana themselves suggest that the value with which they invest individual *mekgwa le melao* varies enormously, but, beyond broad statements ("This *mokgwa* is important"; "We say that we should do this, but it is not so important"), they do not subject substantive norms to abstract or speculative scrutiny in this respect either. If there is any folk theory of normative value to be abstracted from informants' statements, it appears to be based on only two pragmatic rules: (*a*) except for a small core of nonnegotiable ones, the specific value of most norms is meaningfully determined only in terms of the situation in which they are invoked; and (*b*) this value can be derived only in relation to either contingent or opposing norms. In other words, while *mekgwa le melao* encode the manifest elements of the cultural system, their individual meaning and relative value are asserted, evaluated, and realized primarily in the context of social and political action. Of course, the pragmatic and situational emphasis that Tswana place on their normative repertoire is consistent with the nature of the sociocultural order as described in chapter 2; it is a corollary of the enigmatic quality of the lived-in universe and the ideology of individualism that pervades it. But this must not be taken to suggest that *mekgwa le melao* have no determinant effect on behavior or that they do not impart form to the processes that occur within the social universe. As we shall see, the problem of normative determination is a highly complex one.

Normative Transformations

The repertoire of *mekgwa le melao* is not regarded by the Tswana as immutably bounded or unchanging. Rather, it is held to be involved in a constant process of formation and transformation. This process is associated mainly with three orders of events: (1) dispute-settlement processes, (2) legislative pronouncements, and (3) changes in patterns of social relations.

Dispute-Settlement Processes

Tswana readily conceive of the possibility that the outcomes of particular disputes may have the capacity to change the repertoire. Indeed, decisions are sometimes commended precisely because they are anticipated to modify *mekgwa le melao* in a necessary or desired way; we also have documented case histories in which a given award was believed to bring about an unwelcome change (Roberts and Comaroff 1979). In this respect, Tswana appear to share the view of the inter-relation between norm and dispute that is implicit in our own system; that is, rules are typically held to be located within judicial decisions, with the result that innovatory judgments lead to the creation of new rules. In short, they regard the decisions made by chiefs in the same relation to the norms of their society as our judicial outcomes stand to the rules of English law.

At the same time, Tswana do not express uniform attitudes about the connection between judgments pronounced in *kgotla* and social change. Innovatory decisions are often rationalized on the ground that they merely reflect observable de facto transformations. Earlier we alluded in passing to an example that is instructive in this respect:

During the early years of his occupancy of the Kgatla chiefship, which he had assumed in 1963, Linchwe II handed down a series of judgments according to which the unallocated balance of an estate (*boswa*) was to be divided equally among the children of a dead man. This deliberately ignored the norm that the eldest son must receive a major share of *boswa* in order to "look after" the members of the agnatic segment. But the chief legitimized it on the grounds that he was simply recognizing a new trend in Kgatla life, for in recent times eldest sons had shown a tendency to "eat up" the heritable cattle themselves and had not taken any interest in their segments. In these circumstances it seemed pointless, indeed unfair, to perpetuate such an inappropriate norm. It is to be emphasized that Linchwe's decisions were not made in response to the behavior of the specific eldest sons involved in these particular cases but of eldest sons in general. The chief's perception of law and social change—that law is seen to "catch up" with changes after a lapse in time—was similar to that usually held to exist in Western societies (Rose 1956:52).

Numerous Kgatla, however, expressed a view rather different from Linchwe's. They argued that the decisions would *induce* the very state of affairs he claimed to be recognizing. That is, the new norm introduced in the context of dispute settlement was expected to effect an (undesirable) transformation in the social system.[3] In fact, many people explicitly accused the chief—then an inexperienced officeholder—of failing to understand the wider importance of the established *mokgwa*. As we have already explained, Kgatla see a close connection between this *mokgwa* and the principles upon which they perceive their society to be organized. In short, their objections were grounded in an elaborate set of ideas concerning the continuity of their social order. Even today, while it is accepted that Linchwe's innovatory norm is regularly applied, the view is still expressed that it violates one of the essential elements that regulate their universe.

Apart from the assumption that the repertoire may be altered with little difficulty, the opposed views of Linchwe and his critics shared another common denominator. Both views were founded on the notion that dispute processes provide the context in which manifest trends and transformations in social patterns are brought into relationship with the normative order, yet the example indicates that two contrasting notions of causality and determination fall within the compass of Tswana theory; one ascribes normative change to social change, the other reverses this priority. Both are clearly oversimplifications; for instance, despite the belief that innovatory decisions induce transformations, it sometimes occurs that a chief hands down a judgment that, far from being viewed as the valid introduction of a new norm, is widely held to be "not the law." Varying reactions to such innovatory decisions, it seems, depend on factors that may have little to do with the content of the norm itself; they appear to be largely a function of the legitimacy of a particular chief at a particular historical moment. The performance of Tswana officeholders undergoes constant public evaluation, and this process of negotiation determines the extent of the recognized rights that may be realized by them (J. L. Comaroff 1975). Hence a chief whose legitimacy is substantial is likely to have his judicial decisions treated as law-giving pronouncements. On the other hand, an unpopular incumbent, with limited effective authority, may find his judgments perceived as idiosyncratic statements; under these conditions, they have little prospect of becoming accepted as *melao* or even of being executed. In practice, then, the relationship between judicial decision and the transformation of the repertoire may depend substantially on considerations extrinsic to them both. The factor of chiefly legitimacy, not surprisingly, also affects the introduction of norms by legislative pronouncement.

Legislative Pronouncements

Aside from chiefly decisions, legislative pronouncements provide the only context for an explicit modification of, or addition to, *mekgwa le melao* (Schapera 1943a, 1969, 1970). In theory, only a chief can make such pronouncements, although he need not necessarily be their author. In reality, however, a powerful headman (particularly if he lives some distance from the capital) may occasionally introduce specific rules pertaining to the grouping under his jurisdiction.

Before any legislative pronouncement can be made, the proposal should first be discussed informally by the chief and his advisers. If the majority favor it, the proposal will be debated at a gathering of the council of headmen (*lekgotla*). Once accepted at this level, it will finally be considered at a public assembly (*pitso, phuthego*). In formal terms, the chief may announce any decision he chooses at the end of this meeting, and it stands as a *molao* until amended or revoked. Unless it reflects public opinion, however, it will have little de facto chance of being executed, and the chief may suffer some criticism and loss of legitimacy as a result. The quality and quantity of legislative innovation are regarded as important indexes of chiefly success, and the *melao* of popular past office-holders can easily be recalled (see Schapera 1943a).

While chiefly pronouncements are clearly a significant source of *melao,* the likelihood that a newly declared rule will actually be incorporated into the repertoire does not depend solely on its career in the legislative process, for the degree of executive authority enjoyed by the officeholder is also very important. This is exemplified by the case of the Tshidi chief, Kebalepile, who announced three new *melao* at his *kgotla* in Mafikeng during 1969. Kebalepile was going through a critical phase in his career and was being heavily and repeatedly censured for misrule. None of the three norms was ever executed, and when, in 1975, the Tshidi were again asked about them, informants denied that any such *melao* had ever been made.

The Tswana are not conservative about normative change in itself. As in the sphere of ritual technique (J. Comaroff 1974), they display a marked tolerance for innovation. As we have seen, particular modifications may be subjected to critical examination and debate, and the proper procedures for introducing them are carefully protected. But there is little resistance to change for its own sake. Moreover, the undifferentiated nature of *mekgwa le melao* facilitates the introduction and transformation of norms; there seems to be little felt need to test or scrutinize a new one in order to eliminate contradiction, ambiguity, or redundancy in the repertoire as a whole.

Changes in the Pattern of Social Relations

Because Tswana perceive a substantial proportion of *mekgwa le melao* to be implicit in the organization of their social universe, they recognize that the repertoire may change gradually in accordance with emerging social patterns. This was demonstrated in the example of Linchwe's innovative judgment. While some norms may result from judicial decisions and legislative pronouncements, a wide range of them may come into existence simply as a consequence of behavioral regularity. Such emergent regularities may themselves, of course, be an expression of more fundamental changes in wider politicoeconomic conditions.

A corollary of normative transformations occurring in this manner is that the content of the repertoire may not be uniformly perceived or recognized throughout a chiefdom. The Tswana sometimes speak as if *mekgwa le melao* are universally shared; but since the component groupings of their communities change unevenly (J. L. Comaroff 1976), there are politicojural arenas within which differing constructions may be placed on a given norm and on its relevance to modern conditions. While we do not view the different structural aggregates as loci of discrete normative orders (cf. Pospisil 1958a, 1971), it is a matter of empirical observation that certain norms are considered obsolete and disregarded in some units but not in others. Moreover, one seen as outmoded in particular wards may still operate in the chief's *kgotla*. Changes of *mekgwa le melao* in one unit do not necessarily set up a chain reaction among its neighbors or a ten-

dency toward any form of universalization; the Tswana are
ultimately as tolerant of the possibility of diversity as they are
of normative transformation in general.[4]

The Invocation of Norms in Dispute Settlement

It will be plain, both from our account and from the cases
recorded in chapters 5 and 6, that *mekgwa le melao* play an
important part in Tswana dispute processes. Disputants organize their utterances with reference to them, as do third
parties acting in mediatory or judicial roles. The fact that the
repertoire of norms should give form to the argument elaborated in this context is understandable. The selection and
arrangement of relevant messages must derive from some set
of referential principles; and, because *mekgwa le melao* are
held indigenously to regulate both social interaction and the
course of disputes, for Tswana they represent the obvious
source of such principles. It is also clear, however, that the
relationship between rule and outcome is a complex one—a
point that becomes self-evident once it is conceded that disputes are seldom decided by the prescriptive application of
norms alone. We shall consider the logic of normative determination in chapter 7. Here we seek to answer a prior
and more limited question concerning the nature of the normative order, a question that has long confronted legal anthropologists but has never, in our view, been satisfactorily
answered.[5] Given that substantive rules *do* rarely determine
outcomes in a simple, mechanistic fashion, what underlies the
logic of their utilization and invocation? In order to address
this question it is necessary to examine more closely the way
in which argument is constructed, and rhetoric formulated,
with reference to *mekgwa le melao.*

In presenting a case, Tswana disputants typically seek to
contrive what we shall call a "paradigm of argument," that is,
a coherent picture of relevant events and actions *in terms of one
or more implicit or explicit normative referents.* Any such
"paradigm of argument" is sited ultimately in the requirements of a particular case and is not fixed or predetermined. Its degree of elaboration and integration depends on several factors, such as the oratorical abilities of the

litigant, his anticipatory calculations concerning the maneuvers of his opponent, and his own strategic intentions. Moreover, its construction may vary over a number of hearings of the same dispute before different agencies, since the perceptions, expectations, and strategies of the opposing parties may change or become progressively refined. The important point to note is that the complainant, who always speaks first, establishes the paradigm by ordering facts around normative referents that may or may not be made explicit. The defendant, in replying, may accept these referents and hence the paradigm itself; if he does so, he will argue over the circumstances of the case *within that paradigm.* Alternatively, he may assert a competing one by introducing different normative referents, in which case he may not contest the facts at all. At the higher levels, where the mode of settlement becomes one of adjudication, the third party responsible for it (a headman or the chief) may order his decision within the agreed paradigm, choose between the rival ones, or impose a fresh paradigm on the issues under dispute.

One notable feature of Tswana dispute processes is apparently shared with some other African societies (see, e.g., Fallers 1969, for the Soga): although paradigms of argument are invariably constructed with reference to *mekgwa le melao,* direct appeals to the repertoire, involving express statements of rule, are seldom made by disputants. Even where an explicit normative reference is made, it is usually indirect (e.g., "I ask whether it is proper that . . .") rather than direct ("It is the law [*molao*] that . . ."). Generally, the disputants and others involved in a case simply talk about what happened, organizing their statements in such a way as to refer unambiguously, if tacitly, to some mutually understood norm. Thus, the manner in which the facts are ordered informs listeners of the identity of the rule (or rules) in terms of which the paradigm is contrived. These features of argument are readily evident in cases 2 and 3.

Where direct mention is made of the properties of *mekgwa le melao,* it is usually by senior men watching the case in *kgotla* or by the headman or chief hearing the dispute. Significantly, when entering on a discussion of rules, Tswana employ a mode of speech that differs conspicuously from the style they use when talking about everyday events or the conduct of living persons. This mode corresponds to what Comaroff has elsewhere (1975) termed the "formal" code as opposed to the "evaluative" code used in political oratory. It is characterized, among other things, by its stylistic formality and reliance on metaphor and by its impersonal and authoritative quality, which is denoted by appeals to the transcendent legitimacy of shared values ("It is our custom that . . ."; "Tswana have always said that . . ."). In contrast, the "evaluative" code is marked by less formality and by minimal reliance on formulaic or idiomatic expression; it is the explicit language of argument, where the message comes unequivocally from the speaker ("I say that . . .") and conveys his opinion in the unmistakable terms of the first-person singular. Thus, in a dispute concerning, say, marriage, debate over the actions of the parties and the relevant "facts of the case" will proceed in the evaluative style, but any discussion of *mekgwa le melao* associated with conjugal relations, if it occurs at all, will utilize the formal code.

The coexistence of the two codes has significant implications for Tswana rhetorical forms. Most immediately, however, by differentiating talk about rules from argument over events and actions, it distinguishes and insulates the authoritative enunciation of *mekgwa le melao* from the public negotiation of particular rights and liabilities. This is not to say that Tswana cannot (or do not) readily evaluate, debate, and transform their *melao;* we have shown that they do. Nor does it imply that orators may not, in certain situations, seek to relate utterances in the two codes for rhetorical effect (see J. L. Comaroff 1975). But it does mean that, in the everyday context of the *kgotla,* men can confront each other—and sometimes disagree bitterly—over the circumstances at issue in a given dispute without calling into question the integrity of the shared normative repertoire. A degree of "insulation" can thus be maintained between the normative repertoire and discourse that seeks to impose interpretations on events for purposes of influencing the dispute process.[6]

Cases 2 and 3[7] exemplify the way in which paradigms of argument are constructed and serve to illuminate further the part played by *mekgwa le melao* in the dispute process.

CASE 2:   MMATLHONG'S FIELD

Mmatlhong[8] had inherited a tract of arable land from her mother, Kwetse [see the accompanying genealogy], who had received it from her father by way of *serotwana*[9] when she married. Nobody could remember this plot having been cultivated and, by 1960, it was covered by scrub and mature trees.[10] On it lay a pan from which water was perennially obtainable. Kwetse had never used the land but had allowed her brother, Thari, to draw water from the pan. Like her mother, Mmatlhong never cultivated the plot. She had married into another ward and had been provided with a field by her husband. Following Thari's death, Leoke [his ZSS and MZSS of Mmatlhong] had been permitted to draw water from the pan.

Some years later, Mogorosi, Mmatlhong's MZDS, asked her to exchange the field for a beast. She agreed, and the transaction was witnessed by several people. But in all the visits made to the field in the course of the exchange it seems never to have been specified clearly whether or not the pan fell within it. At the time, Leoke was away from home and did not know about the agreement. Nor did any of Kwetse's male agnates witness these events, although they were informed later.

Following his acquisition of the land, Mogorosi excluded others from it and prevented the cutting of bark from the trees. Meanwhile, Leoke had returned. On hearing that his children had been told not to cut the bark, he visited Mogorosi, taking with him a man to whom neither was closely related. The argument that ensued is recounted below, but it was serious enough to persuade the two men to report it to their kinsmen. Both chose senior members of the agnatic segment into which Kwetse had been born. Pholoma [see genealogy], who was consulted by Leoke, initiated informal efforts at conciliation by approaching Mmatlhong and Mogorosi. The latter was asked to allow Leoke to draw water, while Leoke was shown the boundaries of the field by Mmatlhong. On this occasion it was indicated that the pan fell within these boundaries. Leoke reacted by entering the plot and cutting down trees; quite explicitly, he wished to challenge Mogorosi's right to it.

Some time later, at the request of Mogorosi, the members of Kwetse's agnatic segment convened a meeting to discuss the dispute. Raditladi, the senior member, questioned Mogorosi about the terms of the transaction. These appear to have been accepted, although Raditladi expressed regret that none of his agnates had witnessed it. Those present at the meeting emphasized that, while Mogorosi clearly had rights over the land, the two men should use the pan peacefully together. This, however, did not satisfy either of them, and their wives, Masa and Shamme, exchanged abuse and

Genealogy of Leoke and Mogorosi

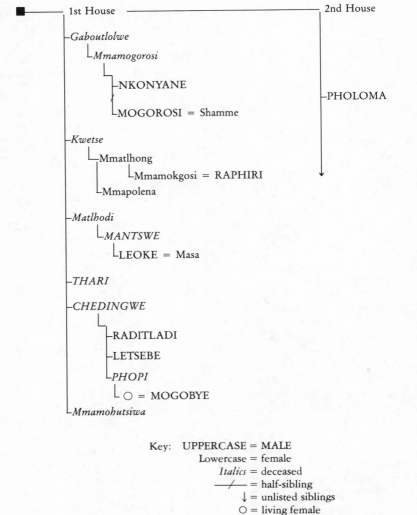

Key: UPPERCASE = MALE
Lowercase = female
Italics = deceased
—⁄— = half-sibling
↓ = unlisted siblings
○ = living female
■ = founder of agnatic segment
1st house = descendants of segment
    founder from his first union
2nd house = descendants of segment
    founder from his second union

blows in the *kgotla*. This convinced members of the segment that a settlement at this level was impossible, and Raditladi informed the ward headman of the issue.[11]

Before further attempts at settlement could be made, some of Mogorosi's goats wandered over to Leoke's homestead, where Masa impounded them. Mogorosi sent a child to fetch them, but Masa demanded that they be collected by an adult. Mogorosi went himself, and they were handed over. This happened again, and Mogorosi again collected them. This time Masa complained that the goats had been after Leoke's billy; but most of them were pregnant, and they were probably attracted to the area by an out-crop of rock salt. Subsequently, the billy wandered home with Mogorosi's goats, and Shamme impounded it. One of Leoke's children went to fetch it, but, like Masa, Shamme insisted that the animal be collected by an adult. Nobody came, so Shamme sent it off toward Leoke's homestead. Some days later Mogorosi's goats again wandered over to Leoke's place. When Mogorosi asked for them, Leoke refused, on the ground that his billy had not yet returned. Soon after, the dispute was heard by the ward headman, Thai Tlhadi.

MOGOROSI: The dispute began over a ploughing field [*tshimo*]. I bought the field from Mmatlhong. I paid [*dueletse*] a large red ox for it. I was with Mmusi. I found that Raphiri had cut some bark from my ploughing field. I told Raphiri not to cut bark again. I was with Mmamotalala when I issued this warning. One day I found the sons of Leoke cutting bark again, and I told them not to cut bark in my field. I told them to tell their father that I had stopped them cutting down trees in my field.

Later, Leoke came to me with Mokgakgele. Leoke asked me why I prevented his children from cutting down bushes. I told Leoke, "I have bought the field, and I need the trees to fence the field." Leoke said to me that the plot I am talking about is the field of Raditladi. I said to Leoke "man" [*monna*].[12] Leoke said: "Do not say 'man' to me. You must say 'man' to my son, not to me!"

I swore at him: I said *"marete"* [testicles]. He replied *"mmago mpapa"* [your mother's genitals].[13] I tried to catch his leg, but he moved away quickly. I tried to take a stick, but Mokgakgele and my wife stopped me. I again swore at Leoke. Leoke replied and said that I was an illegitimate child and did not know my father. He went on to say that I was the illegitimate child of Mantswe [Leoke's father]. I told Leoke that I would make him defecate involuntarily on the next day. The following day I looked for Leoke without success. On the same day, Leoke's wife came to me. When she asked about the quarrel, I refused to answer her.

When this field was allotted to me, the following were present: Mmusi, Segale, Mmatlhong, Mmamokgosi, Mmamotalala, and Shamme. Raditladi said he wished the Modisana family had been present.[14] When Raditladi and my people were present, Leoke's wife poked my wife in the head with her finger. Masa challenged Shamme to follow her outside to fight. Shamme refused. Masa then went and scratched Shamme's face, and she bled. Sebopelo and Mmamotalala separated them.

[One day] Nkonyane informed me that my goats were in Leoke's enclosure. I actually saw them there. My wife sent a child for them, but they sent her away; they said they wanted an adult. I went there and found Masa, Leoke's wife. Masa said my goats were worrying her billy; they are after it. They allowed me to have them, and I drove them away. My goats returned there again, being attracted by the salt lick. I went a second time, and they allowed me to have them. I told Masa that my goats were in kid and did not need a billy.

One day Leoke's billy came along with my goats. I tied it up to prevent it interfering with my goats, as they were in kid. Leoke's son came to fetch it. Shamme sent him back to tell his mother to fetch it herself. She refused to come. Shamme untied it and chased it to its owners. My goats were captured a third time. I went for them, accompanied by Ditswe. When I was there, Leoke asked me about his billy. Leoke said that if he did not find his billy, he would not let me have my goats. Leoke said I should call Letsebe and Raditladi. The goats captured by Leoke are six in number.

Leoke said he could see I wanted us to fight. He also said one of us will die. The goats captured by Leoke are still there now.

LEOKE: During the Christmas month I went to the Transvaal. On my return I found that my sons had cut bushes at Leboeng. The children said that Mogorosi had stopped them cutting down bushes. They said that Mogorosi came to my place and told them to let me know on my return that he would like to see me at his place. When I came, the boy told me. I waited four days, hoping Mogorosi would come and talk to me; but he did not come. On the fifth day I went to his place. I was with Mokgakgele, so that he could become a witness of what occurred between Mogorosi and me. When I got there, I said: "The children say you have stopped them cutting down bushes." He admitted that he had stopped them. He had also stopped Raphiri and Mogobye.[15] I told him he had made a mistake to prevent them. He said it was a field [*tshimo*] and he was going to plough it. I told him it would be understandable if he had stopped them because the field was already ploughed.[16] He said that the plot was a piece of arable land. I told him that the plot belonged to Raditladi's people.

I told him this plot has never been ploughed since before I was born. He said: "Son, tell me when you have finished." I warned him I had not come to fight but to ask where I was supposed to cut bushes. He stood up and looked for a stick. Mokgakgele stopped him. As I went, he swore at me. He said: "Your father's testicles [*rrago marete*], you Mokgalagadi." I told him the man he swore at was actually his father. He said to me: "Your mother's genitals." I told him to say it to his mother. He threatened that if he meets me on my own somewhere he will make me defecate against my will. I came and asked at the *kgotla* if it was proper for him to say he would attack me wherever we would meet.[17] I went and cut trees where Mogorosi had prevented the children from cutting branches. I took the bush away and kept it for a week and then used it. I went back and cut down another and kept that one for two weeks, then used it.

Mogorosi had not actually seen my children cutting down the trees. When they cut down the trees, Mogorosi was at the cattle post. It was the month of Christmas. In February, Mmatlhong sold the field to Mogorosi and received the ox. When Mogorosi bought the field, I was away; Mmusi told me what had been done. Mmatlhong also told me that she had allocated the field to Mogorosi. The following day I went to water the cattle and found that the entrance to my pan had been moved away. I asked Mmatlhong why this was done. I said the pan was mine, allocated to me by Mmamohutsiwa, where Thari had dug before.

[Leoke then went on to detail some of the events that preceded the meeting of the agnatic segment. He ended this passage by saying:] Raditladi asked Mogorosi if he wanted a case [*tsheko*]. Mogorosi said: "Yes, I want a case." Raditladi asked him where his father, Nkonyane,[18] was. Mogorosi replied by saying that Leoke's wife is worrying his wife.

[Leoke explained that he went away again; he then continued:] I returned from Oodi and found that my billy was not in the flock. I heard that it had been serving Mogorosi's goats. Mogorosi caught it and tied it up. When he let it loose, it went away. Mogorosi's goats came to me, and I put them into my enclosure. I asked him why he could not have released it [the billy] when my wife sent for it. I sent him to go and call Raditladi and Letsebe so that he could take the goats in their presence. I asked my wife whether she had ever refused to release Mogorosi's goats. I asked Mogorosi the same question, and he said it had never happened. Later Nkonyane came and said he had come for the goats. I told him they were in the enclosure. He asked me what damage they had done. I said I did not find my billy where it should be. He asked if Mogorosi had borrowed it from me. I said no, and he said "A billy, like a bull, has no fence." I said to him that he could take the goats. Nkonyane asked if I would wait while they went to look for my billy first. They departed, leaving the goats with me. Mogorosi said to Nkonyane: "I told you one of us [Mogorosi or Leoke] would have to move elsewhere or he would die."

[In answering questions, Mogorosi admitted to having started the exchange of abuse, but added, "I am not to be insulted by reference to my testicles." Leoke confessed that his abuse of Mogorosi's mother had been wrong and that he should not have imputed illegitimacy.]

THAI TLHADI [in judgment]: Leoke, we have listened to your case with Mogorosi very carefully. You used very obscene language toward Mogorosi. Therefore the *kgotla* finds you guilty. You will receive four strokes on the back. You, Mogorosi, will receive two strokes.

[After this, the hearing proceeded with a series of statements made in evidence by Mmatlhong, her younger sister, Mmapolena, and her eldest son, Segale. All reported, in a matter-of-fact fashion, the events surrounding the transaction concerning the field, the demarcation of its boundaries to include the pan, and the reporting of these events to Letsebe, the younger brother of Raditladi. Segale added that the land had not been ploughed for a number of years and that Leoke had drawn water without title to it. Leoke interrupted, claiming that he was allowed to use the pan by Mmamohutsiwa, a younger sister of Kwetse. Mmatlhong replied that the trees that were felled had been within the field that she had the right to alienate. Leoke and Mogorosi then exchanged words: the latter argued that he had only stopped the children from taking trees from his field; the former answered that he had cut trees "in order to see what Mogorosi would do." Thai Tlhadi delivered a second judgment, in which he simply stated that the field had belonged to Mmatlhong and that she had transferred it properly to Mogorosi. The pan was within the field, and it was up to him to decide whether to allow Leoke to draw water. Leoke then raised the matter of the goats.]

LEOKE: My billy had not yet been found.

MOGOROSI: I learn that it was seen by Mothagi and my wife, Shamme. [Mothagi confirmed that he and Shamme had seen the animal in the company of Leoke's other goats.]

LEOKE: The billy is now present among my other goats. When it went to Mogorosi's place, it was attracted by the female goats, as most billies are. It was caught and tethered there. I was advised to fetch it. After that, Mogorosi's goats came to my place, and I decided to detain them as he had detained my billy. Mogorosi came to claim the goats, but I did not give them, as my billy was astray. I saw the billy only when the matter had been handed to the *kgotla*.

[Then followed another series of exchanges between Leoke and Mogorosi. Both reiterated the alleged facts concerning the goats, and the former admitted that he still held the six animals. Both accused the other of taking the matter to the *kgotla* without due warning.]

THAI TLHADI [in judgment]: Leoke, we have listened carefully to the arguments between you and Mogorosi. You have caused the *kgotla* to deal with an unnecessary problem. You have fought with Mogorosi and detained his goats. The *kgotla* orders that, from this day, you and Mogorosi should live together in peace. Mogorosi, you may have back your goats. You, Leoke, the *kgotla* orders you to pay the sum of R6 (approximately $7), which is a fine imposed by the *kgotla*.

[The corporal punishment was administered immediately. After receiving his fourth stroke, Leoke arose swiftly. This was taken as a sign of disrespect, however, and a further stroke was administered. Leoke was dissatisfied with this, and with the outcome of the hearing in general, so he took his grievance to the chief's *kgotla*. The hearing there went as follows:]

MOGOROSI: I am complaining against Leoke. Leoke came to my homestead with Mokgakgele. He said I had chased his children away for felling trees. I told him it was true. They were felling trees in my field, which I had bought from Mmatlhong. This field had not been ploughed for some time. I told him they were not the only ones I had chased away. Leoke answered by saying the field belonged to the Raditladi people, not to Mmatlhong's. I replied, saying I had bought it from the owner, Mmatlhong. Leoke said he would understand if I prevented them from felling trees in fields that had been ploughed before, but not where there has been no ploughing. That time, in conversation, he called me "son." I warned him not to call me "son" and swore at him. He swore at my mother, and I told him I would give him a hiding the next day. I stood up to thrash him and grabbed a stick. Mokgakgele and my wife prevented me. He stood outside, insulting me, and called me an illegitimate child, saying I was fathered by his father. [He then repeated the argument concerning the goats, and concluded:] Leoke and I have not fought. Leoke lost the case of the goats. I was allowed to receive the goats. I therefore have no case against Leoke; I have fully settled with him.

LEOKE: I brought this appeal here because I was not satisfied with the decision of my *kgotla*. He had a case, and I was ordered to receive four strokes. After the fourth stroke I arose, and the men of the *kgotla* caught me and thrashed and assaulted me. That is why I have appealed. I was thrashed unlawfully. When I quarreled with Mogorosi, he had not yet cleared the field, which he says he has bought. The claim that he had bought it is only an excuse. I disagreed when Mogorosi claimed that the ploughing field was his, because he had not paid the ox for it as he states.

[In answer to questions, Mogorosi reasserted his rights over the field and the pan. Leoke clarified his statement by saying that he thought the field did not include the pan. He also claimed the exchange occurred in February, *after* his children had been chased away. Mogorosi answered that Leoke was not present at the time of the transaction; it was earlier, when he was in Johannesburg.]

LEOKE: I went to the court and reported my disagreement with Mogorosi and asked the court if it was proper for a man to say to you that he will make you defecate.

[The remaining discussion was devoted entirely to the details of the transaction. Mmatlhong and Mmapolena repeated the evidence they had given at the earlier hearing, and the former stressed her right to alienate the plot. Leoke claimed once again that he had received the pan from Mmamohutsiwa. No new evidence was introduced, and the argument was an almost verbatim repetition of that heard in the ward court. Finally, judgment was given.]

CHIEF: Mmatlhong, I have gone carefully into the case of Leoke and Mogorosi. According to Tswana law, you can sell a field, not a plot of land. Land belongs to the chief. You have broken the law by selling the chief's land. I therefore order you to refund Mogorosi his beast. Mogorosi must receive the beast from you. You, Leoke, will receive the pan. It is yours, do not be worried by anyone about it. The fines imposed on you by the ward *kgotla* will remain as they are. You must carry those out, for you quarreled with the *kgotla* when found guilty.

At the start of the hearing in the ward court, Mogorosi—who, being the complainant, had the right to speak first—began by elaborating a paradigm of argument in relation to an implicit set of norms. He first established that it was a *ploughing* field that was at issue, and he stated the terms of its acquisition with tacit reference to a substantive norm governing exchange. He pointed out, further, that he had warned people who had infringed his rights to the field, and he named a witness who could verify this. In other words, he stressed that, as far as he was concerned, the dispute was mainly about title to the land itself. He then recounted the confrontation with Leoke, which had resulted, in his view, from the violation of his rights. He admitted to having initiated the exchange of abuse, but he implied that this was *not* a separate issue: it was a reaction to his having been wronged. In organizing his statement in this fashion, Mogorosi was anticipating an argument by Leoke to the effect that it was the confrontation, rather than title to the field, that lay at the heart of the case. With regard to the confrontation itself, however, Mogorosi tried to offset the fact that he had begun the swearing by pointing out that Leoke had escalated the abuse and that the defendant's wife had attacked his wife. Finally, he raised the matter of the goats, claiming that Leoke had impounded his animals for no justifiable reason. Again he made precise, if implicit, reference to the rules associated with the infringement of property rights.

In short, Mogorosi's argument contained no explicit reference to norms, but it did depend directly on a series of normative assumptions associated with control over land and animals. It was in relation to these that the facts he adduced were organized. Both his and Leoke's actions were to be understood as having resulted from the contravention of his rights. His primary claim, therefore, was for recognition of his title to Mmatlhong's field and for the return of his goats. He was not asking the *kgotla* to pass judgment on his relationship with Leoke; as he implied in his opening statement in the chief's *kgotla,* he believed that, once the property dispute was settled, nothing more general was at issue.

In reply, Leoke began by disputing Mogorosi's rights to the field. He stated that Mmatlhong had no business alienating the land, as it belonged to Raditladi's descent group. But the logic behind his argument lay in a somewhat different direction. He did not, in fact, question the norm his opponent adduced as governing the transaction. Rather, he claimed that, when he returned home in December (the dates are important here), he found that Mogorosi had told his children and others not to cut bushes. Later Leoke emphasized that the transaction between Mmatlhong and Mogorosi had occurred in February. He also added that at least until the time of the first confrontation the plot was not a ploughing field but a bush tract. In other words, he began not by questioning the norms referred to by Mogorosi, but by disagreeing with him over the *interpretation* of the facts. Nor was Leoke haphazard in the way he developed this: he attempted to construct a picture of Mogorosi's verbal and physical belligerence. The central statement of his argument then followed: "I came and asked at the *kgotla* if it was proper for him to say he would attack me." Here, although the reference to norm is indirectly phrased, it is *explicit* in the sense that the rule invoked can be understood without reference to the specific context or facts of the case.[19] Thus Leoke organized his evidence in such a way as to arrive at, and assert, a competing paradigm of argument. Significantly, he emphasized this by explicitly invoking the relevant norm; he wished to establish control over the proceedings so as to ensure that Mogorosi's violence would become the central issue. The remainder of his argument reaffirmed this. Mogorosi had chased the children away before he had actually received the field and at a time when Leoke still believed it belonged to Raditladi's agnates. (After all, he had been given use of the pan by Mmamohutsiwa.) Finally, in claiming that Mogorosi had initiated the dispute and in outlining the events surrounding the impounding of the goats, Leoke attempted to reinforce the impression that the complainant was a violent man who offended people and interfered with property.

In his judgment, Thai Tlhadi carefully distinguished three separate issues. He first took the question of the exchange of abuse and found Leoke relatively more guilty than Mogorosi. His judgment, which contained no explicit reference to norms, was terse and to the point. He then heard further evidence on the exchange of the field and, again without explaining his reasons, awarded it (and the pan) to Mogorosi.

Finally, he allowed discussion over the goats. Leoke admitted that his billy had returned, but he stressed that this was not the central issue; in any case, it had not returned at the time the dispute was reported to the ward headman. The way that he raised this matter, knowing that the animal was no longer missing, appears to sustain the suggestion that he viewed it as an integral part of his general argument. Thai Tlhadi, however, interpreting the question as a straightforward dispute over the seizure of animals, fined Leoke. The headman's decision to separate the three issues did not suit the defendant, who argued them as a single claim. But, as we shall indicate, this is one of the choices open to Tswana agencies when dealing with multiple disputes.

In the chief's *kgotla* hearing, Mogorosi again chose to assert his rightful acquisition of the land. In laying down the normative basis of his argument, and perhaps anticipating that Leoke would again claim that the plot was not a ploughed field at the time of the dispute, he explained that it was true that it had not been ploughed for a long time, and he implied that he had bought it with the intention to cultivate. He then recounted the events surrounding the exchange of abuse and the impounding of the goats and ended by saying that he no longer had a case against Leoke. Leoke's statement, less cogent than his earlier one, appealed against the "unlawful" extra strokes he had received. He also repeated his arguments about the transaction itself and began building a case similar to the one he had stated previously. After answering questions, he immediately reiterated his explicit enunciation of the norm concerning the threat of violence.

The judgment in this hearing is significant. The chief dismissed Leoke's argument, which focused on Mogorosi's alleged violence, by affirming Thai Tlhadi's decision. In concentrating on title to the field—to which he reduced the dispute—he addressed his remarks to Mogorosi's suit. He began by stating a norm governing the alienating of land that nullified Mogorosi's claim to have effected a valid transfer, and he ordered him to take back the ox. Thus, in judging the case, the chief selected the complainant's paradigm of argument for primary attention. He did this by explicitly invoking a conflicting norm, and awarding against him. As a result, Leoke's right to use the pan was reestablished.

GENEALOGY OF NAMAYAPELA

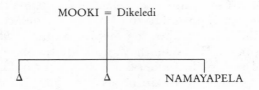

Key: UPPERCASE = MALE
Lowercase = female
Δ = living male

CASE 3:   NAMAYAPELA, THE TROUBLESOME SON

This case arose, as many do, out of the transfer of property across the generations (see chap. 6). Mooki was an ailing and elderly member of the Manamakgothe ward in Mochudi, and his mother had been a member of the agnatic segment to which the headman, Molope, belonged. Namayapela was one of Mooki's younger sons (see genealogy). For several years there had been acute tension between him and his father. Because his other children were away as migrant laborers, Mooki feared that, in the event of his death, Namayapela would seize and waste their portions of his estate. He had therefore tried to arrange an inter vivos allocation to Namayapela, but the latter refused to accept it. The case was heard by the chief's *kgotla*.

MOOKI: I have come with a complaint. My son, Namayapela, gives me a lot of trouble. He has been troublesome for a long time. Recently I told my ward headman, Molope, that I intended to give Namayapela his portion of my estate. The point is to get rid of him, because I fear he would cheat my obedient children in the division of my estate if I did not give him his share now. However, he would not accept it.

I fear that Namayapela may kill me so that he can enjoy my cattle. That is why I want to give him what I think he is entitled to; then I may have nothing to do with him. I want to forestall his chances of doing what he likes when I am gone.

I went to see how the crops were doing after I had reported the case to Molope. When I returned, I went to join a bereaved family. Headman Molope sent Setlhabi to bring Namayapela to him. But Namayapela refused to go. That evening a big noise was heard at my place. Molope sent people to find out the cause of the row.

Molope sent people to go and fetch Namayapela, who was causing the row and intended to kill me. When he made the row, he was looking for me; but he did not get me. People sent by Molope reported that Namayapela had a chisel and a hammer. They tried to take these tools away, but he refused.

During the night I wished to go home to sleep but was advised not to go, as Namayapela was so unruly he could have killed me. The following morning I went home to fetch prayerbooks so that I could lead prayers at the home of the bereaved family. Namayapela told me to sit down; he wanted to tell me something. I refused, as I was wanted at the *kgotla*. His mother and Ramakokwana begged me to listen to Namayapela. I complied and listened to Namayapela. Namayapela asked me whether I enjoyed reporting him to the *kgotla*. My reply was that I could not answer because I was urgently wanted.

When I realized that he was persistent, I ordered him to be quiet. He caught me by the shirt. I lost my temper and gave him a blow. When he tried to choke me, I caught his sex organ, and he let go. He opened up his thighs. Those who were present separated us. Again I reported to headman Molope that Namayapela was assaulting me. Molope reported this to the chief's *kgotla*. Namayapela defies me when I see him, and I am therefore appealing to the chief to help me give Namayapela his share of my estate.

NAMAYAPELA: Mooki is my real father. I have never fought him. It is true I caught him by the shirt with the intention of beating him. I caught him in heated passion. My intention was to persuade him to listen to me. He refused but was persuaded by my mother and Ramakokwana. The hammer and chisel are mine. When I had them in my hands, my father-in-law asked me what I was going to do: was it my intention to commit suicide? I took these tools out of their usual place without thinking of anything in particular.

I have never had any case against my father. My mother said to my father: "You are troubling Namayapela, yet you know his wife is expecting. She would become ill because of the dispute."

Machobele came and said he had been instructed to arrest me; yet he was not aware of the reason. He said I was expected to report at the *kgotla*. I refused to go. Then I asked my father to explain why he conspired against me with Molope, without talking to me first. I refused to accept the cattle my father wanted to give me. I told him that if I am not his son I am not entitled to the cattle. I told him I did not want them.

MOOKI: Namayapela sold cattle without consulting me, and that is another thing that annoys me. He benefits from my cattle, yet he refuses to come when I send for him. That is why I want to give him his share of the estate. I told Molope and my brothers that I want to give Namayapela his share so that he may get away from me.

MOLOPE: Mooki told me that he wanted to give Namayapela cattle from his estate but that Namayapela refused to accept. I sent people to call Namayapela, but he refused to come to the *kgotla.* I hesitated to employ forceful means. When Namayapela refused to come, he told the people I had said that he would rather they carry his dead body to the *kgotla* than get him there alive.

NAMAYAPELA: It is true that I was summoned to the *kgotla* but refused to go. I told Setlhabi, who had been sent to me, that my wife was ill. I never said that I would never go there alive. [Answering a question:] On one occasion I was flogged at the *kgotla* for assaulting a girl who had insulted me. She had referred to my testicles.

DIKELEDI: I know the dispute that exists between Namayapela and Mooki. Mooki is my husband [*monna;* also "man"]. Namayapela troubles his father. Mooki went with him to the cattle post to give him cattle, which would be his share of his father's estate. Namayapela refused twenty head of cattle.
Namayapela sold two head of cattle without consulting his father. He spent the money on a trip to Rustenburg (in South Africa) to buy roofing material. When he went to Rustenburg, he did not consult me either. He does not respect me as his mother. He regards me as any other old woman. When he had hurled his father to the ground, threatening to beat him, I said the best thing was for the two of them to part company. He pointed to me and said: "You aged woman, you will see."
When Mooki called his brothers to tell them that he wanted to give Namayapela cattle, Namayapela refused them on the ground that his elder brother was away. Mooki said that he was not distributing the estate. He wanted to give Namayapela his cattle because he was troublesome.
I told Mooki that it was improper to have a dispute with Namayapela while his wife was expecting, because this would make her ill. I was sympathizing with Namayapela's wife and not with him.
During the night on which Namayapela had a chisel and a hammer, he threatened to commit suicide. He was also asking the whereabouts of Mooki. Because he was making a lot of noise, I told my lastborn that his brother was playing the fool with us. He wants to kill your father. No one can use a hammer and chisel to commit

suicide. Namayapela said he wanted to see what he could achieve by sunset. He said that if he did not achieve anything, he would rather die.

NAMAYAPELA: I am willing to accept the cattle that my father, Mooki, wants to give me so that I may get away from him.

CHIEF: Namayapela, I have carefully heard the case between you and your father. Your father was very polite to you in discussing with you the fact that he wanted to give you your share. You refused to accept the cattle until you fought him.

You are not supposed to make life uncomfortable for your parents. If you are tired of living, you are free to kill yourself rather than make life unbearable for them. You have decided to be rude to your parents. Rudeness, dishonesty, and telling lies do not lead to eternal life. You must honor the word of the chief. Because of your rudeness you refused to respond to the summons by headman Molope and did not appreciate the goodwill extended to you by your father. I find you guilty. For disobeying the summons by headman Molope, I sentence you to five strokes. For refusing to accept the cattle, I sentence you to four weeks' imprisonment. The next week you must go with your father to the cattle post so that he can give you your cattle.

In this dispute the pattern of norm invocation differs markedly from that observed in case 2. Mooki, the complainant, opens by stating that his son has been troublesome for a long time. He appears to have organized his paradigm of argument around the generalized precepts associated with the father-son relationship; he thus refers to his son's recalcitrance and his failure to obey or to inform him of what was being done with family property. Namayapela is portrayed as noisy and unruly and as allegedly wishing to kill his father—the ultimate rejection of the relationship. Throughout, his appeal to norm is implicit and generalized. Mooki explains his desire to allocate to Namayapela a portion of his estate as an effort, made in desperation, to sever their tie. Thus, although this aspect of his argument refers implicitly to a precise substantive norm (a father's right to divide his estate inter vivos), it seeks to summarize, in more general (normative) terms, the state of the relationship.[20] Namayapela had refused the cattle, claiming still to be Mooki's "real" son. But, because of this, his abrogation of filial duties was all the more serious.

Hence Mooki asks the court to order Namayapela to accept the cattle in order to terminate his paternal responsibilities. As far as he is concerned, it is the relationship itself that is at issue. The inter vivos allocation is merely a means to achieve the more general end.

Namayapela appears to have accepted the paradigm of argument established by his father, as is indicated by his opening sentences ("Mooki is my real father."). But, while not disputing the validity of the norms associated with the father-son tie, he makes consistent efforts to place a different construction on the facts of the case. Indeed, his refusal to accept the cattle is rationalized as an attempt to assert his recognition of this father-son relationship, although a succession of witnesses in support of his father appears to make him change his mind in this respect. In his judgment, the chief distinguishes two issues: Namayapela's troublesomeness as a son and his refusal to respond to Molope's summons. He introduces each of them with an explicit statement of norms, the first explicit references heard in the case, and he judges Namayapela guilty accordingly.

Although the speeches in cases 2 and 3 do not include utterances in the formal code (see note 6), they demonstrate that a consistent pattern underlies the deployment of the normative repertoire in the dispute process. It should now be clear that most arguments are organized with *implicit* reference to *mekgwa le melao*. The latter constitute the indigenously acknowledged universe of discourse within which meaningful debate proceeds and the assumptions upon which it is predicated, so that the very construal of allegedly relevant facts necessarily entails tacit allusion to rule. Explication is not required to make this apparent to an audience; given the nature of the repertoire, a well-constructed exposition of information is sufficient. Indeed, redundant statements of *mekgwa* would strike most Tswana as a violation of basic oratorical skills. As this suggests, the express utterance of a norm is a rhetorical act of particular significance. In order to comprehend the logic behind such invocations, however, it is useful to distinguish between those made in argument and those made in the context of a judgmental decision.

It follows, from what has already been said, that a complainant will seldom explicitly invoke norms in the course of stating his case; because he speaks first, his presentation of facts will establish his paradigm of argument and its normative basis. Consistent with this, neither Mogorosi nor Mooki made an express reference to *mekgwa le melao*. Speakers coming later, however, must make a fundamental choice: either they may contest the facts, or they may dispute the norms to which an agreed set of facts is applied. Leoke, for example, did not finally question the factual basis of Mogorosi's representation of their confrontation; instead, he tried to impose a different normative paradigm for assessing it. In doing so, he made the only explicit mention of rules during the argument. Namayapela, on the other hand, did not question the normative paradigm laid down by his father, Mooki. On the contrary, he attempted to introduce additional evidence (his wife's pregnancy), and he disputed the alleged facts inferred by others (e.g., he actually took out the hammer and chisel but for no particular reason; it was not a "fact" that he intended to kill his father). Thus, in case 3, in which a single paradigm was shared by the two disputants, no explicit reference was made to norms and the argument focused on interpreting the circumstances and actions in question.

When we draw these observations together, it becomes evident that norms are explicitly invoked by a disputant only when he wishes to question the paradigm elaborated by his opponent and to assert control over (or change) the terms in which the debate is proceeding. The complainant has no need to do this in the ordinary course of events, because the manner in which he organizes his construction of the "facts" itself establishes his paradigm. Although it did not occur in either case 2 or case 3, a Tswana complainant appears to enunciate a norm (or set of norms) only when he anticipates an effort on the part of the defendant to question his characterization of the dispute itself. (It should be noted that Mogorosi did not do this; his anticipation of Leoke's point was over a question of fact *within* his normative frame of reference. In other cases, however, we have occasionally heard such anticipatory statements.) Hence, *mekgwa le melao* are expressly invoked most frequently by defendants, but a complainant may also do so when he wishes to erode his opponent's paradigm in advance.

In the process of debate, then, explicit normative utterances among the Tswana are associated with efforts to assert control over paradigms of argument. If there is no disagreement over such paradigms—as in case 3 and in a considerable number of other cases with which we are familiar—we may expect there to be no express appeal to *mekgwa le melao.*

The invocation of norms in judgment is directly related to their utilization in argument. In the three hearings that occurred in the context of cases 2 and 3, the judges made rather different types of appeal to *mekgwa le melao.* In case 2, Thai Tlhadi, who distinguished three issues and took evidence on them separately, simply gave his decision on the facts of the case without any reference to the repertoire; the chief, who later treated the same suit as being primarily concerned with the transfer of land, passed judgment in terms of a precise stated norm. In case 3, involving Namayapela, the chief distinguished two issues and expressly introduced the norms relevant to each one.

In the vast majority of cases Tswana judges isolate a single issue within a dispute and hand down a decision in relation to it that makes no explicit reference to any norm. The tendency to order and present judgments in this fashion occurs predominantly when argument takes place within an accepted paradigm and refers mainly to the facts at hand. If, however, the judge determines that there is a plurality of questions involved in the dispute, he may do one of two things. He may hear the whole case and distinguish the relevant issues in his own final statement. In such a situation *he* (like the chief in case 3) orders the debate into two or more frames and enunciates the appropriate norms in order to legitimize the distinction and justify his findings. In doing this, he is rearranging the paradigmatic structure of the arguments and is stating the normative basis of his construction. Thai Tlhadi, of course, also distinguished a number of issues in his judgment (case 2), but he invoked no norms at any stage. There was, however, a significant feature of his handling of the dispute: he actually divided the hearing into three parts. In each he judged on the facts, accepting the paradigm shared by the litigants.[21] Had Thai Tlhadi heard the case as a whole, he would have had to order the arguments before passing judgment; he might then have been expected to clarify and adjudicate the priority of the relevant norms. This is precisely what the chief did in case 2. In treating the dispute as a single issue, he was forced to recognize and assign priority to one of the paradigms elaborated by the respective disputants. In electing to give judgment in terms of Mogorosi's, he stated a relevant *molao* concerning the exchange of land. As it happened, this contradicted the complainant's suit, and he awarded against him. In short, judges invoke *mekgwa le melao* explicitly when they are compelled, or feel it necessary, to distinguish or adjudicate between competing paradigms of argument. These paradigms may be presented to them by the disputants, or they may be elaborated specifically for the purposes of judgment.[22]

Finally, cases 2 and 3 suggest that the invocation of norms varies in terms of two dimensions. The first dimension, the explicit/implicit dichotomy, pertains to ways in which disputants and judges give form to, and assert control over, the course of argument. The second dimension is the specificity/generality of the norms adduced in the dispute process. Case 2 is characterized by argument in terms of the precise, substantive norms associated with the exchange of land and the intention to commit assault. Case 3, on the other hand, proceeds with reference to more generalized, abstract precepts concerning the father-son bond. It is significant that in case 2 the complainant repeatedly stressed that the disagreement was over a *value* and his alleged rights in it; explicitly, he believed that the relationship between himself and the defendant was not itself under scrutiny. Once his property rights had been restored, he had "no case against Leoke." In case 3, in sharp contrast, Mooki placed his *relationship* with Namayapela before the court. The substantive issue regarding the inter vivos property allocation was merely a symptom of the broader problem. This appears to suggest that in cases having to do with the negotiation of relationships and statuses, suits and judgments are ordered in terms of generalized normative precepts; those that entail conflict over rights in a particular value tend to be marked by (implicit or explicit) appeal to highly specific *mekgwa le melao*. When debate embraces *both* relationships and values, as it of course can, then precise *and* generalized references may both be made.

It will be evident, however, that these observed variations —and, more generally, the nature of the normative repertoire and the logic of its invocation—raise a fundamental analytical problem; for if it is true that the manner in which *mekgwa le melao* are deployed varies with the object of debate, it follows that the *form* (or range of forms) of the dispute process is systematically related to the *content* of dispute. It is equally evident, moreover, that this form-content relationship requires to be elucidated before we may usefully consider the connection between rule and outcome or address the problem of determination.

4

As we saw in chapter 1, a number of agencies together provide the institutional context for disputes and their settlement in Tswana communities. Tswana, moreover, share well-established ideas as to how such disputes may be prevented or ought properly to be dealt with when they arise. In all circumstances, settlement-directed activity is said to be the ideal and appropriate response to situations of conflict. Retaliatory violence and forcible attachment of seized or violated property are tolerated within narrow limits but rarely elicit unambiguous social approval. Similarly, although it is recognized that mystical techniques may have to be invoked to establish responsibility for affliction or misfortune, resort to these techniques for purposes of vengeance is strongly discouraged.

The Formal Hierarchy

Settlement-directed discussions may occur in several contexts, and they are subject to widely differing formal and situational constraints. That these constraints differ so widely derives primarily from the fact that efforts ostensibly made to resolve a dispute may involve only the disputants themselves, acting alone, but they may also involve the intervention of a range of third parties. When third parties intervene, moreover, their participation may be essentially passive, being confined to carrying messages between the two disputants, or it may be actively directed toward formulating a solution and urging it upon the individuals concerned. At

higher institutional levels third parties may have the authority to arrive at, and execute, decisions in a public forum; at
lower ones they may intervene only to expedite negotiation
and compromise, and, in doing so, they may overtly align
themselves in support of one or the other of the disputants,
or they may adopt the position of neutral mediator. Under
these conditions, Koch's preliminary distinction (1974:27–
31) between processes of negotiation, mediation, and adjudication would appear to be relevant, at least in the context of the formal hierarchy within which such settlement-
directed activity is indigenously organized.

The Tswana identify four levels at which successive attempts to resolve disputes ought to be made. First, although
an individual should ideally report to senior kinsmen any
incident likely to be a source of conflict, the parties themselves should strive to settle their differences before pro-
voking the active involvement of others. Second, if their initial efforts fail, the disputants must seek the advice and help
of senior agnates and matrilateral kin—fathers, brothers, and
paternal and maternal uncles. If such informal intervention
does not result in a successful resolution, the matter should
then be taken to the headman of the ward of the person
against whom the complaint has been made. Only if the dispute is not settled by the ward headman is it finally taken to
the chief's *kgotla*. These agencies, then, provide a hierarchical
course through which any dispute may proceed; that is, a settlement ought to be sought at each level in turn, and the matter
should not be referred to a higher authority unless resolution
appears impossible.

At the first of these levels, where only the two parties
themselves are involved, the mode of settlement is necessarily one of negotiation. Private meetings between the disputants should be occasions of explanation and apology, at
which offers of compensation ought to be accompanied by
assurances of future amicability and good conduct. When
such bilateral contacts fail to resolve the conflict (or, as is
often the case, serve only to exacerbate it), the kinsmen who
are then approached to mediate have considerable latitude in
choosing a procedure to follow in seeking a settlement. Typically they begin by making informal efforts to persuade the
two parties, either individually or together, to come to terms

with each other before the conflict escalates into a bitter public confrontation. Alternatively, they may suggest convening a formal meeting of the agnatic segment, or segments, to which the disputants belong. A meeting of the segment must in any case occur before the dispute can be taken to a higher level. At the meeting of the segment, the mode of settlement remains one of mediation. The kinsmen who intervene between the disputants may stress the implications of the available courses of action and urge them to follow an approved solution, but they have no recognized authority to impose a decision.

If a dispute is not resolved at the lower levels, it is placed before the ward headman of the individual against whom the original complaint was made. At this level there still remains some procedural flexibility. The respective groupings may make informal appeals to the headman, or the matter may be raised directly in the formal context of the open *kgotla*. Similarly, the headman also has the option of handling the dispute in either a formal or informal manner. He may decide to mediate by suggesting a solution that he considers should be acceptable to both parties; he may even send them away for further discussion among their close kin if he feels that this means has not been sufficiently explored. However, the headman has the authority to convene a hearing and to make an order-in-settlement that the parties must recognize, whether they agree with it or not. When a headman chooses to deal with a dispute in this way, the mode of settlement is one of adjudication. In the face of such a decision, the parties may appeal against the outcome and take the case to the chief. Once this has occurred, the latter must hear the report of the headman who dealt with the matter before listening to the accounts of the respective disputants and their senior kinsmen. Like the headman, the chief (or his representative) may try to effect a mediated settlement,[1] or he may proceed directly to make a final decision, which he can enforce if necessary. In other words, negotiation, mediation, and adjudication, as modes of conflict resolution, stand in a fixed *ideal* relationship: negotiation should first be attempted at the lowest level before resort is made successively to mediation and adjudication at the higher ones (cf. Gulliver 1979:22). On the other hand, in everyday dispute-settlement processes, negotiation does not automatically give way to mediation and adjudication if initial efforts at resolution have proved fruitless; it is thus an oversimplification to correlate agencies and procedural modes in any rigid fashion.

Processes and Procedures

The formal hierarchy thus provides the institutional framework within which disputes are managed, but Tswana recognize the existence of a range of procedural flexibilities that may be manifest in the processual course of any particular case. Apart from the room for maneuver allowed to headmen and chiefs in their attempts at adjudication and mediation, flexibility is especially conspicuous at the lower levels, where the disputing parties may exercise considerable freedom in deciding whom they will approach to intervene. The formal model itself permits some degree of latitude, of course, because most disputants will have several senior paternal and maternal kin to select from. In practice, moreover, they do not confine themselves to such kinsmen, for whom they choose depends also on the different preliminary goals for which the third parties are recruited.

These preliminary goals, as they are indigenously perceived, are broadly divisible into three categories. First, an individual may approach another person simply to discuss an incident or a relationship about which he or she feels uneasy; that is, a confidant may be sought for purposes of *perceptual clarification*. At this stage, the individual will strive to organize his own definition of the situation so as to determine whether he has, in fact, become involved in a dispute. In some cases he may actually desire to initiate such a dispute and may precipitate it, either by acting in a hostile manner or by exploiting a chance occurrence in order to rationalize the conflict. Here the confidant may be sought by the prospective disputant for the purpose of self-justification and for help in organizing his construction of the circumstances. Whatever the specific motives behind such exploratory consultations, many cases, later marked by clearly stated differences between the opposing litigants, begin when each tries to structure ambiguous perceptions by discussing them with a third party. The identity of the individual approached may sometimes be a matter of chance; he may be the first person with whom the disputant comes into contact after a worrying incident. But the element of chance does not diminish the significance of this first contact. The response of the confidant—whether it is one of passive agreement, confirmatory aggression, or disagreement with the disputant's interpretation—is often important in determining whether the matter will be pursued or forgotten.

Second, a disputant may wish to *seek a settlement* and may recruit a neutral mediator in order to expedite his efforts. In these circumstances the third party is likely to be an individual regarded as being both fair and skilled in the arts of mediation and informal settlement. If the disputants are kin, the mediator may be a man whose relationship to the two parties is recognized to be equally close (or distant), for if he is closer to one than to the other, the possibility that he can successfully intervene is slight; more often than not, a person related to neither disputant is chosen.

Third, intervening parties may be sought for *strategic purposes* by a disputant as his supporters in the prospective confrontation. Here recruitment will tend to be confined to persons with whom the disputant has particularly close ties and/or recognizes reciprocal obligations. Such parties are expected to take his side in the dispute, both in the formal arena of the *kgotla* and outside. Each disputant will attempt to extend his field of support as widely as possible and will strive to include within it men of political influence, prestige, and skill in litigation. Where the two disputants are linked by bonds of kinship or coresidence, the competitive recruitment of partisan followers assumes crucial significance, since both will be drawing largely from a shared field.[2]

These three sets of goals are not exclusive of one another; in a particular situation, a disputant may seek third parties in order to satisfy some or all of them, and the capacity in which a third party actually intervenes is not always unambiguous or enduring. Moreover, the goals may emerge either in sequential order or simultaneously. In the former case the same individual may be selected to fulfill the roles implied by each goal, starting as a confidant, becoming a neutral mediator, and ending as a supporter of one of the disputants. Where all three goals are expressed simultaneously, however, a disputant may seek different people for the various roles. In fact, some Tswana appear to view this as an optimum strategy, as case 4 demonstrates.

CASE 4:   MMA-M AND THE DEPUTY CHIEF[3]

At Good Hope, the capital village of the Botswana Rolong, Mma-M, the chairman of the Village Development Committee (V.D.C.), complained that the deputy chief, Rre-B, had impugned her reputation and integrity during an incident that occurred outside the Tribal Offices in 1975. Rre-B had been holding some V.D.C. funds, for which he had repeatedly been asked. When Mma-M demanded that he finally hand them over, he refused and claimed angrily that she was accusing him of theft. In his denunciation of her, Rre-B accused Mma-M of dishonesty and venality. As a number of informants indicated, this conversation seems to have expressed long-standing tension between the traditional authorities and V.D.C. officeholders.

Immediately after this quarrel had taken place, Mma-M, who was widely recognized as a dynamic and able politician, left the office to seek the head teacher of the local primary school and secretary of the V.D.C. As soon as she found him, she proceeded to describe the incident and to recall the number of contingent events she thought had some bearing on it. At first her account consisted of a disorganized series of statements in which she brought up random aspects of the dispute. As she spoke, however, she appeared to order her construction of the situation, and she ended by remarking that this was certainly a case for litigation. The teacher, whose participation was limited to questions of fact and to periodic acknowledgement of her emerging position, assumed a compliant posture throughout. At the conclusion of the meeting Mma-M, having thanked him for listening and advising her, walked directly to the village bottle store, where she had seen the truck of one of the ward headmen. The latter, Rre-P, whose home was some distance from Good Hope, was highly respected for his wisdom and capabilities as a mediator in disputes.

Mma-M took Rre-P aside and asked him if he would "offer advice" to herself and the deputy chief on the question that had arisen between them; because his seat was far away, he would never be required to hear the case in his formal capacity. Rre-P agreed to accompany her to the Tribal Office, but, by the time they arrived,

Rre-B had already left. Mma-M prevailed upon the secretary to send a message to him, and he returned an hour later.

Mma-M began by outlining the incident that had given rise to her complaint. While she was doing so, Rre-B rose angrily and began to walk out. Rre-P admonished him and told him to sit down, which he did. Five minutes later, however, he left for good. Both Mma-M and Rre-B then set about recruiting supporters, and, within two days, the dispute became a *cause célèbre*. A week later the district commissioner, himself a Morolong, was approached by Mma-M to intervene; Rre-B had managed to include the chief among his following, so that the two men who alone were authorized to preside over the Customary Court (i.e., the chief and the deputy chief) had become directly involved as partisans. Because it threatened to become a sensitive issue for the administration, the district commissioner chose to hear the matter informally. In making her statement, Mma-M emphasized that she had taken initial advice from a responsible local man (the teacher) and had then sought mediation from one with a reputation as an arbitrator (Rre-P); both, in fact, appeared as witnesses to testify to her activities in this respect.

In deciding in Mma-M's favor, the district commissioner praised her responsible efforts to settle the matter privately and quickly. Several Rolong, when discussing the case, stressed that she had won an impressive victory against powerful opposition *because* she had been careful to proceed in a morally commendable fashion while simultaneously recruiting support of considerable quality and quantity.

The hierarchy of agencies may define the formal features of the process of dispute settlement, but, clearly, both the procedural course and the nature of any particular dispute will depend on a range of variables that are external to it. Perhaps the two most significant of these are the nature of the relationship between the parties involved and the litigants' goals, as expressed in the object of dispute.

Among the Tswana, relatively few disputes arise out of isolated incidents in which unrelated strangers become temporarily associated only in the specific context of litigation. Disputants are usually known to each other even if they are not bound by kinship or coresidence. The nature of their relationship may, however, vary widely. At one ideal-typical extreme, this relationship may be highly *determinate;* that is, its content is derived from, and is primarily restricted to, recognized and specific obligations, whether transient or enduring.[4] At the other extreme, the parties may be involved in a *generalized* bond in which kinship and coresidence are overlain by relations of mutual or complementary obligation, cooperation, or even hostility. Between these polar extremes, then, relationships fall along a continuum defined by the extent to which their content is generalized beyond the purely determinate.

Cutting across the relational dimension is the dimension of litigants' goals, the nature of which significantly influences the object of any dispute and, hence, both its procedural and its political career. The litigants' goals may, again, be ordered along a continuum, here defined in terms of their specificity or generality. On the one hand, they may be directed primarily at settling an issue that has arisen in relation to a particular value, such as the chance destruction of crops by cattle or the ownership of an item of property. Under these conditions, few considerations beyond the immediate circumstances of the incident may be brought to bear upon the dispute, and its settlement may be uncomplicated and swift. On the other hand, litigants' goals may be more generally directed at the negotiation of the relationship itself. This may involve, for example, efforts to sever the bond completely (see case 3), redefine its jural nature (case 9), or reorder the relative rank implied in it (see chap. 6). In such cases, the value *ostensibly* under dispute is of minimal significance in its own right, although it may constitute the focus around which arguments are organized. Indeed, the disputed object may have little or no intrinsic worth. As we have pointed out elsewhere (1977a), a conflict over a household utensil may be treated with the utmost seriousness by a Tswana chief's *kgotla,* while one concerning a large family herd may be settled with little difficulty by informal negotiation or mediation. Neither the gravity of a dispute nor the intensity with which it is fought is thus necessarily determined by the material value of the object or right in question, since this may represent merely the symbolic context for confrontation over a more fundamental, and quite different, substantive issue.[5] It is important to stress here that processes that occur within the hierarchy of settlement agencies do not always concern the resolution of disputes alone, for litigation may also provide an arena for the public enactment and recognition of relations whose content is a function of prior political interaction.

The indigenously perceived factors determining litigants' goals are extremely varied. Important among them, however, are the respective career situations of the disputants and the social context in which the conflict arises. Thus, for example, an individual who finds himself desperate for money with which to discharge debts or to deal with pressing obligations may be eager to see any dispute quickly resolved through the offer of an acceptable sum by way of compensation. In contrast, another may be at a stage of his career at which he sees advantages in playing a prominent part in protracted litigation before a large public. In such circumstances a dispute may allow him the opportunity to demonstrate his political acumen and the strength of his support or enable him to test and reaffirm relationships with both followers and opponents. In terms of the analysis of the dispute process itself, however, the crucial issue is not one of motivation per se; it lies, rather, in the implication of litigants' goals of different orders once they have crystallized and emerged.

The fact that both phenomenal dimensions—litigants' goals and relations—are subject to wide variation and themselves subsume diverse factors[6] may suggest that it is impossible to abstract a pattern underlying the course of everyday disputes. A systematic relationship obtains, however, between the two continua that describe, respectively, the quality of the social link between the two parties and the nature of their intentions. Indeed, the relationship is such that a model may be constructed to account broadly for the diacritical tendencies characteristic of Tswana procedural and processual forms. This model is presented in figure 1.

As this model indicates, the two dimensions intersect in such a manner as to generate four possible situational complexes: (1) that in which dispute over a specific value arises between persons involved in an essentially determinate relationship; (2) that in which confrontation over a specific value occurs in the context of a generalized bond; (3) that in which determinately linked persons contest the nature of their relationship; and (4) that in which the nature and quality

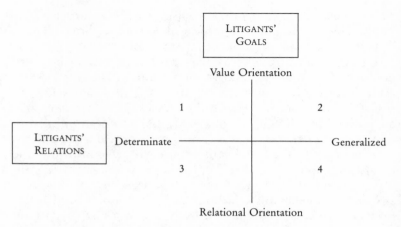

FIGURE 1. MODEL OF PROCESSUAL FORMS

of a generalized bond itself becomes the object of conflict between litigants. These four complexes may be lineally arranged as follows:

$$1 \rightarrow 2 \rightarrow 3 \rightarrow 4$$

This progression in turn describes the systematic variation of dispute processes in terms of a number of closely related features that underlie their form and content.

The first of these features, *procedural flexibility,* increases consistently in the direction of (1) to (4). When a dispute falls into the first category, it is likely to be settled very much in terms of ideal procedures. Even if it concerns property of considerable value, it may readily be disposed of by direct negotiation or by means of informal third-party mediation. When conflicts are of types (2), (3), or (4), however, there will be a growing tendency on the part of disputants to exploit procedural flexibilities. Thus, in a case of type (4), each may attempt to use the lower-level agencies to gain maximum strategic advantage rather than to achieve a settlement of the conflict per se. Similarly, the participation of the higher authorities may be the subject of competitive efforts on the part of the litigants; for example, one who seeks the broadest possible arena in which to confront an opponent (for there may be strategic benefit in first revealing one's suit in the highest [internal] forum) may try to have the ward headman intervene informally in order to secure a direct referral of the case to the chief's *kgotla*.

Second, the determinant significance of *circumstantial factors* surrounding the precipitating incident decreases along this linear path, while that of the *prior history* (and the temporal duration) of the particular dispute increases concomitantly. This is not to say that such circumstantial factors do not provide a focus for argument in cases of types (2), (3), and (4); they are, however, both in the exposition of suits and in statements of judgment, increasingly treated as symptomatic rather than etiological. Third, and following directly from this, there is a tendency for the *object of the dispute* to become more generalized along the same path; this, of course, is implicit in the constitutive parameters of the model itself. Thus, in conflicts of type (1), the definition of the issue at hand is usually clear and unitary, while in those of type (4) it is generally ambiguous and multistranded, as, for instance, when close agnatic rivals accuse each other simultaneously of slander, theft, subversion of jural rank, and other forms of improper conduct. As this suggests, the linear progression from (1) to (4) also implies the increasing possibility that the disputants will differ over the definition of the nature of the dispute and hence may engage in competing efforts to impose their own *paradigms of argument* upon the case (cf. chap. 3). (It follows, obviously, that the tendency to invoke norms will also increase concomitantly.) This is particularly so when it has been initiated, by one or the other party, for specifically political ends that transcend the narrower contingencies of the incident or issue itself.

It is possible for any dispute to move from one category to another during its career as litigants reformulate their goals, strategies, or relations. When this occurs, the procedural nature of the case will be transformed along the lines implied by the model. It is to be emphasized, however, that the model is not in itself intended as an explanation of processual forms. It is, in the first instance, a descriptive device for typifying the different modes of dispute and for ordering and categorizing the particularities of everyday processes in terms of general principles of form and substance. This will become especially significant in chapter 7, when we seek to relate rule and process and the logic of dispute to the constitution of the sociocultural order. At this stage we are trying simply to identify the relevant categories and, to this end, shall provide illustrations of the tendencies we have isolated.

Modes of Dispute

As we noted earlier, the Tswana regard themselves—and are regarded by others—as having a proclivity for litigation and a sustained and abiding interest in it. Nevertheless, while cases of type (1) may provide a source of passing gossip, they are, save in exceptional circumstances, seen as unremarkable; they are a taken-for-granted feature of everyday life and social relations. A typical example of cases of this type, often cited by informants in the course of discussion, is provided by an instance of the random destruction of crops by cattle. This frequently occurs when young boys drive herds to waterholes.

CASE 5:   THE TRAMPLED FIELD

One morning, while Roberts was talking to an elderly man at Mochudi, the Kgatla capital, they were joined by one of the man's sons. The latter reported that their cattle had trampled a field of young maize planted by another [unrelated] man, whose agricultural holding outside the village abutted their own.[7] The father set out at once for the field, some miles away, where the neighbor was waiting. When he arrived, this man pointed out quite extensive damage in one corner of his field. An apology was immediately offered, but a bag of grain was demanded as compensation. This was agreed, and the old man returned to Mochudi. The bag of grain was delivered to the claimant's homestead, without formality, some days later.[8]

Such cases are rarely, if ever, exploited for wider political or social ends; if one party strives to do so, cogent moral sanctions may be brought to bear upon him by members of the community. From the perspective of the litigants, patently, neither the nature of the relationship between them nor the circumstantial factors will usually be ambiguous enough to permit anything but settlement-directed activity—except at the risk of a loss of personal reputation and legitimacy. In the very logic of their construction, then, these cases largely preclude the exploitation of procedural flexibility; the disputants' room for maneuver is, by definition, severely constrained. Moreover, the history of relations between the two parties prior to the precipitating incident is unimportant. Circumstantial factors thus appear to determine the course of the process. Here they represent the etiology of the conflict; that is, they are not seen to be symptomatic of anything else. Similarly, the object of dispute is restricted to the issue of apology and compensation for the loss of a specific value; and, since it is unambiguous, the paradigm of argument does not come into question. The only possible difference between the parties may arise over the extent of restitution; provided it is reasonable, however, and within the broadly established limits, the wronged individual may expect to receive what he requests.

Cases of type (2) again involve disputes over a particular value, but they occur in the context of a generalized relationship between the parties. As in those of type (1), any such dispute may be settled quickly and quietly, with little recourse to the hierarchy of agencies, but here the tendency to exploit procedural flexibility is greater, as case 6 illustrates.

CASE 6:   THE DISPUTED HOUSE

Rre-M, a headman among the Botswana Rolong, owned a house situated about 200 yards away from his homestead in Good Hope village. His twenty-year-old [first] son, F, claimed that he had been given this house by his father, an assertion supported by his mother. Rre-M, however, rented the property to two sisters, who lived there and operated a shebeen on the premises. In 1975, F expressed the desire to occupy the house, as his natal home was overcrowded. He said that his father had consented to this but had done nothing about it for several months, despite F's repeated requests.

Finally, F decided to precipitate a dispute and bring the matter to a head: he threw a stone through one of the windows of the property. Rre-M, who wished to hush up the incident, sought a settlement through direct discussion, but F immediately approached third parties; he specifically wanted to prevent his father from making further empty promises. His first confidant, the tribal secretary, warned him that, while he was justly angry, he would gain little from a public confrontation; once drawn into open conflict,

Rre-M would ensure that the case would be taken to the chief, his longtime ally. The second person whom F chose to approach was his mother, Mma-F. She offered aggressive encouragement and persuaded him to pursue the case further. Mma-F, moreover, advised her son to avoid private third-party mediation on the ground that Rre-M would either ignore it or use it to his own advantage; hence F should petition his kin to hold a family meeting as soon as possible.

The family meeting was duly held, but it only exacerbated the dispute. Rre-M made an angry speech in which he claimed that his son had behaved improperly, having been goaded on by Mma-F. The latter, he asserted, was in fact exploiting the situation to initiate a quarrel with him over their domestic relations. F, on the other hand, was careful to stress that his complaint was addressed specifically to the question of the house. Rre-M then said that the case should be taken directly to the chief, and he refused to have anything more to do with the family meeting. [Because he was the headman, litigation at the ward level was bypassed.]

In the chief's *kgotla*, F reiterated that his actions were intended simply to ensure that his father would fulfill his promise and procrastinate no further. In reply, Rre-M again claimed that his wife had advised his son improperly; but he did not repeat the argument that a more fundamental conflict underlay the dispute. Rather, he stressed that F had been wrong to take action, as he had done, when the problem could have been resolved by direct and amicable discussion. In announcing his judgment, the chief admonished F and supported Rre-M's view that arrangements with respect to the house should be settled between the disputants themselves. The majority of the villagers believed that the decision was inadequate and that it reflected the alliance between the chief and Rre-M. Rre-M's dilatory behavior toward his son, they argued, should also have been negatively sanctioned by the chief.

A greater degree of procedural flexibility is evident in this case than in case 5. Having deliberately precipitated the dispute process by his act of violence, F resisted direct negotiation or third-party mediation and, after taking advice, called immediately for a family meeting. He hoped that the matter would go no further, once his father had been censured for his breach of promise, and he did not mind being reprimanded for his own behavior. Rre-M, in contrast, first tried to negotiate with his son in an effort to prevent the incident from becoming an object of public attention. When this failed, however, he ensured that no settlement would emerge from the family meeting; for in that context the consensus seems to have been in favor of F. Hence he sought to have the case heard by the chief, on whose sympathies he knew he could depend. Both disputants, in other words, attempted to manipulate the hierarchy of agencies to maximum strategic advantage.

In this case, moreover, the paradigm of argument and object of dispute came briefly into question. While F asserted throughout that he was concerned only with the tenure of the house, Rre-M, in the family meeting, introduced the wider issue of domestic conflict. Both F and his mother understood from his speech that he would pursue this line of argument in the chief's *kgotla*.[9] But Rre-M chose not to do so. Differences over the paradigm of argument and the object of dispute were thus taken no further, and debate was confined to the litigants' behavior with respect to the house and its tenure. Similarly, apart from Rre-M's outburst at the family meeting, discussion centered on circumstantial factors rather than on the prior history of the conflict. The latter came under scrutiny only in passing, when Mma-F's involvement was raised.

It would appear, therefore, that the exploitation of procedural flexibilities, disagreement over the paradigm of argument and the object of dispute, and the significance of the prior history of social relations (at the expense of circumstantial factors) tend to be more marked here than in cases of type (1); but, as case 7 shows, they are less marked than in cases of type (3), in which disputants contest the definition of a determinate relationship.

CASE 7:   THE SHARECROPPING DISAGREEMENT

In 1970 a dispute over a field arose between Rre-L and Rre-S, unrelated commoner members of different Tshidi wards in Mafikeng. According to Rre-L, the field belonged to him; he had allowed Rre-S to share-plough it for one season in return for 25 percent of the yield. Rre-S, on the other hand, claimed that he had been allocated the plot as his own by Rre-L, who had been acting on behalf of his senior FBS. The latter, the senior member of the agnatic segment that controlled most of the surrounding land,[10] had migrated to seek employment. After the field had been harvested, Rre-L asked Rre-S for his portion of the crop. He was given one bag of grain and told that he would receive no more.

Rre-L, who was poor and relatively uninfluential, was inclined to let the matter rest, for Rre-S was not only rich and powerful, with a reputation for being troublesome, but also counted among his allies several prominent men in the capital. When Rre-L's own crop failed, however, he approached his wealthier younger half-brother, Rre-N, for aid. On hearing that Rre-L had not been paid, Rre-N urged him to pursue his claim and took him to see his friend Rre-M, a well-known and influential rival of Rre-S.

Rre-M immediately offered to accompany Rre-L to see Rre-S in Mafikeng. The latter had done nothing about the matter, since he chose to act as if no dispute existed. When he was visited by the two men, he made this view explicit. He had been allocated the field by a responsible authority: Rre-L had been acting, as he was entitled, for the man who controlled the land in the area. His only con-tractual obligations toward Rre-L were thus those of a nonresident recipient of a plot; i.e., he was not to leave it unused, and he was bound to ensure that his enterprises did not disturb other land-holders. Indeed, he had been generous in offering a bag of grain as an unsolicited gift. As his contractual relationship with Rre-L had never involved a cooperative farming agreement, he had no more liability. When it was clear that Rre-S was not interested in any further mediation, Rre-M invited him to come to a meeting at Rre-L's place to sort out the dispute, but he refused. If a complaint was to be brought against him, he said, a formal report must be made to his ward headman. The two visitors were told un-ceremoniously to leave before Rre-L had even had an opportunity to state his side of the case.

Rre-L, again at the prompting of his brother, then called a meet-ing of their agnatic segment, at which it was decided to petition the provincial headman[11] to intervene. It was commonly held by those present that a direct complaint to Rre-S's ward headman would not be fruitful, as the defendant had "eaten" this man.[12] When the provincial headman was approached, it was explained that, because the disputed field and Rre-S's other holdings were in his area, Rre-L had felt it desirable to bring the case to him first. Like some other provincial headmen, this man was also a section headman at the capital, and Rre-S's ward happened to fall within his unit. In formal terms, the complainant was approaching him in his capacity as pro-vincial headman. But Rre-L and his allies were quick to note that the fortuitous overlap of roles might be exploited as a means of circumventing the ward headman's jurisdiction.

The provincial headman agreed to hear the case and summoned Rre-S. The defendant, however, sent back a message conveying his refusal to appear. In stating his grounds, he chose to ignore the fact that the headman had jurisdiction over the province and argued that a dispute could not come before a superior [section] *kgotla* prior to being heard at the ward level. By now, Rre-L was committed to pursuing the case. The provincial headman instructed him to go to the ward headman, as it would be a lengthy and difficult process to bring Rre-S forcibly to his own *kgotla* first; in any case, the complainant could always appeal.

The case was duly taken to the ward headman, who found in favor of the defendant. Thereafter, the complainant appealed formally to the section [provincial] headman, who upheld his suit. Finally the case was taken to the chief on the initiative of Rre-S. But the chief turned down this last appeal. In the course of the settlement process, both sides recruited support of considerable, and roughly equivalent, strength. The opposing arguments remained broadly the same throughout the three hearings: Rre-L outlined the circumstances under which he had first entered the share-ploughing agreement with Rre-S and stated that he had not been paid. While he did not debate his opponent's assertion that he was entitled to allocate the land in the area, he was careful to establish that the disputed field was known to local people as a holding that had been cultivated before by himself and his agnates. Not only had Rre-S been in breach of contract, he claimed, but he had also behaved badly in refusing the offer to negotiate. In contrast, Rre-S continued to suggest that there was no dispute [*ga gona tsheko*]: he had simply been allocated a field by a proper authority. [Some attention was paid in his statement to the devolution of this authority to Rre-L from his FBS.] He had satisfied his contractual obligation in this respect and had ploughed the land successfully, giving the complainant a bag of grain out of generosity. The latter, however, had become greedy and jealous and had made a false claim.

The essence of this case, then, lies in the competing constructions placed on the nature of their contractual relationship by the respective parties. Present and future rights in the disputed values—the field and its product—are ultimately entailed in, and contested in the rhetorical terms of, this question.

The extent to which procedural flexibilities were exploited by the litigants is patently greater in case 7 than in cases 5 and 6. Rre-L initiated the dispute-settlement process when, at the prompting of his brother, he sought mediation by a third party in an effort to recover his alleged share of the crop. Rre-S, the defendant, had up to that time assumed a posture of strategic inactivity and denied that any dispute existed; for, had the matter been allowed to lapse, he would have gained considerably from the entire venture. Rre-L, of course, did not permit this to happen. In the course of seeking redress, he first summoned his agnates, to recruit their support and discuss strategy, and then attempted to bring Rre-S before the provincial headman. This was an explicitly opportunist measure designed to circumvent the jurisdiction of the ward headman, whom the defendant had reduced to clientage. Consistent with his own position, however, Rre-S refused to be drawn; in order either to discourage the complainant from pursuing his suit or, failing that, to ensure that the case would be heard initially in circumstances favorable to himself, Rre-S insisted throughout that Rre-L report the dispute directly to his (Rre-S's) ward headman. His refusal to attend a meeting at Rre-L's homestead or to appear at the provincial headman's *kgotla* underlined his unwillingness to enter the judicial arena under anything but the most advantageous conditions. In other words, both parties tried to employ established areas of flexibility (including appellate provisions) and adventitious factors (such as the conjunction of the section and provincial headmanship) in their effort to assert control over the course of the dispute-settlement process.

Case 7 also demonstrates the operation of the other elements, especially in comparison with cases 5 and 6, drawn from types (1) and (2). The circumstantial factors surrounding the dispute itself were of conspicuously less significance here than in those cases. Hence, while the precipitating incident involved the nonpayment of an unspecified amount of grain, this act had little intrinsic meaning *except* as a corollary of previous interaction between the two men. And, inasmuch as both of them were primarily concerned with defining the nature of their relationship (and, by implication, the circumstances of its genesis), much of the argument was explicitly addressed to the historical dimension of the conflict. Each party, moreover, invoked contingent past events in attempting to establish their cases: the defendant took care to confirm that authority over the area had devolved legitimately to Rre-L from his FBS, while the complainant had witnesses state that the contested field was known publicly to have been held and cultivated by him and his agnates.

In case 7, as in cases 5 and 6, there was little real or enduring difference between the litigants over the object of dispute. Despite Rre-S's strategic denials of the existence of any such conflict, they agreed on the essential facts of the case: Rre-L acknowledged that he had the right to allocate land and that he had entered a contractual agreement over the use of the field, and Rre-S admitted that he had rejected the request for the bags of grain. Implicit in both suits was the view that the object of dispute concerned the contractual terms of the allocation and, by extension, future rights in the land. But here, for the first time, each party strove to impose his own paradigm of argument on the debate. Each invoked a set of norms appropriate to his construction of the situation and then proceeded to interpret the (agreed) facts in terms of these organizing precepts.

Cases of type (4) represent the furthest extreme in the linear progression described by the model. In them, as we have already suggested, there are both the potentiality and a marked tendency (a) to exploit procedural flexibility, (b) to emphasize the prior history of the conflict and ignore its immediate circumstances, and (c) to contest the object of dispute and the paradigm of argument. Several of the disputes discussed in later chapters are of this type; one of them (case 9) is here summarized as an appropriate example.

CASE 8: MOLEFE AND MADUBU

Molefe, a Mokgatla of the Masiana *kgotla* in Mochudi, established a liaison with Madubu, a Ngwato woman, in about 1945. The circumstances in which this occurred are not entirely clear, but Madubu was taken away from her home village by Molefe before any formal marriage negotiations or exchanges had taken place. Molefe, moreover, kept her away from his own ward because his father, Mankge, had wanted him to marry someone else and was expected to be angered by this turn of events. After a while, however, Mankge became reconciled to his son's actions and began to treat Madubu as a daughter-in-law, eventually arranging a residential site for the couple in the larger Tlagadi ward of which Masiana forms a part. No bridewealth passed between the two sets of kin, who seem to have had little contact until the dispute was later taken before the chief's *kgotla*.

Although they lived peacefully for some years, Madubu bore no children and, about 1953, Molefe persuaded her to permit him to enter a secondary union with her younger sister. Despite the refusal of her kin to consent to this, the young woman came to Mochudi, where she bore Molefe a daughter and a son. But the new domestic arrangements soon led to quarrels and disagreements, which were exacerbated when, after Mankge's death in 1956, Molefe went to live with his father's third wife, Mmaseteba. By 1959 he had ceased to maintain Madubu or her sister.

In that year, Madubu complained of neglect to members of Molefe's descent grouping and, later, to Motshegare Ramalepa, the headman of Tlagadi. Motshegare, who had a long-standing relationship of hostility with the men of the Masiana *kgotla,* immediately expressed sympathy for Madubu's plight. He ordered Molefe to sell a beast to maintain her. But Molefe did nothing to comply with this order until required to do so by the chief.

In 1961 Madubu made a further complaint, this time to Segonyane, Molefe's yB. The latter took her to Letsebe, the senior member of their agnatic grouping, who summoned Molefe to a meeting attended primarily by his close agnates. Letsebe opened the meeting by confronting Molefe with Madubu's claim of neglect. To this he replied that he had left her with six bags of grain when he departed recently for his cattle post with Mmaseteba. Discussion later turned to the general state of the relationship: Molefe asserted that it had broken down and that Madubu should be sent back to her home. The meeting ended when all the men present agreed to this.

Madubu, however, protested again to Motshegare Ramalepa at the Tlagadi ward, and he agreed to hear the case formally. [The transcript is to be found in case 9.] In summary, Madubu claimed that Molefe was her husband and that their marriage had been properly negotiated. [She described in detail her version of its arrangement.] The relationship had broken down because of Mmaseteba. Significantly, the women involved in the case— Molefe's sister and Mankge's surviving wives, including Mmaseteba—all supported Madubu's assertion of her wifely status on the ground that it had been publicly accepted. In contrast, Molefe held that Madubu "is only a woman who lives with me," not a wife, since neither formal negotiations nor a promise of bridewealth had been entered into. In his judgment, the ward headman censured Molefe for his neglect, which had been made all the more serious by the fact that he had ignored the earlier order to support Madubu. He decided, furthermore, that the latter *was* Molefe's wife and that a divorce case would be heard by the chief. Consistent with this, he fined Letsebe R4 [$4.60] for "not controlling your children and for granting a divorce in your *kgotla.*" [Among the Kgatla, divorce orders can be made only by a chief.]

Subsequently, when Madubu argued her suit in front of the chief, she reiterated her claims concerning Molefe's desertion, stating that her "witness is headman Motshegare Ramalepa." Again, much of her case revolved around the history of their union—its legal establishment and public recognition; Molefe went into equal detail in order to deny that a marriage had ever taken place. Molefe seems to have recruited more support in preparation for this hearing. On this occasion a number of witnesses, including two of Madubu's kinsmen, agreed with his construction of the nature of their relationship. The chief, however, judged the union to have been a marriage and, in granting a divorce, ordered a division of the property acquired by the couple over the past eighteen years.

Because it is the relationship between the parties, rather than any particular event or action, that is at issue in cases of type (4), there is rarely an isolable precipitating incident or a clearly identifiable point at which the settlement process is set in motion. In case 8, Madubu's decision to seek redress seems to have been prompted by a cumulative frustration at Molefe's behavior and at his failure to respond to her private complaints. Once the settlement process had been initiated, moreover, its early stages bore little resemblance to the formal pattern. Neither disputant attempted to negotiate with the other directly or even through a mediator, and, when Madubu took action, she recruited neither her own kin nor a neutral arbitrator to intervene informally. She appealed to Molefe's agnates and then petitioned the Tlagadi ward headman to order her husband to support her. (The partisan involvement of Motshegare Ramalepa throughout the dispute is a particularly striking departure from the stated ideal.)[13] In contrast, Molefe, like Rre-S in case 7, avoided direct participation in the settlement process and disappeared to his cattle post.

Further exploitation of procedural flexibility occurred when the dispute began to proceed up the hierarchy of agencies. Molefe wished to have it dealt with at the agnatic-segment level. Knowing of Motshegare's antipathy toward

him, and fearing that his defiance of the earlier order would
reduce his credibility, he sought to avoid having the case
taken before the headman or the chief, in whose *makgotla* he
was likely to sustain a costly defeat. Hence he tried to ensure
that his close agnates would cooperate with him in contriving
to terminate his bond with Madubu. At the meeting of the
segment he first rebutted the accusation of neglect and then
turned his attention to the nature of the relationship. Those
present did not challenge either aspect of Molefe's argument.
On the contrary, they appear to have shared his hope that, by
construing the dispute in the way they did, and by deciding
publicly to return Madubu to her home, the matter would be
quietly disposed of in his favor. Moreover, despite Madubu's
dissatisfaction with the outcome of the meeting, Letsebe did
not report the case to Motshegare, as he should, ideally, have
done. It was left to the complainant to elicit the intervention
of the ward headman.

Motshegare Ramalepa had been in open sympathy with
Madubu's predicament ever since she had first approached
him a year before, and much of her strategic effort depended
on deploying his support in the public arena. Using his room
for maneuver to help her, he summoned Molefe to appear
before his court and engaged in a ploy the effect of which was
to give Madubu the maximum advantage from the legal process. Although he could not try a divorce case in his own
right, he immediately *defined* the dispute as falling within this
category and, therefore, as requiring referral to the chief. In
doing so, he was acting quite within his bounds, and he emphasized this by confining the hearing at the ward level to the
question of neglect. At the same time, of course, he was
offering cogent legitimacy to Madubu's construction of the
relationship and preparing the ground for a successful appearance before the higher authority. To reinforce this, he
fined Letsebe for exceeding his jurisdiction; this would make
it difficult for the chief not to treat Madubu as Molefe's wife
unless he first reversed Motshegare's decision on this count.

Hence, by ordering the dispute into two separate issues,
Motshegare ensured that Madubu would benefit first from
his own instruction to Molefe to make financial reparation to
her and, second, from a divorce case in the chief's *kgotla,*
which could produce a substantial property disposition in her

favor. Of the two, the latter was of greater moment, and it was effected by using an agency of the hierarchy to define the dispute in a manner partisan to one of the litigants rather than to settle it. In other words, while the ward headman has no officially decisive role in the settlement of divorce cases, his intervention served here to transform the conflict between Molefe and Madubu into such a case. The importance of the headman's intervention on behalf of the complainant was clearly expressed in her opening statement before the chief: "My witness is headman Motshegare Ramalepa." Procedural ambiguities, and their competitive manipulation by the various parties, underlie the strategic character of the settlement process; because litigants generally strive to *win* cases rather than to conform to some abstract ideal that celebrates the desirability of conflict resolution per se, this is hardly surprising. Madubu's behavior illustrates the point clearly. Had she simply wished to end her relationship with Molefe in an amicable spirit, she might have accepted the outcome of the meeting of the agnatic segment. After all, this was no different from the outcome in the chief's *kgotla* as far as the future of the relationship was concerned; in both, the decision was to terminate it. And, indeed, this was what Madubu desired; otherwise she would not have sued for divorce. But the point of pursuing the case via Motshegare to the chief's *kgotla* in the way she did was specifically to win a property disposition, not simply to resolve the dispute by dissolving the relationship.

In cases of type (4), the significance of circumstantial factors is relatively limited; most argument is addressed to the history of the relationship between the parties. The lack of a single precipitating incident, as we have noted, emphasizes this tendency. Both Molefe and Madubu were concerned first and foremost to impose their respective definitions on the nature of their bond, and both discussed its formation and development in some detail in order to do this. Each of them, moreover, treated the particularities of the other's behavior as symptomatic of a more general condition—the breakdown of their relationship.

Finally, the division between the litigants with respect to the object of dispute and the paradigm of argument is potentially greatest in cases of type (4). For Molefe, the object was simply to have Madubu recognized as "only a woman who lives with me"; given this status, he had discharged his obligations toward her. Madubu, however, sought initially to establish that she had been deserted; but, once the meeting of the agnatic segment had set aside her claims, she sued simultaneously for neglect and divorce. In other words, her position changed during the settlement process: at the outset she attempted to have her marriage recognized in order to persuade her husband to return and look after her; later she sought to have it recognized in order to obtain a divorce and, hence, a property disposition (see chap. 5). The contrast is patent: Molefe saw the dispute as an opportunity to redefine the relationship as a casual liaison and to terminate it with minimal cost to himself; Madubu ostensibly viewed it as an opportunity to restore the conjugal bond and, when that failed, to achieve a materially advantageous dissolution. Consequently, the litigants tried to impose their own paradigms of argument upon the conflict. At the first meeting Molefe succeeded in doing so; his agnates accepted that no marriage had occurred and proceeded to interpret his behavior accordingly. In the two *kgotla* hearings, however, Madubu's paradigm—which was predicated on the assumption that a valid marriage had existed—was established, largely on the initiative of Motshegare Ramalepa.

The logic that underpins our model of dispute-settlement processes and the progression of types to which it gives rise depend on two fundamental features of Tswana law. First, outside a limited range of delicts in the public domain,[14] most cases are initiated by a complainant rather than by a neutral party or a central authority; as a result, the definition of disputes is generally determined in the first instance by the litigants themselves. Second, notwithstanding the functionalist assumptions that continue to pervade much of legal anthropology, the parties involved in litigation are primarily concerned to emerge victorious, not simply to ensure that conflict is resolved and that amicable relations are restored. Admittedly, the restoration of amicable relations may be an objective of one or both of the disputants, but it is not a necessary or even a frequently expressed motive.

Given these two considerations, it will be apparent that the model shown in figure 1 does not merely subsume the ideal-typical range of forms that dispute processes will take. It also illuminates the manner in which actors may perceive the normative and strategic dimensions of these processes and, therefore, the configurations of choice that present themselves to the relevant parties. Most obviously, perhaps, the progression of types constitutes a movement from specificity to generality and, concomitantly, toward greater ambiguity: cases of type (1) concern specific actions or events; those of type (4), the management of social relations. From the participants' perspective, the growth of ambiguity implies ever increasing room for maneuver, for competing constructions of reality, and for the manipulation of procedure to gain strategic advantage. It is this potentiality that is expressed in the tendencies described by the model, and it underlies both the variations of content associated with Tswana dispute processes and their normative bases.

In chapter 7, where we consider the relationship between rules and the determination of outcomes, we shall examine the wider implications of our model for understanding the logic underlying the different modes of dispute. Before doing so, however, we turn our attention to two substantive areas of dispute and its management: marriage and the devolution of property and status. Earlier, in chapter 2, we explained why Tswana perceive their social universe as intrinsically enigmatic, competitive, and individualistic; we also showed that the negotiation of unions and of status relations represents the stuff of everyday managerial processes in that lived-in universe. It is therefore particularly appropriate to exemplify the sociocultural logic of dispute with reference to these two domains.

5

It is a commonplace today to observe that the anthropological analysis of marriage owes its major conceptual debt to Western jurisprudence. As Kuper (1970:466) puts it,

> Modern social anthropology has stressed the jural approach whose starting point is the dictum that "marriage is a bundle of rights." Marriage is generally reduced, for purposes of anthropological analysis, to the transfer of a set of rights in a woman and the creation of new linked social statuses.

As an established orthodoxy, then, the so-called "jural approach" envisages marriage as a process consisting primarily in the generation and exchange of liabilities and entitlements (see Fortes 1962:3 ff.; Leach 1955 passim). By extension, its associated prestations are typically held to mark the reciprocal passage of these legally sanctioned rights (see, e.g., Mitchell 1963:32).

Ethnographic accounts of marriage-type relationships among the Tswana provide no exception to this characterization. Thus, for example, while neither expressly acknowledges it, Matthews (1940) and Schapera (1940b) ground their respective descriptions of conjugality among the Rolong and Kgatla firmly in the categories of Western jurisprudence. Essentially, this implies two assumptions: first, that a precise distinction is made by Tswana between approved

---

Our discussion of Tswana marriage in chapter 5 is a synthesis of three earlier essays: Roberts 1977; Comaroff and Comaroff 1981; and J. L. Comaroff 1980. It should also be noted that our description of the process of marriage formation is a summary one, since this process has been described in detail by Schapera (1938, 1940b) and by Matthews (1940).

and disapproved forms of mating; second, that the appropriate procedures of conjugal formation have the capacity to create a legally valid union and thereby to remove all ambiguity in respect of its status. In short, the Tswana are usually portrayed as sharing a clear and uncomplicated perception of marriage and its definition—one, it seems, that is remarkably like our own. Once the required succession of (right-creating) incidents has been properly undertaken, an approved bond exists and legitimate cohabitation may proceed.

This approach would appear prima facie to have much to commend it. Apart from circumventing a number of arid definitional problems, it reflects the fact that Tswana *do* stress the formalities associated with the conjugal process in classifying and conceptualizing heterosexual bonds. At the same time, however, informants rarely suggest that the occurrence of these formalities necessarily confers *validity* upon a union or that the marriage relationship is typically an unambiguous one. On the contrary, it is often difficult to ascertain whether a particular couple is in fact married—or, more generally, to determine the status of their bond. Further, the ambiguities that pervade the creation and categorization of such unions are not regarded as transient or anomalous by the Tswana themselves; unions are viewed, rather, as potentially negotiable in the natural order of things. This is most clearly expressed in the jural arena, where the customary courts regularly hear cases involving rival efforts by litigants to define and construe heterosexual bonds to their own maximum personal advantage. What is more, the dispute-settlement agencies themselves operate with a patently flexible and pragmatic notion of conjugal legitimacy. Ironically, then, it is in the "legal" context that the irreducibility of marriage-type relations to simple jural formulation becomes most obvious. In order to demonstrate this irreducibility and to examine its corollaries for our understanding of marriage, we begin by describing the conjugal process and the indigenous classification of unions.

The Formation and Definition of Unions
The Classification of Unions

The Tswana classify heterosexual unions along a continuum delineated by duration and jural state. At one extreme are transient relationships in which couples merely cohabit intermittently over a short period, with neither party making any enduring commitment to the other. If the arrangement develops into an established liaison, it may be described by the term *bonyatsi,* which is usually translated as "concubinage." If the man and woman stay together more permanently but do not initiate any procedural formalities, they may be said to be "living together" (*ba dula mmogo*). Once official negotiations are set in motion, however, the union is on the way to becoming a "marriage" (*nyalo*). At the other pole of the continuum stand those relationships that have passed through all the various stages of the conjugal process.

Despite the apparent precision with which the continuum is ordered, everyday terminological usage does not distinguish clearly between the different forms of mating. Hence, for example, when a man speaks of his *mosadi* ("woman"), he may be referring to a partner of long standing or to a woman with whom he is having only a fleeting affair. Similarly, the term usually translated as "to marry" (*go nyala* [m.]; *go nyalwa* [f.]) may be loosely used to describe the creation of either an approved conjugal tie or a less formal liaison. The Tswana, of course, impute sharply contrasting social, material, and jural implications to these different kinds of bond, but in the context of everyday utterance such contrasts are latent rather than overt. It will become clear that the endemic ambiguity of these terms has a particular semantic value; their capacity to obscure distinctions is closely linked to the fact that, while the formal classification and definition of heterosexual unions are unequivocally shared, the status of many of them is open to negotiation for much of their existence. Moreover, the continuum itself will be seen to represent the range of possible constructions that an individual may seek to impose on a specific union. This characteristic of the continuum in turn is to be understood with reference to the process by which a legitimate union is ostensibly established.

The Formation of Unions

In common with patterns found in many African societies, a Tswana union is held to mature slowly, progressively attracting incidents as time passes. Traditionally, the first element of the process, at least as it is formally conceived, involved a spouse being selected for a man by his guardian and close kin, who undertook negotiations (*patlo*) in his name. (Today most men choose mates for themselves and later seek the approval of their close kin.) It is not agnatic *units* that participate in such negotiations, however, but those *individuals* who constitute the effective ego-centered kindreds of the respective parents (see Kuper 1970:468, 479). Typically, some of the paternal and maternal uncles of the couple are included among them. *Patlo* proceedings are concluded with the acceptance of a gift (*dilo tsa patlo; mokwele*)[1] by the guardian of the woman, who thus expresses his agreement to the marriage.

The transfer of *dilo tsa patlo* is taken to signify the commitment of both partners and their kin to the union. It also entitles the couple formally to sleep together in the woman's homestead at night (*go ralala*), provided they are regarded as sufficiently mature by their guardians. In the past this stage might continue for several years, and it often developed gradually into uxorilocal residence. In fact, children were often born to the couple before the next phase of the process was initiated. Among the Kgatla this continues to be the case, albeit to a limited extent; in contrast, Rolong seldom observe *go ralala* formalities today. Furthermore, while cohabitation should not occur before the conclusion of the *patlo,* this seems to be complied with only rarely by modern Tswana.

The next phase of the marriage process should be the removal of the woman to a homestead prepared for her in the man's natal *kgotla*. It is said that, in the past, this was supposed to be preceded by further formal visits to the *kgotla* of her guardian, in the course of which representatives of the wife-takers would make ceremonial requests for a *segametse* ("drawer-of-water"). There has been a growing tendency, however—especially evident among the Rolong—for the conjugal home to be established with little formality or ceremonial.[2]

Finally, bridewealth (*bogadi*) should be transferred to the woman's guardian at this juncture or some stage thereafter. It usually consists of two to six head of cattle, but it may also include small stock or cash. The mobilization of the animals is usually undertaken by the prospective husband himself, possibly with the aid of his father or his mother's brother. In theory, too, he may use some of the bridewealth received for his cattle-linked sister in making his own marriage payments, although this seldom occurs in practice (see chap. 2); the unions of siblings, or the exchanges they involve, are, by and large, not carefully synchronized among the Tswana. Similarly, distribution patterns are straightforward: the woman's father will receive the stock and earmark them for her linked brother; if her father is dead, they will be integrated directly into her brother's herd, since these beasts should be used to look after her, particularly in the event that her own union is prematurely dissolved. Perhaps the most noteworthy feature of bridewealth arrangements in these chiefdoms is the widespread tendency to delay the exchange. Neither Kgatla nor Rolong insist that it be made either at, or soon after, the creation of a union (see Matthews 1940). Both the amount and timing of *bogadi* are left entirely to the discretion of wife-takers. Not only are they nonnegotiable, but it is generally regarded as unseemly for the parties to allude even indirectly to such matters. And, as we saw earlier, many men delay the transfer at least until their children begin to marry (see below).

The final element in the establishment of a union, public recognition, is unlike the others in that it is not formally marked by a specific incident or event. In particular, there are no elaborate *rites de passage* to acknowledge the formation of a new bond. The transfer of bridewealth may occasion feasting, but this usually occurs late in the developmental cycle and serves, in reality, to define a union, qua marriage, as the *outcome* of a relationship over time (see below). It is also not infrequent for public opinion, where it is directly expressed at all, to be less than unanimous, for disagreements can and do arise out of competing interests in such a union. Nevertheless, it will become clear that Tswana courts, in deliberating upon a marital dispute, set great store by the way in which the relationship in question is regarded by kin and by local groupings. They appear to attach very limited weight to ceremonial formalities or exchanges in making their decisions.

The marriage process, then, contains a number of constituent elements: (1) the *patlo* negotiations; (2) the transfer of *dilo tsa patlo;* (3) *go ralala,* which permits nocturnal cohabitation but not coresidence; (4) uxorilocal residence and the birth of children, followed by the establishment of a permanent household in which the couple assume conventional conjugal roles; (5) the transfer of *bogadi;* and (6) public recognition. None of these elements, however, with the limited exception of the *transfer* of bridewealth, serves invariably or unambiguously to define or confer validity upon any particular union.[3]

Thus *patlo* and *dilo tsa patlo* are neither sufficient nor necessary conditions of conjugal legitimacy. Among the Tshidi, in fact, they occur in less than 20 percent of all unions. Moreover, in 60 percent of domestic disputes in which a marriage was judged to exist in Mafikeng in 1969–70, one of the litigants argued unopposed that *patlo* had not taken place and/or that *dilo tsa patlo* had not been transferred. More significantly, however, neither element is *assumed* indigenously to have the capacity to constitute a union; what is more, their absence does not preclude the possibility of establishing that a particular couple is married. The former situation is illustrated in part by the example of two full sisters who were living in their father's homestead among the Botswana Rolong in 1975. *Dilo tsa patlo* had been presented on behalf of both and, in each case, the (prospective) husband had become a migrant laborer before a conjugal homestead had been set up. One regarded herself, and was regarded by the community, as married; the other was held unequivocally to be unmarried. The difference between the two lay in the fact that the first sister sustained contact with her absent mate, while the second did not. In this community, furthermore, many unions that had not involved these formalities were widely recognized as marriages. At the same time, it is not uncommon, in the context of dispute, for disagreement to arise over whether *patlo* negotiations had been completed in respect of a particular bond (see case 9). Indeed, we have heard men, both in court and outside, interpret a casual chat before a public meeting as *patlo* and have heard others deny that a formal meeting apparently convened for this type of negotiation had been "successful." Similarly, a funerary gift or a bottle of brandy consumed together is sometimes agreed to have been *dilo tsa patlo,* while a sheep passed formally between two men may be construed as a quite different transaction.

As among the Sotho (see Murray 1976:104), coresidence

is not a prescriptive condition of a valid marriage either. Hence, couples separated for lengthy periods, especially as the result of the man's working as a migrant laborer, may still be considered married. In addition, where a man and a woman cohabit sexually but live apart, an enduring union may be construed as being in the process of formation; typically, when asked to explain their predicament, they will say that practical contingencies have prevented them from establishing a marital homestead but that they plan to do so soon. Conversely, conjugal status is never achieved by coresidence alone: a couple may be "just living together" (*ba dula mmogo hela*). Even when a new household has apparently been created, the respective kin may later debate whether they had recognized it. Nonetheless, the fact of coresidence and the assumption of conventional domestic and affinal roles clearly influence the manner in which the bond is perceived by others. Another factor of material importance in categorizing the status of a union is its duration; for the longer it persists, the more likely it is to be accepted as a marriage, and the less prone it becomes to reinterpretation and negotiaton.

As we have already implied, the remaining two elements —the passing of bridewealth and public recognition, particularly on the part of kin and neighbors—seem to be of greater moment in defining a union, a view in which Tswana themselves readily concur. It will become clear, however, that the element of public recognition is seldom invoked unless a crisis arises and a union is threatened; even then, recognition may not be unanimous. In other words, public recognition is usually a jural factor only in deciding what a union *was,* though in this respect it is certainly crucial. However, it does not, of itself, represent a definitive criterion in determining the status of an existing bond. *Bogadi,* on the other hand, is treated as the single nonnegotiable element of the conjugal process. While its nonpayment does *not* necessarily mean that a couple will be regarded as living in concubinage, its transfer is held to constitute a marriage. It is also true that, once bridewealth is *agreed* to have been passed, a union is seen unequivocally as such.

Nevertheless, it is an oversimplification to view *bogadi* primarily as an arrangement that exists for the purpose of creating or legitimizing conjugal bonds. Apart from all else, its capacity to validate unions is mediated by two factors. First (although it appears to occur infrequently), Tswana may debate retrospectively the status of animals passed between two men (see case 25), arguing that they were *mafisa* (loan cattle) or *marebana* (compensatory payments for seduction) rather than bridewealth. The conditions of transfer would appear to allow, rather than eliminate, such ambiguities. Second, and more significant, there is the tendency to defer the presentation of the cattle. This tendency, too, would make little sense if the sole purpose of the transfer of cattle were to secure jural legitimacy.[4] Of course, such deferral does not in itself negate the promise of payment or the recognition of debt implicit in the existence of a union; and, while the union endures and is not disputed, this promise is tacitly perpetuated. Still, *bogadi* is associated with domestic and reproductive rights in a woman (see below); as long as it has not changed hands, these rights may, in fact, be called into question. The tendency to delay payment therefore renders the status of many unions negotiable; where the existence of a marriage is denied, it follows that both the affinal tie and the bridewealth debt may be disavowed. In other words, the pattern of deferred transfer creates a potentiality for the manipulation of marriage and affinity that may be exploited by a Motswana in the management of social and political relations. This does not mean that the conjugal bond is inherently fragile or that the parties to a union invariably repudiate the debt and the mutual obligation involved. On the contrary, many unions are never disputed, and the *bogadi* debt is generally fulfilled at some point if a relationship endures. But, ultimately, the jural significance of bridewealth in conferring validity lies in its presentation rather than in a promise that may later be successfully repudiated under a number of conditions.[5]

Several important points emerge from this outline of the marriage process, the most significant of which is the fact that the validity of a union does not depend on the occurrence of any particular procedural or ceremonial formality. It is, rather, the subtle interrelation of these elements, and their expression in public recognition, that ultimately defines such a union. And, as the decisions of Tswana courts indicate, the question of definition requires to be determined in the light of the facts of each particular case; the incidents of the marriage process do not themselves embody or subsume any substantive norm or norms that can be applied deductively and precisely in order to evaluate the status of a relationship. In short, these elements are simply not reducible to a jural device for the legitimization of unions. The only incident that is (theoretically) above all debate is the *passing of bogadi,* but the frequency with which its transfer is delayed emphasizes the potential negotiability of marriage. In other words, Tswana arrangements would appear to contradict much of the conventional wisdom concerning African marriage, for the cultural logic that underpins conjugal formation here seems to stress the perpetuation of ambiguity rather than its elimination. This ambiguity is expressed in the tendency to *avoid* imposing public definition on ongoing relationships, a tendency that is sustained by relevant (everyday) terminological usage. In fact, there are only two situations in which the status of a union may specifically come into question: either when it is under threat of termination or redefinition or when the children it has produced reach the age at which their marriages assume political or material significance.

Many of the essential features of the marriage process as we have described it thus far are clearly illustrated by the case of Molefe and Madubu, introduced briefly in case 8 in the preceding chapter and now described more fully.

CASE 9:   MOLEFE AND MADUBU[6]

It will be remembered from case 8 that Molefe, who belongs to the Masiana *kgotla* in Mochudi, is the eldest son of Mankge by the latter's first wife, Mokhute. Madubu comes from Mookane, a small settlement in the adjoining Ngwato chiefdom. They met while Molefe was working at his father's cattle post in the extreme north of the Kgatleng. Molefe soon decided that he wanted to marry Madubu, but there were difficulties in the way of this. Mankge had already chosen a prospective wife for Molefe and would not agree to the match with Madubu. Mankge's choice was Thothome, a girl from the Monneng *kgotla* and a member of the descent group from which Molefe's own mother had come.[7]

Despite his father's disapproval, Molefe went ahead and himself conducted negotiations with Madubu's kin through a Mongwato friend of his, Lekula Mannaesi. Although accounts of these negoti-

MOLEFE AND MADUBU: DRAMATIS PERSONAE

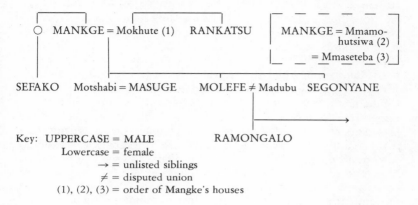

Key: UPPERCASE = MALE
     Lowercase = female
     → = unlisted siblings
     ≠ = disputed union
     (1), (2), (3) = order of Mangke's houses

ations differ, it seems clear that they broke down and that Molefe took Madubu away without her parents' permission in about 1945. He took her first to the cattle post and then to live near the ward at Mochudi into which his elder sister, Motshabi, had married. He kept her away from the Masiana *kgotla,* however, because of Mankge's disappointment. But, after a while, Mankge seems to have become reconciled to the fact that Molefe would never marry Thothome, and he began to treat Madubu as a daughter-in-law. She and Molefe were received together at Mankge's homestead by Mmamohutsiwa, Mankge's second wife (Molefe's mother was long dead), and Mankge gave her a present of some cloth. He eventually approached Motshegare Ramalepa, headman of the Tlagadi ward, and asked for some land for the young couple to build on. The allocation was made and a homestead built. Some say that at this stage further steps were taken to obtain the agreement to the marriage of Madubu's kinsmen and that Rankatsu Monametsi, Molefe's maternal uncle, sent representatives to Mookane to attempt this. But, when the dispute later arose, Madubu's senior kin strongly denied before the chief that these overtures had been successful. Certainly no *bogadi* was transferred. Nonetheless, it is clear that Molefe and Madubu were allowed to set up a home together in the Masiana *kgotla.*

Molefe and Madubu seem to have lived peacefully together for a while, but Madubu bore no children and, about 1953, Molefe persuaded her to allow him to enter a sororatic relationship with one of her younger sisters.[8] But, when Molefe approached Madubu's kinsmen to ask permission to do this, it was refused. Madubu's maternal uncle stated that such a relationship must await a proper marriage between Molefe and Madubu. Nevertheless, Molefe took the younger sister home with him to Mochudi, where she bore him a daughter and later a son, Ramongalo. Although Madubu initially agreed to this sororatic relationship, it led to disagreements and quarrels between the two sisters and between Molefe and Madubu. These initial difficulties were added to when, after Mankge's death in 1956, Molefe went to live with his father's third wife, Mmaseteba. (This was a potentially permissible leviratic arrangement, but the members of Molefe's descent group never agreed that he should enter into it.) By 1959, Molefe had wholly ceased to maintain Madubu and her younger sister. During that year, Madubu complained of neglect to members of Molefe's descent group and to Motshegare Ramalepa, and the latter ordered Molefe to sell a beast to clothe her and feed her. Molefe complied only later, when the matter was taken to the chief; but he subsequently made no sustained effort to maintain Madubu.

In the following year Madubu made a further claim of neglect while Molefe was away, living at the cattle post with Mmaseteba. She went first to Molefe's younger brother, Segonyane, who took her to the senior surviving member of the descent group, Letsebe. Letsebe, reluctant to act in Molefe's absence, sent Segonyane to fetch him back from the cattle post.

When Molefe returned, a few members of the descent group and some other kin met at the Masiana *kgotla* to consider the dispute. Among them were Letsebe, Segonyane, Molefe's sister, Motshabi, and her husband, Masuge. Letsebe began the discussion by confronting Molefe with Madubu's claim of neglect, to which he replied by saying that he had left her with six bags of corn when he set off for the cattle post.[9] Talk then turned to the general state of the relationship between Molefe and Madubu, the former asserting that it had broken down completely and suggesting that Madubu be sent back to her kinsmen at Mookane. All the males present were in agreement about this, and the decision would probably have been carried out had not Madubu protested to Motshegare Ramalepa at the Tlagadi *kgotla*.

Motshegare consented to hear Madubu's complaint, and the proceedings in the Tlagadi *kgotla* were recorded as follows:

MADUBU: Molefe has left me in our home and is staying with his mother.[10] Now he has turned her into his wife. It is because of her that I will have to leave his house. Molefe has built a house for me, but he took all the household goods to his mother's place. He does not support me; he eats, sleeps, and washes his clothes at his mother's place.

Molefe sleeps with his mother in the same house. Three years have passed since he deserted me. I do not deny Molefe the right to a marriage with two women, but I do not like my rival to be his mother. He can rather marry another wife. I am Molefe's wife. My marriage was arranged by Lekula Mannaesi. Lekula said he would pay *bogadi* on behalf of Molefe. He was sent by Rankatsu Monametsi. After my marriage arrangements were completed, Molefe took me to his cattle post. This was in 1944.

MMAMOHUTSIWA: I know Madubu to be my daughter-in-law because Molefe once came to his father and told him that he had seen a wife he wanted at Mookane. Mankge replied that he had already found Molefe a wife. Mankge then went to tell Rankatsu that Molefe did not want the wife he had found, and Molefe confirmed that he had found one at Mookane.

Molefe then went away, and, when he came back, he brought this woman with him. Rankatsu had refused to undertake any marriage negotiations because Molefe had disappointed him by refusing the wife Mankge had found. Molefe brought her and put her into Motshabi's yard.

MOLEFE: Madubu is only a woman who lives with me in the yard. I do not love her any more. I have had many troubles with her. The first quarrel we had was about the children she had chased from my home.[11]

Lekula is my friend. I asked him to find me a wife, but the woman's father refused. This woman I am with now was not formally negotiated for. I once fell in love and took her away with me. I told them to make negotiations for our marriage in 1942.

MMASETEBA: Molefe is my son, and Madubu is my daughter-in-law. I have not drawn Molefe away from Madubu. Molefe has no belongings in my home. Molefe brought his belongings and even Motshabi's money to my house and told me he had fought with his wife. Later he came back and took all these things away. There is nothing in my house of Molefe's.

LETSEBE: In May, Segonyane and Madubu came to see me and told me that she was not being supported. I sent Segonyane to go and call Molefe. On the third day Madubu came again with Masuge and told me that Molefe did not support her. I told her I had sent for him. She answered that she could not wait for the time Molefe would take to come here. I told her I could do nothing about it while Molefe and Segonyane were absent. I told her to wait.

MASUGE: When Molefe came, he told us that when he went to the cattle post he left six and half bags of corn for her, and he was surprised when she claimed that he did not support her. Madubu answered that she had opened the sixth bag when Molefe went away. Molefe said even then there would still be a lot, because the pot she was using was very small.

LETSEBE: I told them that I wanted to hear their opinions. Molefe answered he had nothing to say, except that he wanted to take Madubu back to her people. I agreed with Molefe, because I did not know her. She was only brought to me by Segonyane, who told me she was his brother's wife.

MOLEFE MATLHAGE (a senior member of the Masiana *kgotla*): I say that he knew the woman. All he wanted was to be rid of her. He overlooked the authority of the Masiana *kgotla* and thus has made the case more serious.[12]

MOTSHABI: Letsebe said he wanted Molefe to send her away. He asked someone to accompany them so that Molefe should not beat her on the way home. Those who were present when he took this action were Letsebe, Monametsi,[13] Masuge, and Segonyane and myself. Madubu said that she understood she was to be taken back home; but she first wanted to make a case, because Mmaseteba had taken her husband.

MATHIBEDI (senior member of the Tlagadi *kgotla*): Was it right of you, Letsebe, to grant a divorce in your *kgotla* as you did?

LETSEBE: I just agreed to be a witness.

MATHIBEDI (questioning Segonyane and Motshabi): What relationship had Madubu to you?

SEGONYANE: I know her to be Molefe's wife.

MOTSHABI: I know her to be my brother Molefe's wife.

[Some discussion of Molefe's property then follows.]

HEADMAN MOTSHEGARE RAMALEPA: I am glad to listen to your case, but I want to draw your attention to the fact that men in this *kgotla* have been cheating women.

Molefe, you lied to me and said that you would go back and stay with your wife, but you did not do that.[14] I fine you four head of cattle for having stolen this woman. I direct you to give a big ox to be used for buying the woman's clothes. Your divorce will be heard and judged by the big *kgotla*, not me.

You, Letsebe, because the children are yours, I fine you R4 for not controlling them and for granting a divorce in your *kgotla*.

The following account was then recorded when the dispute came before the chief.

MADUBU: I am bringing an action against Molefe. I am bringing an action against him because he deserted me. My witness is headman Motshegare Ramalepa. Molefe deserted me in our home. He went away with his father's third wife. She is the one who separated us. I am appealing to the *kgotla* to help me by preventing Molefe [from] enjoying all the fruits of our wealth without giving me a share. I also wish to find out whether it is proper of Molefe to desert me to go with his father's third wife. Molefe has taken his father's wife; that is why he has deserted me.

I am starving, I have nothing to eat. It is the sixth year since Molefe deserted me. Even when I am ill he does not care to see that I get medical treatment. He does not even care about our children.[15] Eventually I was forced to report to his *kgotla* in Masiana that he had deserted me and was living with his father's third wife.

Molefe is my husband. He got married to me in the Ngwato area. Our marriage was according to Tswana law [*ka lenyalo la Setswana*]. He married me but did not pay *bogadi*. He promised my parents that he would pay during the course of our marriage. Molefe was with Lekula when he negotiated with my parents. Lekula is a Mongwato. There was no Mokgatla save for Molefe himself. My parents agreed that Molefe should marry me all the same.

[Madubu speaks of the livestock held by Molefe. She then continues:]

Lekula negotiated my marriage with Molefe. Lekula is a Mongwato, not related to Molefe. Probably a friend of Molefe's. Lekula said he had been sent by Molefe to ask my parents to allow me to marry him. No Mokgatla came to negotiate for our marriage. Molefe pointed out that according to Kgatla custom people married first before paying *bogadi*. While I was still at home, no relative of Molefe came to confirm that they wanted us to marry or that *bogadi* would be paid after marriage.

The Bakgatla people did not go to fetch me as their daughter-in-law. Rankatsu never came to my home. When I still lived happily with Molefe, Mankge used to call me daughter-in-law.

On my arrival, I found Mmamohutsiwa, my mother-in-law. I was introduced to her as daughter-in-law. We lived together peacefully for twelve years. For the last eight years we have been living in separation. I gave birth to our youngest child in Mmamohutsiwa's home. When Molefe deserted me, I was living in our marriage home, that is, the home we built together. When we were allotted the land on which to build our home, Mathibedi and Mogotsi were present.[16] In fact, they are the ones who allotted the plot to us. I am quite convinced that I am married into the Masiana ward. We got married in 1944 and were separated in 1955.

MOLEFE: I did not get Madubu from her parents. I got her from her home, and her parents did not know about it. I disagree with Madubu when she says that Lekula negotiated on my behalf. I fell in love with Madubu while our parents were still alive. I stole her in 1945. I never said anything about *bogadi* to Madubu's parents. I did not tell my father anything when I came with Madubu. We went to the cattle post instead of coming home. I told my sister Motshabi that I had brought a woman with me. I did not tell Mmamohutsiwa. I disagree with the statement made by Madubu when she says that we lived in my parents' home when we came from the cattle post.

[Molefe speaks of property accumulated while he was living with Madubu, then continues:]

The misunderstanding between us started in 1953. Madubu went to her home to work on the lands so that she could be given some corn. She left me at our lands, and I was with her sister. She spent the remainder of 1953 at her parents' home, only to come back at the beginning of winter in 1955. She found us harvesting. She said she had been sent to collect the children. When Madubu came, she found that her sister had a baby boy by me. She expelled her sister and the baby without asking my opinion.

I looked after my father's third wife. I started doing so after Mankge's death. I look after her by ploughing for her. I disagree with Madubu when she alleges that I do not look after her. I also disagree when she says that I am distracted by the fact that I look after my father's third wife. It is true I do not plough my father's fields.

Madubu is not telling the truth when she says Lekula was the man who acted as a link in our marriage negotiations. I actually stole Madubu away. I was quite aware of the law [*molao*] when I stole her. I did not tell my father when I came with Madubu. When we came on the first occasion, we went to my father's home. I did not introduce my father to her after my arrival. When I arrived home with Madubu, I found Mankge, Mmamohutsiwa, and Segonyane. I did not introduce Madubu to Mmamohutsiwa. I hesitated to introduce them because Mmamohutsiwa did not like Madubu. I did not introduce Madubu to other members of the Masiana *kgotla,* nor did I tell my father's elder brother. I was afraid of members of our *kgotla,* so I did not introduce Madubu.

I have a baby whose mother is Madubu's sister. I love this baby as well as its mother. Madubu sent away both the baby and the mother, and I went and fetched it. I sent to fetch this child so it could come and live with its father. The baby that Madubu's sister had by me is a boy. His name is Ramongalo. Ramongalo is a name that is common among my people, the Bakgatla. My other child is a girl and was born before the boy. I have not yet asked Madubu's parents if I can marry Madubu's sister. I have paid several visits to the Ngwato area to see Madubu's sister. I have already mentioned that the dispute between me and Madubu started after she sent away her sister and baby.

MOTSHABI: Molefe told me about Madubu while she was still at her home. He asked me to go and see her. I declined because Molefe had already promised to marry another woman here in the Bakgatla area. I feared that it might appear as if I was encouraging him to turn down the woman that our parents had arranged for him to marry. One day Molefe came to my home to introduce Madubu to me. After Molefe had introduced Madubu to me, I went to tell my father about the fact that Molefe had come with a wife. They were staying with me.

Mmamohutsiwa came to see Madubu, but our father did not come because he did not like the marriage. Later my father came with a present for his daughter-in-law. Molefe and his wife went back to the cattle post only to return later. They indicated that they had come to stay. This time they stayed at my father's home. Molefe and Madubu were entertained by my father as his own children, and they were using the same cooking facilities. Later they went to the lands.

SEGONYANE: I was not told anything about Madubu's arrival. Molefe introduced me to her when I found them together at the cattle post.

Molefe did not tell me anything about the child which Madubu's sister had by him. I gathered from the last words said by my father before he died that Molefe's son should be given cattle.

ODIRELENG MABUA (a paternal kinsman of Madubu): I heard a rumor that Molefe was proposing to marry Madubu, but before I confirmed this rumor Madubu had disappeared. I did not know where she had gone to. Lekula is the one who negotiated on behalf of Molefe. When I returned from military service at the end of World War II, I met Molefe. After that I was told my daughter had been stolen. I was made to understand that she was at Mochudi in the Kgatla area.

BALEKANYE MAKGOENG (Madubu's mother's brother): I do not know anything about the marriage between Madubu and Molefe. I only heard by the way that Madubu was married to a Mokgatla. I was told this when I arrived from Johannesburg. In 1953 Madubu and Molefe visited my home. Madubu told me that, since she did not have children, she had decided to take her sister so that her younger sister could bear children for her. I asked Molefe whether he was married to Madubu and he denied it. I asked him how he could marry Madubu's sister before he married her. I told Madubu that I would have to discuss it with Madubu's parents before any decision could be made.

We met and discussed the matter, and we told Molefe that he could not marry Madubu's sister before he married Madubu. Molefe agreed with us and returned to his home, promising to come back later to arrange to fulfill his promise. We told Molefe that we wanted the children sent to their maternal grandparents because Molefe had not married their mother. We sent Molefe back home to urge his parents to initiate proper negotiations for marriage between him and Madubu.

We were surprised, later, to see Madubu come to fetch the children. When Madubu came to fetch the children, she did not consult with us. We are also surprised to find ourselves gathered here for what is alleged to be a divorce case. Molefe has not acted according to our custom by stealing both Madubu and her younger sister. Molefe lived with Madubu for several years. He stole her, and [they] lived with [each other] as husband and wife.

SEFAKO PILANE: Molefe, your father, Mankge, is my mother's younger brother. I regard Madubu as my daughter-in-law and also as my grandmother, because she is married to my uncle's son. Though we do not know how the marriage started, Mankge ultimately accepted Madubu as his daughter-in-law. I even had to give a sheep for Molefe and his wife Madubu as I was expected to do when my uncle's son got married. I was doing so in my capacity as the nephew. I did not help in the building of their home, because they lived in the Masiana *kgotla*.

THE CHIEF: Molefe and Madubu, I have listened to your case attentively. Molefe, you stole Madubu and lived with her for eight years. You point out [that in] the beginning your father was not keen on Madubu but ultimately accepted her as your wife. I gather from your relatives that Madubu is known to be your wife. Motshabi, your sister, Segonyane, your younger brother, Sefako Pilane, your father's nephew, and Mmamohutsiwa, your father's wife, all speak to this. For those reasons there is no doubt in my mind that Madubu is your wife.

You are now declaring before this *kgotla* that you wish to divorce her. You must divide everything that you acquired in the last eighteen years between yourself and Madubu. You must share your thirty-six head of cattle. You, Molefe, will get twenty-six head, while Madubu will get the remaining ten. Out of the seven sheep, you will give Madubu three and you will take four. As for the donkeys, each of you gets half of them.

The nature of the case, placed first before Motshegare Ramalepa and then before the chief, was effectively determined by the meeting of the agnatic segment and by Madubu's reaction to it; for at this level the essential issues underlying a generalized relationship of hostility were distilled into the question of whether Madubu had been properly married, and this distillation, in turn, was largely the result of the litigants' strategic efforts to impose their respective paradigms of argument on the dispute.[17] The arguments adduced in the various contexts, moreover, indicate that the normative referents around which Molefe and Madubu organized their suits derived from the elements of the marriage process described above. These arguments, and the response of the authorities to them, illuminate Tswana perceptions of the jural character of marriage.

The complainant considered five of the elements in her effort to construe the relationship as a marriage. Thus she suggested (1) that *patlo* negotiations, involving her kinsmen, had taken place at the request of Rankatsu, Molefe's MB;[18] (2) that *bogadi* had been promised; (3) that she and Molefe had lived together on a (patrivirilocal) site allocated to them by the headman; (4) that they had adopted the conventional roles of husband, wife, and affine for a substantial period; and (5) that she had clearly been accepted by Mankge and members of the Masiana *kgotla* as an incoming wife and had been introduced to Mmamohutsiwa as a daughter-in-law. In asserting that Madubu was merely his concubine, Molefe also ordered his statements in terms of these elements. He argued that the *patlo* negotiations were unauthorized and had ended without success (i.e., no *dilo tsa patlo* had been transferred) and that no *bogadi* had been pledged. Moreover, he had *not* introduced Madubu to his father or to Mmamohutsiwa and the Masiana *kgotla,* so that she could not have been accepted as his wife. (While Molefe was opposed on this question by some of the witnesses, he had the support of Letsebe[19] and of Madubu's kin from Mookane.) By implication, then, Molefe was intimating that the element of coresidence was merely the corollary of an enduring concubinage relationship.

All this suggests that neither litigant believed that the validity or jural definition of the union hinged directly on any single formal incident; apart from everything else, it is now clear that the occurrence of such incidents is often difficult to prove. Indeed, had the actors themselves shared a narrow jural view of validity, Molefe must have won the case, for, despite Madubu's lone protestations to the contrary, it was agreed that *patlo* negotiations had not been completed and that the promise of *bogadi* had not been made. As we have repeatedly stressed, however, the adjudication of validity does not depend on a legalistic deduction, and the intrinsic jural weight of the individual elements is always limited. It is thus significant that the chief paid no attention to the occurrence or absence of ceremonial formalities in the course of delivering his judgment; even though Madubu had been "stolen," her acceptance by Molefe's kinsmen and members of the Masiana *kgotla* was sufficient ground for construing her relationship with Molefe as a marriage.

In summary, the Tswana tend to view a union as a marriage when it is recognized as such (or, at least, is not questioned) by the persons who occupy the social space immediately surrounding the couple. The problem then arises: Why is the conjugal process held to consist of a series of formal incidents if these incidents have such limited jural significance? The answer derives from the fact that these incidents, though they are not attributed the capacity to establish legitimacy, are deployed rhetorically as normative referents in the context of dispute—the primary context in which the status of unions is regularly considered. (Hence the various mentions of Tswana "law" by the litigants in case 9.) It must be stressed, however, that the incidents are utilized in a highly specific fashion; together they constitute a total *gestalt* in terms of which a *composite* image of any union is typically drawn and evaluated. The closer a particular bond is made to conform to this *gestalt*—by careful construction of evidence of its recognition, of coresidence, of the assumption of conventional conjugal roles, and so on—the likelier it is to be defined as a marriage. It follows, too, that countersuits will seek to contrive just the opposite total impression. Again, all this is aptly illustrated by the arguments presented in case 9. Outcomes depend, in this respect, on the court's estimation of fault: the apparently rightful or wrongful actions of the respective parties are held to reflect the veracity of their rival constructions. The elements themselves, then, subsume the normative indices through which the complexities of a current relationship—and of past interaction—may be reduced, debated, and, when necessary, classified with reference to the continuum of unions outlines above (pp. 133–34). (It is in this sense, patently, that the continuum represents a range of potential constructions that may be placed on most bonds.) But since these normative indices are elements of a rhetorical order rather than clauses in a legal code, they cannot be applied with deductive exactitude. This may explain, in part, why everyday unions are not readily classified or easily defined, despite the fact that Tswana appear to entertain a common conception of the formal conjugal process. The shared conception of conjugal formation represents a normative statement of a culturally inscribed code; the ambiguities surrounding definition refer to the management of existing relations.[20] When unions endure and their status is not called into question, little spontaneous effort is made indigenously to classify them, a tendency that the nonspecificity of everyday terms (e.g., *mosadi, nyalo,* etc.; see above, p. 134) would appear to facilitate. Indeed, the absence of formal bridewealth negotiations, *rites de passage,* and other expressive manifestations of status transformation[21] together underlie the avoidance of definition and the perpetuation of ambiguity.

The Definition of Marriage and the Disposition of Property

An obvious corollary of the negotiability of Tswana unions is the ease with which different constructions may be, and are, placed on heterosexual relationships.[22] Even where the definition of a particular union is *not* the specific object of management, however, it may change in the public eye as the state of the relationship alters. As long as a man and woman live together amicably, their bond is usually assumed to constitute a "marriage" or, at least, to be in the process of becoming one. Once the relationship sours, however, and begins to break down, there is a tendency for it either to be dismissed as an informal union or to become the focus of rival efforts to impose meaning upon it.[23] The history of the relations between Molefe and Madubu illustrates how parties may revise their perceptions of a union over time. When in 1959, Madubu initially complained that Molefe was neglecting her, neither Molefe nor his agnates denied that she was his wife. Indeed, before the chief's *kgotla,* where he was taken for failing to carry out Motshegare Ramalepa's first maintenance order, the defendant stated that Madubu was his wife and that they had been married for fourteen years; yet, two years later, he tried to justify his conduct on the ground that he had never been married to her. Similarly, the views of some of his agnates changed, although not always in the same direction, over an equally brief period. The Tswana appear to see nothing incongruous in the fact that perceptions of a relationship are subject to revision in this way—a fact that only reiterates the danger of trying to cast Tswana marriages in a Western legal mold.

If the definition and classification of particular marriage-type relationships are rarely the object of spontaneous speculation or abstract intellectual interest among the Tswana, they do assume practical and material importance in critical situations, i.e., when the dissolution of a union is threatened and/or when the affiliation of its progeny becomes of consequence. In these contexts, both status and rights over property hinge directly on the way the union is categorized, particularly by the ward headman and the chief. If it is identified as a marriage, large numbers of cattle (or sums of money) may be awarded to the woman in the event of a divorce, and the maintenance of children born to the couple will continue to be the responsibility of the husband, to whose agnatic grouping and ward they belong and in whose estate they have rights of inheritance. If, on the other hand, the relationship is characterized as concubinage or simply as a fleeting liaison that has ended in the impregnation of an unmarried woman, the property disposition will be significantly less substantial and other consequences will be less enduring (Comaroff and Roberts 1977b).[24] The man may be ordered to pay a fine in compensation for the pregnancy, but no division of his assets will be required; moreover, the affiliation of, and control over, the children will rest with the woman's father or, if he is dead, with her brother. Cases 10 and 11 demonstrate the material implications that follow from the classification of unions by dispute-settlement agencies.

CASE 10:   MAGGIE'S STATUS[25]

Ramasu, a Mokgatla, met Maggie, a girl from Gaborone, in 1964. He was then living with a woman in Mochudi, and Maggie herself had two children by another man. Although the circumstances under which they met and began to live together remain a subject of argument, it seems clear that Ramasu promised to marry Maggie. He spoke to her father, Motseko, about this, and subsequently installed her and her children in his homestead with the first wife.

For a while the relationship remained amicable, and Maggie bore two more children, one of whom did not survive long. But she soon began to complain to her father that the first wife was treating her as a servant and that Ramasu was neglecting her. Motseko visited Mochudi and spoke to him and some of his senior kinsmen, but his efforts to resolve the dispute were unsuccessful, and Maggie left Ramasu's homestead.

In 1968, Maggie took her complaint of neglect to the chief's *kgotla*. When the matter was heard, she told the chief how Ramasu had promised her marriage, how he had agreed to accept her two earlier children as his own, and how she had gone to live in his homestead with the first wife. She then claimed that the first wife soon began to treat her as a servant and that Ramasu began to neglect her, following the second pregnancy.

Ramasu defended himself by denying that Maggie was his wife. He said: "I know this woman from Gaborone, and was in love with her. I have a child with her, but she is not my wife according to the law. She is just a concubine [*nyatsi*]." He then described how he had employed her as a servant for his wife and how she had gone away when the wife was no longer satisfied with her.[26]

The chief ordered Ramasu to pay Maggie R80 (about $92)—the

contemporary monetary equivalent of four head of cattle, which was then the standard fine for impregnating an unmarried girl—and allowed him to pay this sum at the rate of R14 a month.

It should be noted that, broadly, the same elements of the marriage process are manifest in this case as in case 9, except that here it is the woman's rather than the man's agnates who recognized the bond as a marriage. Moreover, a promise of *bogadi* seems to have been made in respect of Maggie, which was not the case with Madubu. Yet Maggie was held to be a servant involved in a casual relationship, while Madubu was accorded the formal status of a wife.

CASE 11:   TOLLO AND MOTLAKADIBE[27]

Motlakadibe is the eldest daughter of Ratsie, a Tebele immigrant who married a woman from Rampedi ward and settled there. Tollo, a member of the Morema ward, initiated *patlo* negotiations for her in 1942, while Motlakadibe was still at school. On his side, these negotiations were conducted by his ZH, Segale, and, on Motlakadibe's, by a maternal uncle, Ramoka. Soon after, it was arranged for Tollo to "find his way into Motlakadibe's hut," and, before her education was finished, his kinsmen asked if she could accompany him when he went abroad to work. This was agreed to by her parents, and the couple spent approximately seven years in the Transvaal. No *bogadi* was presented for Motlakadibe. While they were away, they managed to buy some cattle and a plough. Five children were also born, and, when they returned, they settled down to manage the cattle and cultivate a field together among Tollo's kinsmen. They had not been back long when relations between them became strained. There were repeated quarrels, and Tollo accused Motlakadibe of having affairs with other men, particularly Setshwane Setshwane, whose home was in Moganetse ward, not far from Rampedi.

In the late 1950s Motlakadibe left Tollo and returned with the children to her father's homestead in Rampedi. By now, Ratsie was dead, and Motlakadibe and the children were given succor for most of the period 1959–60 by her maternal kinsmen and her younger brothers. Pheko, her MBS, sold two beasts to provide food for her and her children, and her youngest brother, Wete, then working at the mines, sent at least R20 for their maintenance. All this time no word came from Morema *kgotla* about the breakdown of the union.

The dispute was eventually heard in the Morema *kgotla* toward the end of 1960, after Motlakadibe's kinsmen had themselves complained. When the matter was heard, Motlakadibe told of her marriage to Tollo and of his subsequent neglect. But Tollo responded by denying that they were married and claiming that Motlakadibe was just a concubine whom he had impregnated.

The headman dealt with the dispute as a case of impregnation and ordered Tollo to pay four head of cattle plus an additional R20 for the maintenance of the children. [This sum seems to have been related to the amount that Wete provided for the same purposes when Motlakadibe was back in the Rampedi ward during 1959–60.]

Motlakadibe's kinsmen then took the dispute to the chief's *kgotla,* complaining that the matter should be treated as a broken marriage and not as a simple case of impregnation. Before the chief, the dispute was introduced by Thage, one of Motlakadibe's maternal kinsmen. He told the *kgotla* of the original negotiations and how permission had been granted for Motlakadibe to accompany Tollo to work abroad. He then went on to describe how the couple had returned and started to cultivate a field together, and he said that he had been surprised to see Motlakadibe return alone with her children to Rampedi, without any word from the people of Morema. Finally, he mentioned how her kin at Rampedi had been obliged to maintain her and her children. Thereafter, Motlakadibe spoke of the property that she and Tollo had accumulated during their time together, objecting that Tollo had marked them with the brand of his ZH, Segale. She ended her account by telling the court of her quarrels with Tollo; his neglect, she argued, had obliged her to return eventually to Rampedi.

Tollo attributed the souring of their relationship to Motlakadibe's affairs with other men. The final break had come when Motlakadibe had refused to sleep with him, ostensibly to force him to present *bogadi.* In this context, the defendant did not attempt to argue, as he had done in the Morema ward, that the dispute was simply one of impregnation. When pressed by the chief, he admitted that Motlakadibe was his wife.[28]

In judgment the chief clearly accepted Motlakadibe's definition of the relationship. Since it had obviously broken down, they should now divorce. He ordered that the children be looked after by their mother and that Motlakadibe should retain the field to cultivate for them. The nine head of cattle that remained of the herd accumulated by the couple while they were abroad were to be divided: six were awarded to Motlakadibe, and three were left with Tollo.

In both cases 9 and 10 the opposed parties tried to impose differing definitions on the union in order to gain or retain control over property. In each instance the man sought (at least for as long as possible) to construe as a casual relationship what the woman construed as a marriage. But this is not always the case, for sometimes the man asserts the existence of a conjugal bond (and hence the need for a formal divorce) in order to gain control over the children, while the woman may reject this if she is prepared to forsake a property disposition so that the children may be affiliated to her own grouping. The express goals of the two parties in any particular case will depend on a number of situational factors: the extent of the assets involved, the age of the children, the attitude of the woman toward retaining the status of a *lefetwa* ("one passed by"), and the particularities of the social environment in which the couple are located, to mention just four. Broadly speaking, however, where the interests of the parties are *complementary*—i.e., where one wishes to retain the children while the other prefers to keep or gain property—their bond may simply dissolve by mutual consent, possibly accompanied by discussions between the relevant kin. Significantly, its definition, in these circumstances, may never be considered; for the distribution of assets is agreed to. But where interests are *divergent* and the assets cannot be amicably divided, the case will usually develop into a *kgotla* proceeding. In such disputes, debate invariably turns on whether or not a marriage existed, for the classification of the union becomes an index for the way in which its human and material product is to devolve. In its legal aspect, then, Tswana marriage may be understood less as a jural state than a jural potentiality. As one member of a taxonomic set (see pp. 133–34, above), it provides a normative means of designating relationships, usually at their end, in terms of which the negotiation of interests, rights, liabilities, and statuses may be ordered.

The Creation and Transfer of Rights

The negotiability of the conjugal bond has a number of implications for the way in which rights are created and transferred in marriage among the Tswana. It is usual, in describing African marriage, to view it as involving the gradual, but usually quite precise, transmission of rights in a woman from her guardian to her husband as prestations and obligations pass in the other direction (see Evans-Pritchard 1951:97). Thus Kuper (1970:476–77), in his study of the culturally cognate Kgalagadi, portrays marriage in much these terms, although he does note that areas of ambiguity may arise in the process. Among the Rolong and Kgatla, however, the transfer of rights does not occur in quite such an orderly and predictable way, although Tswana informants, in describing ideal arrangements, sometimes imply that it should.

In theory, the initial acquisition of rights to sexual access, embodied traditionally in *go ralala*, is associated with the successful conclusion of negotiations and marked by the presentation of *dilo tsa patlo*. Then, when the woman is removed to a homestead in her husband's ward, jural control and the responsibility for maintaining her pass to her spouse, though her guardian retains a strong residual interest in, and right to protect, her welfare. At this stage, she should be provided with a house, arable land, and the nucleus of a herd to succor her children. When *bogadi* is presented, membership in the husband's agnatic descent grouping and incontestable rights in his estate are conferred on children born to the woman. If the marriage ends in divorce, this process should ideally be reversed, with the wife returning to her own agnatic segment and natal ward, vacating the house she has occupied and the field she has cultivated. Thereafter she is under the guardianship of one of her own agnates. Of course, she may have been awarded a substantial property disposition by the chief, and this will be used for looking after her. (Arrangements for raising and maintaining the children, who remain members of the husband's agnatic group, tend to vary according to their ages and needs.) This ideal pattern is associated by Tswana themselves with the agnatic principles they see as ordering social relations in their society.

Quite apart from the fact that many unions are formed, and persist, in the absence of several elements of the marriage process—and, hence, without the balanced exchange of rights and prestations—the normative basis of the conjugal rights themselves is less than straightforward. Thus, for example, control over rights to sexual access in an unmarried

woman should rest entirely with her guardian, yet unauthorized access does not give him any claim to compensation—provided no pregnancy results. A man found having
sexual intercourse with a spinster may be chased away and
even thrashed, but it is only if she is impregnated (i.e., where
her child-bearing capacities are violated) that an action may
be instituted (Schapera 1933, 1938). Similarly, the passage
of rights to sexual access should follow upon the presentation of *dilo tsa patlo,* but in practice the formation of a
heterosexual relationship that involves cohabitation seems
typically to precede, and in many cases to prompt, the initial
negotiations toward the formation of a marriage. Even where
dilo tsa patlo has been transferred, the man on behalf of whom
it was presented enjoys limited rights of sexual access. He
may have intercourse with, and impregnate, the woman; but
he cannot seek restitution from another individual who
sleeps with her, for that prerogative remains with her guardian until she is removed to the conjugal homestead; it is
only at that point that the husband's right to sexual access,
and the corresponding exclusion of other parties, is protected
by an entitlement to compensation for what would be termed
"adultery" in Western legal terminology. Even then, the man
has to establish the existence of a marriage in order to exercise it; where *bogadi* has not passed, this may not be easy to
do. In short, rights in a woman's sexuality are not transferred
in a precisely ordered fashion. Indeed, the ambiguities surrounding them disappear finally only when bridewealth
changes hands (see Schapera 1938:139), and this may occur
long after she has become sexually inactive. Until then these
rights may be, and often are, called into question (Comaroff
and Roberts 1977b).

Similarly, *bogadi* may theoretically be necessary to secure
the progeny of a marriage as members of the husband's
agnatic grouping and as his heirs, but there are ambiguities
associated with the application of this rule also. Even before
the transfer has been made, the (virilocal) coresidence of
their mother and her mate, whether or not he is their genitor,
implies de facto that guardianship of the children passes to
him. Although close links will usually be maintained with
their mother's kin, and they will generally spend periods liv-

ing with them, these children will grow up as members of the man's *kgotla*. He may in fact allocate them property by way of inter vivos devolution and, as they mature, incorporate them in household property and productive relations. Boys will principally be associated with the management of the (sociological) father's herds, girls with cultivating the fields and preparing food for the domestic grouping. So long as their parents live amicably together, the children's membership in the man's agnatic segment cannot be challenged without causing severe friction and eliciting the rebuff that the (implicit) promise of *bogadi* will be fulfilled. Even when *bogadi* is presented for the daughters, it cannot be appropriated by their mother's kin except at the risk of initiating a dispute, unless their father sees this as a judicious moment to discharge his own obligations (which many men seem to do). The result is that the question of bridewealth and of the affiliation of the children remains implicit until it is either resolved, by the transfer being made, or brought into the open, by conflict over the parents' relationship. Nor must it be assumed that, where *bogadi* has not passed, the maternal kinsmen will claim the children as members of their descent grouping. There are obvious and fundamental cultural reasons for them not to do so (see chap. 2); moreover, in the purely pragmatic terms in which such matters are often indigenously rationalized, to claim the children would require the provision of material support and the extension of rights of inheritance. Mothers' brothers frequently display a marked reluctance to bring a sister's child into (potential) competition with their own sons for resources devolving agnatically. On the other hand, there are circumstances in which claims to the affiliation of a sister's children are seen by those involved to be both socially appropriate and materially attractive (see case 25).

Although Tswana tend to speak as if only the payment of *bogadi* has the capacity to *guarantee* the affiliation of children, there is little consistency in the decisions made by Tswana dispute-settlement agencies on this question. Sometimes a judgment may correspond with the stated norm, as in case 11, where, despite the fact that the couple were found to have been married, the children were, in the absence of *bogadi,* returned with Motlakadibe to Rampedi and have since grown up as members of that *kgotla.* But the outcome in case 12 was markedly different.

CASE 12:   RAMAJA AND MMAKGOTHA'S CHILDREN[29]

Ramaja, a man from the Ramadiakobong ward, began negotiations to marry Mmakgotha, from Ramasilela, in about 1951. *Dilo tsa patlo* was presented, and not long afterward her parents allowed him to take her to Johannesburg, where he was working. In 1953 she returned to her parents to have her first child. Later she went back to Johannesburg for a while, but returned again to the Kgatleng, where she bore twins. In 1958, while still at home, she was made pregnant by a man from Tlokweng, and her relations with Ramaja seem to have deteriorated rapidly after that. She bore another child with the man from Tlokweng, and, in 1964, Ramaja brought her before the chief's *kgotla,* complaining of these births. Following the original negotiations, no further steps were taken, and no *bogadi* was presented.

Introducing his grievance at the chief's *kgotla,* Ramaja related how the negotiations had been completed and how her parents had allowed him to take her to Johannesburg. He then went on to say that he had been able to forgive her the first pregnancy by the man from Tlokweng but not the second. Mmakgotha confirmed what Ramaja said about the negotiations [*Ramaja o ne a mpatla sentle ka molao, a ba a gorosa dilo tsa patlo*]. She explained the birth of the children by the man from Tlokweng by saying that Ramaja had neglected her while she was at home. Other witnesses confirmed the negotiations, and Ramaja's relations told how they had taken corn to feed Mmakgotha while Ramaja was in Johannesburg (thus seeking to negate the charge of neglect). In answer to a question from the court, Ramaja explained that he had taken no action against the man from Tlokweng because he had "not yet presented *bogadi*"[30] for Mmakgotha.

The chief placed the blame for the breakdown on Mmakgotha for bearing children with another man while she was Ramaja's wife. Ordering the couple to part, he directed that Ramaja's children should belong to his descent group and that those by the man from Tlokweng should go with Mmakgotha.

In case 12, then, the nonpresentation of *bogadi* did not prevent the children of the union from being affiliated to the man's agnatic grouping and becoming his heirs; yet in case 11 the implicit promise of payment was insufficient to effect the same outcome. Therefore, while the transfer of bridewealth may render the issue of affiliation less negotiable, affiliation and transfer are not immutably linked: right and prestation are not elements in a simple exchange relationship.

Further evidence for this assertion is provided by the Tshidi chief's *kgotla* in Mafikeng. In 1969–70 two cases in which bridewealth had not passed ended with the man's gaining control over the children. The reasoning behind the decision was broadly the same in each: both relationships had broken down irrevocably, but the respective husbands had behaved properly throughout and had made provision for their dependents. While it was not clear which of the formal incidents had occurred, the court accepted the husbands' versions that most had. It had no grounds, moreover, to doubt that they had intended to pay *bogadi.* Since the women were at fault, the chief upheld the plea that a marriage had existed in each instance and that the children should be affiliated to their fathers' groupings. Yet, during the same period, the court dismissed a claim by a litigant that he had paid *bogadi.* Despite his production of witnesses, the chief accepted the woman's father's plea that these had been *marebana* (a pregnancy compensation) offered in private settlement. He observed that the man had not behaved as a husband and that the relationship failed to conform to customary expectations; a marriage, therefore, did not exist, and the animals could not have been *bogadi.*

Finally, the rules governing the redistribution of rights following divorce, as indigenously stated, are superficially clear-cut. On the termination of the marriage, the woman must return to her own agnatic grouping, whose members should sustain her. The rights to the dwelling, arable land, and cattle that she had enjoyed while living with her husband are to be withdrawn when she departs their joint household. Yet Tswana also express the apparently conflicting and equally imperative norm that a responsible son must make sure his mother is provided with a house, a field, and cattle to maintain her (see Schapera 1938). Save in exceptional circumstances, that son, of course, is a member of his father's agnatic segment and remains so irrespective of what happens to his mother on the dissolution of her *marriage.* The established tendency of chiefs to make substantial property dispostions in favor of a divorced wife further complicates the normative basis of redistribution.

In pragmatic terms, consequently, the actual rearrangement effected in cases of divorce depends less on normative priorities than on a number of situational variables. The first of these is the presence of children and their age and sex. If the woman already has adult sons, she is likely to stay on among them, continuing to be maintained in the ward of her former husband. She may remain in her homestead or move to another built by the sons, but she will usually retain the same field and enjoy the benefits of the cattle previously allocated to her house. The absence of adult children, however, increases the probability of her moving back to her agnates, although she may later return, with her sons, when they are old enough to build for and maintain her. A second variable is the woman's relations with her husband's coresident kin; the more amicable they are, the greater is the likelihood that she will remain with her affines. This variable is also linked to the question of fault. If a woman is seen to have been a good wife, and the husband is seen to have behaved badly toward her, her affines will discourage her especially strongly from leaving; but if she is commonly held to have been responsible for the breakdown of the union, her return home is almost inevitable (in many such instances she will have departed the conjugal residence by the time the divorce is formally dealt with).

These primary considerations, as well as other circumstantial factors, are reflected in the outcomes of everyday divorce disputes, with the result that no unequivocal rules or simple regularities emerge from them with respect to the rearrangement of rights of guardianship over women or property. Compare the following two cases.

CASE 13:   MOAKOFI AND NKIDI

Moakofi married Nkidi from Mapotsane in the early 1940s and took her to live among his agnates at Madimeng *kgotla* in Mochudi. Four children were born to them in the first ten years of the marriage. Moakofi worked abroad as a wage-earner much of the time, and, during the periods of his absence, Nkidi was looked after by his father, Bogosi. It appears that Nkidi was always well provided for while her husband was away.

In 1963, during one of Moakofi's periods of absence, Nkidi was impregnated by another man and gave birth to a fifth child. When Moakofi returned, this matter gave rise to a dispute, which was heard by the ward headman and then by the chief. Several men were mentioned as possible fathers of the child, but Nkidi insisted that it was Letshwiti, a childhood sweetheart of hers. This issue was never conclusively resolved, but it seems likely that the genitor was a close agnate of Moakofi's. Although efforts were made to repair the relationship between Moakofi and Nkidi, matters continued to deteriorate after this incident, and it soon became generally known that Moakofi had a concubine, with whom he spent most of his time.

In 1965, Nkidi lodged a complaint at the chief's *kgotla*,[31] claiming that she was being neglected. Bogosi made strenuous efforts to rebut these charges, but the chief, who treated the union as a marriage, told him to set aside beasts for Nkidi's future maintenance. Then, early in 1966, Moakofi petitioned the chief's *kgotla*,[32] arguing that Nkidi had returned to her own segment and was no longer behaving as his wife.

The chief, observing that the marriage was at an end and that both parties had lovers, ordered them to part. Nkidi was instructed to return with her fifth child to her own agnates, while the homestead was awarded to Moakofi. ("The house and yard is yours, Moakofi. Nkidi will go back to her father.") The cattle that Bogosi had been ordered to set aside on the previous occasion for Nkidi's maintenance remained with him.

Even though Nkidi had grown sons, then, she was sent back to live among the members of her own descent grouping. The primary reason for this was that the genitor of the fifth child, and her current lover, was a close agnate of Moakofi's. For her to have stayed on in the ward under these circumstances would have perpetuated existing tensions. In the event, the normative precept that a divorced woman must relinquish her dwelling, arable field, and the cattle set aside to feed her was reflected in the outcome—but as the result of a circumstantial social factor rather than a jural imperative.[33] In other instances, as in case 9, between Molefe and Madubu, the woman may stay on in her husband's ward despite the stated norm.

CASE 14:   MPHAKGA AND MMALEGWALE

Mphakga, from the Kgosing ward in Mochudi, went to live with Mmalegwale at her father's homestead in Monneng *kgotla* following preliminary negotiations. Four children were born to them, *bogadi* was presented, and Mmalegwale was finally taken to live at Mphakga's homestead in Kgosing. Little is known about the early years of their marriage because they spent most of the time out at Mphakga's father's cattle post, but by 1958 relations between the two had become tense. Mphakga had tired of Mmalegwale and tried to introduce another woman into the homestead. He had repeatedly beaten Mmalegwale seriously, and she, in turn, is said to have resorted to sorcery against him. Several attempts were made by the respective kinsmen to repair the marriage, and, on one occasion, Mphakga was thrashed in the *kgotla* for excessively beating his wife.

In 1958 or 1959 Mmalegwale fled back to her own kin with the four children. Nobody came to claim her back, and, in 1965, her FoBS, Letshwai, brought the matter to the chief's *kgotla*.[34] When it was heard, Mmalegwale complained of ill treatment and neglect, while Mphakga countered with accusations of sorcery. He told how food she had prepared had made him sick and that parts of this food had been identified by a Kgatla *ngaka* [priest-doctor] as the meat of a human or a baboon. Mmalegwale admitted resorting to sorcery but insisted that she had done so to restore Mphakga's love and not to harm him. Mphakga confessed in the *kgotla* that there was another woman, whom he hoped to marry.

The chief ordered the two to divorce. He told Mmalegwale that she should remain on in the homestead with the children and that the cattle that Mphakga had accumulated should be for her house. The chief observed that, while Mphakga could have a new wife, he could not expect to use any of these for her.

For a few years following this order, Mmalegwale remained on in the homestead with her children, but, by 1970, she had returned to live among her own agnates. Over this period, Mphakga had lived with several other women, most of the time away from Mochudi at his cattle post.

In making this decision, which bears little apparent relationship to the stated norms, the chief seems to have been influenced by Mphakga's fault and by the need to protect the children of the first house against those of any other woman Mphakga might marry. By leaving wife and children in the former husband's *kgotla,* the chief provided a continuing reminder of the entitlement of the members of this house to be maintained from Mphakga's property and ultimately to inherit it. Given Mmalegwale's admission that she had tried sorcery against her husband, it is perhaps surprising that she was allowed to stay on. Informants suggested, in fact, that it was tension arising out of the threat of her sorcery that ultimately forced Mmalegwale to return home.

The diversity of possible arrangements is exemplified further by the case of Motlakadibe (case 11), who was returned home after the *kgotla* hearing but retained both the right to cultivate a field and eight head of cattle. Taken together, then, cases 11–14 reinforce the view that the rearrangement of rights after a divorce, like their transfer during the marriage process, does not follow a normatively preclusive or rigidly prescribed order. In practice, judgments in divorce proceedings with respect to such rights appear usually to combine the allocation of fault with the effort to provide for the woman and children; where possible, too, the dispute-settlement agencies seek solutions that, from their perspective, may reduce tension and sustain existing amicable relations.

Significantly, the redistribution of rights is not always confined to divorce proceedings. Some of the redistributions typically mandated in such proceedings also accompany the dissolution of casual relations,[35] despite the fact that here, in theoretical and normative terms at least, the rights that are redistributed were never created or transferred in the first place.

CASE 15:   THETHE AND RAMOTHAGE

Ramothage met Thethe in Rustenburg [Transvaal] in 1953, promised to marry her, and took her back with him to Mochudi without telling her parents. They lived together there until 1960, when Ramothage went to work in Francistown. When he got back, in 1964, there was another woman in the picture, and he began to neglect Thethe. Despite his personal promise of marriage, no negotiations were ever carried out between the two families.

Thethe herself brought a complaint against Ramothage before the chief's *kgotla*. In doing so, she told of Ramothage's promise to marry her, but she admitted that, according to Kgatla law, she was not married to him. Telling the couple to part, the chief told Ramothage that Thethe should retain the house he had built for her and the field they had cultivated together.

Here the dispute-settlement agency clearly treats some of the important rights associated with marriage as attaching to the formation of "disapproved" unions also; for when the relationship between Ramothage and Thethe was terminated, Thethe retained the right to occupy the homestead and culti-vate the field in spite of her admission that she had not been married. Case 15, like some of the earlier ones, underlines yet again the difficulty of establishing criteria according to which a hard and fast line between approved and disapproved unions may be drawn outside the specific context of particu-lar cases.

In the light of the Tswana conceptualization of the con-jugal process, it is hardly surprising that right and prestation are not linked in a straightforward exchange relationship. Yet Tswana differ little from African peoples who assert that an enduring union gives to a husband both uxorial and genetri-cial rights over his mate and gives to her the legitimate ex-pectation of material, social, and judicial support. However, Tswana tend to hold that these entitlements are created, in the natural order of things, as a relationship matures—a view vividly demonstrated in case 9. Their mutual allocation is held to flow directly from the commitment of the relevant parties to each other and to the union, *not* simply from an a priori definition of its status. The Tswana perspective may be summarized thus: the substance of a bond cannot be de-termined, in advance of interaction, by the mere passage of prestations or other formal procedures; rather, the content of such interaction, over time, gives form to the relationship and the reciprocal expectations and entitlements that it will involve. Hence, while a union endures, these expectations and entitlements become manifest in the ordinary course of everyday life. Only when the union is threatened do the questions of jural status and liability arise. In other words, conjugality is seen by the Tswana more as a state of becoming than as a state of being. Consequently, they regard most unions as potential marriages as long as they persist without threat. This goes some way toward explaining why the status of a union is never spontaneously subjected to classification; it would patently be antithetical to the indigenous conception of conjugal development.

Conjugal Management and the Social Order

The various features we have described thus far—the irreducibility of the conjugal process to simple jural formulation, the negotiability of its component elements, the culturally validated and terminologically inscribed ambiguity of the relevant statuses, and the generation of right and liability as an intrinsic property of the maturation of relationships— would appear to fit closely together. All of them are, in one sense or another, corollaries of the individualistic quality of Tswana marital arrangements, a quality that clearly has its roots in the constitutive logic of the sociocultural system and the manner in which it imposes itself on the lived-in order. As in the Arab context, where patrilateral parallel cousin unions generate a highly individuated and individualistic social universe (see Barth 1973; Murphy 1971; Murphy and Kasdan 1959, 1967; Peters 1980), those who inhabit the Tswana world tend, for reasons spelled out in chapter 2, to perceive it as pragmatically ego-centered and competitive (see Schapera 1963a:161, 169). It is unnecessary to tread again the analytical ground covered earlier, except to underscore two points that illuminate the jural, social, and political character of marriage and, therefore, its negotiation in the context of dispute.

The first point derives from the fact that the constitution of the Tswana system negates the social boundaries of relational categories, the elaboration of structurally defined corporations, and the emergence of alliance units. Since there are no property-holding groups beyond the household, or lineages with an enduring segmentary formation, the marriage process is patently not an affair of large aggregations with complementary interests in regulating cohabitation, status, procreation, and affinal exchange. In other words, few constraints contingent on a structure of corporate relations are imposed on individuals as far as their conjugal careers are concerned; the parties to the establishment of a union are restricted to, at most, a few close kin, just as the liabilities that develop later are enforceable only at the initiative of a very limited range of people. Nor is there any reason why the centralized institutions of government should seek to exercise rigid control over the creation of marriages and the a priori assignment of jural statuses. These institutions are vested in persons organized, in sociocultural terms, in precisely the same manner as any other grouping in a chiefdom.

The second point follows from this. Because the onus of contriving a social network is inexorably thrust on the individual, the negotiation of affinal bonds is a critical element in the construction of any personal career, whether it be entered into by design or default (see chap. 2). Now it will be recalled that, in the context of everyday life, the effective kinship universe consists of an ego-centered kindred (*losika*),[36] a complex field of multiple relationships[37] that are intrinsically contradictory and demand reduction and construal. Indeed, it is this pattern that underlies the enigmatic and managerial quality of the Tswana social world. As a categorical order, the *losika* encompasses the relational classes of agnation and matrilaterality, which embody the cultural—and normatively recognized—opposition between competition and rivalry (i.e., political antagonism) and support and complementarity (i.e., moral and material protagonism). This opposition, in turn, gives form to a set of manifest social values whose realization depends in no small measure on conjugal management; for marriage provides a recognized medium within which agnatic rivalries can be reduced to matrilateral complementarities (see Schapera 1957b, 1963b; Kuper 1975a and b; and chap. 2, above) or by which individuated alliances can be mobilized and perpetuated beyond the agnatic domain. The value of such alliances, as far as Tswana are concerned, is substantial. Not only are they a source of support against agnatic competitors; they often yield considerable economic and political benefits as well. In fact, Tswana regularly attribute success, measured in wealth and position, to the efficacy of matrilateral connivance. Thus, apart from affording sexual and reproductive rights, domestic labor, and a productive base for a couple, the social utility of any union is seen to inhere in the relations to which it potentially gives access, which may then be managed to advantage. This is reflected in, and further illuminated by, the ideal-typical career path of conjugal biographies, at least from the standpoint of Tswana men.

Most men first enter a union early on in their adult lives. In some cases a father may seek to arrange his childrens' marriages, deploying them for *his* strategic purposes; if so, the independent marital careers of his sons may have to await his aging or death. When a man does set the conjugal process in motion on his own account, he may seek out a few women in turn and tentatively explore the prospects and implications of the various attachments and affinal relationships. As long as a liaison has not produced children or substantial wealth, it remains relatively easy to dissolve it without cost. Consequently, a man still relatively inexperienced in the subtle complexities of social management may enter a number of possible unions but then withdraw when it becomes apparent that they are insufficiently attractive. The subjective terms in which such judgments are made depend largely on the context-specific values that particular persons strive to gain from particular relationships: some Tswana today establish such relationships primarily for affective reasons, with little regard for their strategic dimensions; others are more concerned with the creation of advantageous alliances. Nonetheless, but especially under the latter conditions, conjugality and affinity (pace Fortes 1962:2) are dialectically related. Unions are sustained—they continue to *become* marriages— as long as the affinal bonds involved bring value to the parties involved or promise to do so in the future. As J. L. Comaroff has argued elsewhere (1980:186):

> Just as there may be a close interdependence between the genesis of a union and the anticipation of a worthwhile affinal link, so successful alliance and conjugality are seen . . . to be entailed in one another: while a specific alliance yields the returns normally expected of affinity, the union concerned will be sustained and allowed to mature into a marriage. (In fact, this occasionally occurs even where a couple have parted, for the fiction of conjugality may still rationalise an alliance.) Conversely, if that alliance is terminated by one or both parties, the union, *qua* marriage, is generally brought to an end as well. Sometimes the man and woman actually separate . . . but, even where they do not, the former allies might withdraw their recognition from the bond, which thereby becomes construable

only as a casual one. Of course, the partners themselves may persuade their respective kin to invest in an affinal link; here, too, the interdependence of marriage and affinity is stressed. It is in this sense, therefore, that they are connected in a dialectical . . . fashion. Neither is necessarily prior to, or can exist apart from, the other: the management of a conjugal-type relationship, its emergent definition and the negotiation of affinal alliance are reciprocally constitutive elements of a single process.

In early adulthood, then, ambitious young men may exploit the negotiability of marriage arrangements to the full, allowing unions to mature if they prove satisfactory and rejecting them as casual liaisons if they do not. On occasion, however, they become trapped in one from which they would rather escape (see case 16), a predicament that may persuade or compel them to abandon further managerial enterprises in the conjugal field. Moreover, Tswana recognize that different types of marriage carry varying degrees of risk; those involving previously unrelated partners are usually easier to terminate without cost than are those established within the matrilateral domain, and it is invariably impossible simply to dismiss any union with a close agnate as a lapsed informal bond. This fact may explain why men frequently settle down first with unrelated women and tend only later to seek a close kinswoman.

It should be stressed that, whatever the prior relations between spouses, the longer a union endures, the more difficult it is to gain release from it without either cost or the involvement of the dispute-settlement agencies. This does not preclude an individual from arguing that a particular union, despite its having persisted for a decade or more, is *not* a marriage. Whether or not this claim leads to public confrontation will depend on whether the interests expressed by the two parties in the context of dissolution converge or diverge. As we have seen, where such interests diverge, the rhetorical terms of debate (and judgment) are given by the taxonomy of unions, which encodes the normatively recognized implications of different kinds of bonds and their contingent liabilities. Thus, for example, if a man wishes to lay claim to the children while terminating his bond with their mother, he may seek a formal divorce, especially if he is wealthy enough to withstand a property disposition in her favor. (The readiness of chiefs to award property to the woman may make the cost of divorce a major constraint for men who wish to attempt this.) If he does not wish to claim the children, or is unable to do so for some reason, he may attempt simply to end the relationship without further ado, as did Molefe after several years (case 9). But the initiative for negotiation does not reside with men alone; a woman or her agnates may institute proceedings rather than accept the man's withdrawal on his terms. On the other hand, as long as unions persist without tension or divergent interests, as many do, their status is not questioned, whatever jural incidents have or have not occurred. In other words, enduring unions become marriages by implication. It is in this sense, to re-iterate, that marriage represents a jural potentiality rather than a jural state. Its meaning, in cultural terms, depends upon its location in a total set of categories, and these, in turn, establish the range of constructions that may be placed on any union when its social and material currency becomes the object of negotiation.

Case 16, which occurred in a Rolong community, exemplifies some of the principles underlying the management of marriage and affinity.

CASE 16:   KABO'S CAREER[38]

When he was in his early twenties, Kabo, a royal, entered a union with a commoner woman, Paulina, and they established a home at his cattle post. Informal *patlo* negotiations were initiated but, according to informants, were not completed. While it is not clear whether a promise of bridewealth was ever made, Paulina was certainly allocated a nearby field to cultivate. No children were born to the union, however. Kabo and Paulina's wealthy father, Silas, had always been on good terms, and, when the liaison was established, the two men arranged a cooperative farming enterprise. By the terms of this agreement, Silas used Kabo's land and some machinery he had recently inherited, and, providing the necessary labor and management, Silas shared the yield with the younger man.

Kabo had a partly derelict house in Kgosing, the chiefly ward, but he did not bring Paulina to live in it. At first he spent most of his

time with her at the cattle post and visited the capital only intermittently. After three or four years, however, he began to participate more actively in the affairs of the chiefly *kgotla* and stayed for
longer periods in Kgosing, where he rebuilt his homestead. Soon
he began to take an interest in Mmaseremo, his FFFBSSD.
Although no formal negotiations took place on this occasion,
either, the couple began to live together in Kabo's house, and three
sons were born to the union in rapid succession.

Kabo gradually allowed the bond with Paulina to lapse. Both he
and Silas admit to having discussed the matter, but little seems to
have been done about it. Kabo claims to have said that there had
been no marriage; and the question of formal divorce appears not
to have arisen, possibly because there were few assets, either material or human, over which disagreement could occur. More important, however, is the fact that Silas had little to gain from a dispute:
he was enjoying a substantial profit from the cooperative farming
venture, which Kabo took care not to terminate for another two
years. Moreover, Paulina soon entered into another liaison and
went to live with her new partner at his village (outside the capital).
Silas immediately took the opportunity to enter an agricultural
contract with him as well, so that the lapse of the prospective affinal
tie with Kabo involved no major material loss. Kabo also appears to
have encouraged Paulina's new liaison. He, too, had benefited from
his relationship with her, and its amicable termination meant that
he could now concentrate his marriage strategies in a new, and
more appropriate, direction.

In establishing himself at the capital, Kabo became a trusted
adviser of the chief, his classificatory FBS. The father of Mmaseremo, Keme, a classificatory paternal *and* maternal uncle, was
also a powerful royal adviser, an influential public figure, and
the head of a large ward. Keme and Kabo became close allies; the
former had no personal ambitions with respect to the chiefship, but
he persuaded Kabo to think of himself as a future officeholder.
Indeed, Keme's behavior toward Kabo conformed largely to the
indigenous normative model of the MB-ZS relationship—in fact, it
was in these terms that the two men mutually labeled their bond.
The union between Kabo and Mmaseremo was successful for many
years. Although no *patlo* negotiations had taken place or *bogadi*
been transferred, the couple assumed the conventional conjugal
roles of husband, wife, and affine, and nobody questioned the
status of their bond.

During the following eighteen years or so, Kabo gradually became one of the most powerful men in the chiefdom, and, when the
incumbent chief died, childless, a faction supporting his claim to
office quickly asserted itself. It is impossible to recount the events

surrounding the succession, save to say that, in the process, relations between Kabo and Mmaseremo became strained. Kabo had entered a liaison with a younger (junior) royal, Tuelo, whose brothers had become his particularly close allies and were leading members of his faction. Keme had disapproved of this alliance, fearing (he claimed) that Kabo's reputation would suffer if it were commonly known that he had recruited young and immature advisers. Kabo, in turn, suggested that Keme had become senile. (He certainly was very old by now and was incapacitated for much of the time.) At first, Kabo sought to maintain both sets of alliances, but, as Keme became more critical of him, he decided that the support of Tuelo's agnates was of more consequence than that of the ailing elder.

Kabo wished to bring matters to a head; he therefore transferred bridewealth for Mmaseremo and then let it be known that he wanted to divorce her. The *bogadi* transfer was intended unequivocally to assert control over the three children, for, apart from the indigenously stressed desirability of a chief's having sons, the youths were fast approaching marriageable age. But Mmaseremo, advised by her father, confronted Kabo with the fact that she did not wish to be divorced. Keme himself then took matters further by spelling out to his son-in-law the dangers inherent in his strategy. The case would have to go to the local commissioner, since there was no chief in office and nobody else could or would hear it. The commissioner was unlikely to grant a divorce, for Mmaseremo's behavior had been impeccable and she would, moreover, publicly forgive Kabo's adultery. Under these conditions, he stood the risk of appearing either a fool or a miscreant if he pursued the case. In any event, his chances of becoming chief would suffer.

Kabo discussed this with several of his allies, including Tuelo's brothers. The consensus of the advice he received was to leave the matter in abeyance, at least until the succession was decided. About three months later, Kabo was designated as chief. At his installation, murmurings about the trouble between him and his affines were everywhere to be heard. Indeed, though her three sons were present, Mmaseremo did not appear in public that day.[39]

Elsewhere it has been demonstrated that the life-cycle of Tswana individuals regularly tends to follow a path marked by a gradual reduction of ambiguity in the relations (and unions) in which they are involved. This reduction of ambiguity results in part from the progressive growth of constraint and, in varying measure, from an act of volition; but it is a process that often ends with the transfer of *bogadi,* a

symbolic moment of final self-definition within the social
field (see J. L. Comaroff 1980 and chaps. 2 and 6).[40] Here,
however, we are concerned less with the social logic of political biography than with the nature of marriage itself. By now
the structural, jural, and social aspects of Tswana marriage
ought to be clear, but one concluding point requires to be
made.

It must be emphasized that the procedural incidents associated with marriage are not intrinsically either ambiguous
or definitive; their jural character is determined not by their
substance (in fact, they are little different from those found in
many other societies) but by their social value. That this is so
resides, as we have seen, in the fact that these incidents together represent a paradigmatic *gestalt* in terms of which litigants may argue—and chiefs adjudicate—about relations,
rights, and obligations. In appearing to treat these incidents
as negotiable, Tswana courts are merely responding to the
culturally validated perception of a pervasively experienced
reality: that the management of marriage and affinity, in an
endemically shifting social universe, is a fundamental feature
of the construction of everyday interaction. The manner
in which disputes are repeatedly presented—a manner that
reflects the efforts of litigants to contrive and encode relationships and statuses—compels them to recognize this reality (Comaroff and Roberts 1977b). In short, a preclusive a
priori jural definition of unions would make little sense in
such a sociocultural context. Indeed, were it to exist, it would
be extremely difficult to explain; to assume that it should
exist would be merely ethnocentric. Moreover, the emerging
tendency among modern Tswana to choose partners on the
grounds of romantic attachment does not itself affect the
jural nature of marriage or render it less negotiable; for while
the manipulation of heterosexual unions might as a result
derive increasingly from personal emotion rather than political ambition, the potentiality for management depends on
sociocultural principles, not on behavioral motivation.

6

In chapter 5 we showed how the status of a heterosexual bond may be subject to negotiation and redefinition as the configuration of interests in it changes over time. Moreover, as we sought to demonstrate there, the taxonomy of unions represents a culturally inscribed order in terms of which conjugal and affinal relationships can be meaningfully constituted and managed. All this in turn implies that the designation of any such relationship represents a symbolic statement of its status and hence of the mutual expectations and liabilities that it involves at any point in its career. The fact that the social universe of the Tswana is experienced at the phenomenal level as enigmatic and shifting is important here. Reality, as one Rolong informant suggested, "is never what it seems; you think one thing and find out it's another, and then another." Under these conditions, the normative definitions embodied in the taxonomy of unions represent a series of fixed paradigmatic points, a symbolic grammar, in relation to which reality may continually be constructed and transformed.

This view may profitably be extended to the analysis of property relations. For example, the capacity in which a Motswana holds a number of cattle, or the nature of a particular transaction, may always be construed in a variety of culturally recognized ways and may repeatedly be revised in order to express contemporary interests or relations. Because the status of property holdings and exchanges conveys a range of messages concerning social linkages and individual rights, their definition and designation are always critical to the parties involved. In this chapter we consider these features of Tswana property arrangements in the context of the devolution process and the management of material interests, particularly as these are related to the dispute process.[1]

The Devolution Process

In our own society, incidents of property devolution associated with death tend to be differentiated clearly from distributions taking place on other occasions; it is as if they were discrete and totally unconnected transfers. Despite its questionable utility even for our own purposes,[2] lawyers and anthropologists have sometimes elevated this folk distinction—and, in particular, the association between death and "inheritance"—to the level of an a priori assumption in their comparative analyses of devolution systems. This has certainly been the case in earlier descriptions of Tswana arrangements. Thus, in *A Handbook of Tswana Law and Custom,* Schapera describes death-centered devolution in a chapter on inheritance and deals separately with the division of cattle among the houses of a polygynous domestic unit, the *tshwaiso* and *serotwana* customs (see below), and the distribution of assets following a divorce; nowhere does he explain the relationship between these different forms of devolution.

Instead of representing an aggregate of disconnected incidents, Tswana property devolution requires to be seen as a process linked to the developmental cycle of the family. It is not an event associated exclusively, or even primarily, with death. In order to trace this process, it is necessary to break into the developmental cycle at some stage. The most convenient one, perhaps, is the point at which a man has entered a union and established a homestead independent from (but ideally adjacent to) that of his father. The latter probably still survives, and the newly created household will be a nuclear unit composed of the man himself, his mate, and, possibly, some children born to them while the couple were living uxorilocally or at the homestead of the man's father prior to the completion of their own. At this stage the man is likely to have a small but identifiable herd of cattle and other stock. There is no need to examine the way in which this herd has been built up, since this will be implicit in the way the herd itself devolves.

The initial phase of the formal devolution process is associated with a man's first union. At this point a portion of the herd and a tract of available arable land should be designated and set aside for the benefit of the woman's house. The tract of land (*tshimo ya lapa*) is thereafter cultivated by the couple, and the produce is used to feed the members of her house. When a surplus occurs, any cattle or small stock acquired with it are credited to this house. In the same way, the cattle (*dikgomo tsa lapa*) are used to provide milk for the children, draft oxen for ploughing the field, and ultimately, perhaps, *bogadi* cattle for the sons of the house. Whatever the subsequent history of this and later unions, these *dikgomo tsa lapa* continue to be associated with this first woman's house and the children born to it. If subsequent wives are taken, the cattle cannot be reallocated to their houses. Separate allotments of land and cattle are made to each new house as it is formed, and the direction of devolution of further portions of the man's estate is thus determined.

The next step is associated with the birth of children. It is common usage, particularly among the Kgatla, for a man to earmark a cow, under an arrangement known as *tshwaiso,* for each son at the time of his birth. The cow so earmarked, together with its issue, is then regarded as permanently allocated to that child. With good fortune, the cow and its calves will form the nucleus of a growing herd for the individual concerned. Even a man with few cattle will seek to *tshwaisa* a beast for each of his sons. Richer men may make bigger allocations by earmarking for each son all the calves born in the year of their birth or, in the case of the very wealthy, all the stock kept at a particular cattle post. If a *tshwaiso* animal dies without issue, it should be replaced. Ideally, a man should also *tshwaisa* a cow for each of his daughters, and this is typically done by Kgatla who have enough cattle to make this possible.

Dispositions under the *tshwaiso* arrangements represent an important element in the overall pattern of devolution, and, in many estates, a majority of the cattle are distributed in this way. In any case, by the time a man's children are approaching maturity, the division of a considerable portion of the estate has already been ordained. The process continues as the children enter their own unions. When a daughter does so, her father should, among the Kgatla, provide beasts known as *serotwana*. These cattle accompany her on her departure from her natal home and contribute to the maintenance of the household that she and her husband establish. When she dies, the *serotwana* cattle devolve upon her children, preference being given to her daughters (Schapera 1938; Roberts 1970).[3]

At some point in her marital career, too, *bogadi* will also be presented for a daughter, and, again, the devolution of these cattle is fixed from this time. Traditionally, sons and daughters in a given house are "linked" in pairs during childhood by their father; thereafter, linked siblings remain in a special relationship with each other. Thus, for example, a man is expected to look after his linked sister in later life, especially if she should be divorced and should then return to live among members of her own agnatic segment (see chap. 2). Ostensibly in recognition of this obligation, the greater part of the *bogadi* presented for a woman should be transferred to the herd of her linked brother; in theory, he will use these beasts and their increase to maintain her if necessary. Of course, when the boys marry, additional bridewealth may have to be found for their unions, unless the transfer of *bogadi* is delayed.

As a man's sons mature, responsibility for managing his herd falls progressively upon them. If they have their own cattle posts, the father may give some beasts to each one to look after on his behalf. In cases where the herd is large, each may also be given a post to oversee. If a son shows care and skill in their management, the father may actually transfer ownership of the stock to him; moreover, instructions to this effect are generally conveyed well in advance of his death. Later, in his old age, the man may inform his sons and some senior maternal kinsmen about the disposition of the residue of his property. Typically, he will direct that it be divided among immature children or those whose *tshwaiso* beasts have not prospered. The Tswana maxim, *lentswe la moswi ga le tlolwe*—"The voice of a dead man is not transgressed"—suggests that instructions given before death are taken seriously by survivors.

By the time a married male household head dies, therefore, most of his estate has been transferred to, or is in the process of devolving upon, the next generation. It is only

with respect to unallocated cattle that the direction of devolution remains to be determined.[4] When Linchwe II became chief of the Kgatla in 1963, well-defined rules provided
for the division of this balance:[5] the eldest son was entitled to
the largest portion, while the younger ones should receive
increasingly smaller shares in declining order of seniority. At
least since the reign of Linchwe I (1875–1924), daughters
had also been entitled to benefit from the unallocated residue, but they rarely did as well as the boys, and no daughter would ever receive as many cattle as the eldest son.
Nevertheless, the exact amount any child was given had to be
agreed on in each individual case, subject to the established
principle that the senior male heir always received the largest
(Schapera 1938:230–31; Roberts 1970). While no two estates were ever exactly the same, a division made in 1957
by Chief Molefi, Linchwe's father, may be considered to
reflect typical patterns. Case 17 confirms that, in 1957,
younger siblings could expect to receive a substantial share of
the unallocated balance and that the preeminence enjoyed by
the eldest son was little more than a token.

CASE 17:   THEBE'S CATTLE[6]

THEBE'S GENEALOGY

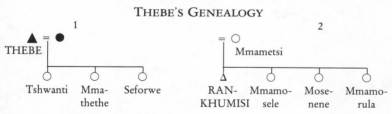

Key: UPPERCASE = MALE
       Lowercase = female
         Δ, O = living male, female
         ▲, ● = deceased male, female
         1, 2 = 1st house, 2nd house

Thebe was survived by three daughters (Tshwanti, Mmathethe, and
Seforwe), the children of his long-deceased first wife, and by a son
(Rankhumisi) and three daughters (Mmamosele, Mosenene, and
Mmamorula), the children of his second wife, Mmametsi, who was
still alive. A dispute arose as to the manner in which Thebe's stock
should be divided. The matter was taken before Chief Molefi, who
distributed them as follows:

FIRST HOUSE		SECOND HOUSE	
Tshwanti	10	Rankhumisi	11 (plus the wagon)
Mmathethe	8	Mmamosele	8
Seforwe	8	Mosenene	8
		Mmamorula	8

The surviving widow, Mmametsi, was given eight cattle and the sheep and goats. The decision, in other words, awarded the eldest son only slightly more than the amount received by the other children.

The rules governing the distribution of the unallocated balance were changed by Linchwe II in the first year of his incumbency. Instead of resorting to direct legislative action, however, he introduced these changes through the division of two estates belonging to senior men of the chiefdom. In both instances, ignoring the existing norm that the eldest son was entitled to the largest share of the undistributed balance, he divided the cattle equally among the deceased's children:

CASE 18:   DIKEME'S CATTLE[7]

DIKEME'S GENEALOGY

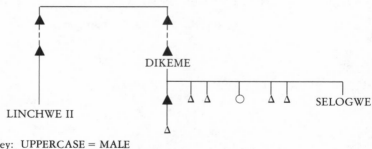

Key: UPPERCASE = MALE
    Δ, O = living male, female
    ▲ = deceased male

    ⋮ = unlisted generations

Dikeme was one of Linchwe's classificatory paternal uncles. He had been dead some time without anything being done about the unallocated balance of his cattle. Shortly after Linchwe became chief, he was asked to divide this balance, which consisted of thirty-five head. Dikeme had seven children who lived to become adults: six sons and one daughter. One of these sons had predeceased him but was survived by a son of his own. Linchwe allotted five beasts to each of the surviving sons, five to the daughter, and five to the child of Dikeme's deceased son.

CASE 19:   RANKO'S CATTLE[8]

RANKO'S GENEALOGY

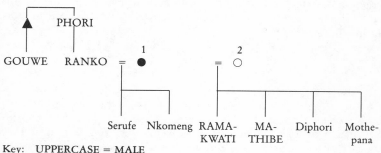

Key: UPPERCASE = MALE
Lowercase = female
○ = living female
▲, ● = deceased male, female
1, 2 = 1st house, 2nd house

Ranko's father, Phori, was born in Ramadiakobong ward but moved later to Morema ward and lived there for the rest of his life. Some say he was taken there as a child, while others suggest that he went as an adult, after his initiation and admission to an age-regiment. Whatever the actual circumstances, Phori established his marital household in Morema ward, where Ranko was born.

When Ranko himself entered a union, he built himself a homestead in Morema. Two girls, Serufe and Nkomeng, were born to this marriage. Following the death of his first wife, Ranko contracted a second union, which produced four more children who survived to become adults: two boys, Ramakwati and Mathibe, and two girls, Diphori and Mothepana. As is common when Kgatla males establish successive houses, relations between the children of the two wives were strained. While Ranko still lived, therefore, Ramakwati and Mathibe settled back in Ramadiakobong ward, where Ranko's father had once lived.

Following Ranko's death, the two girls of the first house complained to the Morema ward headman, Mothei, that Ramakwati was "eating up" the cattle Ranko had left and that they had received no benefit. Serufe argued that the cattle should now be allocated so that she and her sister could be given some. Accordingly, Mothei, in his capacity as headman of the ward in which Ranko had lived, set aside a day on which Ranko's remaining stock would be distributed. He arranged for them to be collected together and informed the senior members of Ramadiakobong, where Ramakwati and his brother were living. Ramakwati and the Ramadiakobong men found these arrangements unacceptable. They replied that, since Ranko was truly a member of Ramadiakobong, it was up to them to organize the division. They did not, however, object in principle to the idea that the girls should have a share. In the face of these disagreements, the respective ward heads took the matter before the chief.

When the dispute came to be heard in the chief's *kgotla,* it was presented in the following manner:

GOUWE (Ramadiakobong ward headman and Ranko's FoBS): I bring this matter before the chief. Ranko is not a member of Morema ward but of Ramadiakobong. Ranko died while living in Morema. Although he paid tax in Morema, the truth is that he is a member of Ramadiakobong. He is my uncle's [*rremogolo*] son. I am bringing this case [*tsheko*] as his father.

[After giving further information on the question of Ranko's tax, Gouwe continued:]

I was told by Ramakwati. He said I was wanted so that I could be there when Ranko's cattle were distributed. At that time the cattle had already been collected by members of the Morema ward. I replied that it was wrong to call me when the cattle were ready for distribution; they should have consulted me even before they were collected together.

Ramakwati told me that his sister had said they wanted to be given some cattle as well. He told me that he has said he was not against this but wanted to settle the father's debts first.

MOTHEI (headman of Morema): Ranko was my son. I am concerned with this matter as a headman. He pays tax to me and not to the Ramadiakobong ward. The source of the dispute is his estate [*boswa*]. Those who are quarreling are Ranko's children. They are quarreling over his estate. Ranko was married to two wives. There were two children born to the first wife, and both of them are girls. There were four children of the second wife, two of them boys and two girls. The children born to the second wife do not want to share the estate with those born to the first. The two boys are members of the Ramadiakobong ward, while the girls born to the first wife are members of Morema. I do not know who separated them.

When the cattle were assembled there were found to be thirty in all. Linchwe divided them equally, so that each child received five beasts.

These two decisions were greeted with dissatisfaction at the time they were made. Nevertheless, Linchwe persisted in dividing any unallocated balance equally among siblings when estates were brought to him for division. His practice seems to have acquired acceptance in the Kgatleng, if not positive approval. In March 1973, informants quoted this mode of division as the established norm.

In the light of contemporary usage in most Tswana chiefdoms, one further phase must be added to this description of the process of property distribution. According both to earlier accounts[9] and to elderly living informants, the direct implications of divorce for the devolutionary cycle were insignificant in the past. When a woman was divorced, she returned to her own agnates to be looked after, and, irrespective of issues of fault, orders under which cattle from the husband's herd might be transferred to her were seldom made. Informants say that she would simply return with her *serotwana* animals and, perhaps, a further beast "to carry her household goods." As we saw in chapter 5, however, substantial awards are often made today in favor of divorced women. Indeed the socially accepted norms in most chiefdoms prescribe this unless the responsibility for conjugal breakdown can be laid solely at her door.[10]

The beasts the wife is granted on divorce should eventually devolve upon the children of her marriage. If she is childless, however, the stated norms seem to vary. Among the Kgatla and the Rolong, it appears to be recognized that these beasts should devolve on members of her own descent group. In practice, even if the woman *has* children from the marriage, stock taken with her when she returns to her natal home are often lost to the husband's agnatic unit. Thus, the occasion of divorce has become a further stage in the devolutionary cycle at which property may effectively be transferred out of the segment.

The proportion of any estate that is allocated at each stage of the devolution process will vary according to circumstance, since a number of intervening factors must be taken into account by those involved. While we have insufficient data to permit an acceptable statistical calculation of diachronic patterns of distribution, the division of Mankge's property, set forth in case 20, would appear to provide a typical illustration.

CASE 20:   MANKGE'S CATTLE[11]

MANKGE'S DESCENDANTS

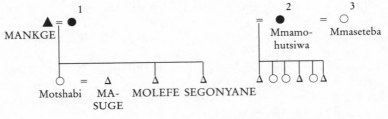

Key: UPPERCASE = MALE
Lowercase = female
Δ, O = living male, female
▲, ● = deceased male, female
1, 2, 3 = rank of houses

Mankge had entered unions with three women. The first, the mother of Motshabi (f.), Molefe (m.), and Segonyane (m.), was long deceased. After her death, Mankge had married Mmamohutsiwa, who bore him a further three boys and three girls. The third wife, Mmaseteba, survived him but remained childless.

By the time Mankge died, he had distributed twenty-seven cattle among the three houses and had earmarked another sixty-four *tshwaiso* beasts for his various children. Some months before, he had also given instructions to Motshabi, Molefe, and Motshabi's husband, Masuge, to the effect that fifteen cattle should be divided among the children of Mmamohutsiwa after his death (three to each of the three boys and two to each of the three girls). These children had fared less well than those of the first house under the *tshwaiso* arrangement. Once these various allocations had been made, the unallocated balance of Mankge's herd amounted to fifteen beasts. Thus, approximately 22 percent of the estate devolved by way of house allotment, 53 percent under the *tshwaiso* arrangement, 12 percent as a result of a testamentary action, and 12 percent according to the norms applicable to any unallocated balance.

Four aspects of these arrangements must be stressed. First, the processual dimension of the system of devolution ensures that property passes gradually from one generation to the next instead of being transferred on a single occasion. Tswana are fully aware of this processual dimension and, from their own perspective, suggest that there are advantages in it. Informants tend to state explicitly that the disposition of assets by stages and the inter vivos distribution of the major part of an estate are likely to reduce the frequency of disputes. In normative terms, the smaller the amount remaining as an unallocated balance, the better; indeed, people speak with approval of the individual who manages to arrange the division of his property well before his death. Moreover, success in this respect is a patent source of satisfaction to those who achieve it.

Second, the system is not one of universal inheritance by which all, or even the greater part, of a man's property is transmitted to a single heir; on the contrary, it involves distribution among *all* his children. Furthermore, there is no certainty as to which child will emerge with the largest overall share. Much may depend on good fortune under the *tshwaiso* arrangement; for example, the *tshwaiso* beasts of a younger sibling may, and in many cases do, prosper and multiply better than those of the eldest son. In fact, Kgatla—and, to a slightly lesser extent, Rolong—appear to be quite conscious of the fact that the eldest son is by no means assured of the major portion of the estate.

A third aspect of this system is that property does not necessarily devolve exclusively within the agnatic segment. As informants recognize, any cattle passing to a daughter are lost to the segment unless she remains unmarried. Such outward transfers are occasioned by *serotwana* and *tshwaiso* dispositions and by the fact that in many Tswana communities, even before Linchwe II's decision, daughters received some part of the unallocated balance. As we have noted, of course, the unit will also lose some of its stock when property is awarded to a woman on the occasion of a divorce.

Finally, despite its relative unimportance in strictly material terms, the division of the unallocated balance (*boswa*)[12] is viewed indigenously as a distinct and especially crucial part of the devolution process. Significantly, the eldest son is known as *moja boswa* (literally, "the eater of *boswa*"), a term that reflects the traditional recognition that, in marked contrast to inter vivos transfers, he was always entitled to the largest share of *boswa*. This rule is justified by informants on the ground that it is he who assumes overall material responsibility for surviving members of his father's agnatic segment (see chap. 3). Now, if the system of inheritance were death-centered and most of a man's property devolved at this point, the emic explanation would make sense in economic terms; for the eldest son might expect to receive enough of an additional portion with which to discharge the obligations entailed by his status. But death is *not* the moment at which the greater part of a man's estate devolves upon the next generation. As cases 17–19 indicate, only a small proportion may remain over by way of a residue when he dies, and the extra share allocated to the *moja boswa* may amount to only a token one or two cattle. In short, there is no guarantee that the eldest son will emerge with the largest percentage of his father's estate, nor do Tswana insist that he ought to. It is with respect to *boswa* alone that his preeminence is emphasized and rationalized in terms of familial duties. As we pointed out earlier, this arrangement appears to represent a normative contradiction: on the one hand, the status and heritable entitlement of the *moja boswa* is linked to a stated material obligation; yet, on the other, the ideal pattern of devolution *should* ensure that he does *not* actually receive the wherewithal to fulfill it. This contradiction was highlighted by the Kgatla reaction to Linchwe II's innovatory decisions: people argued against them on the basis that an eldest son would no longer have the assets with which to carry out his responsibilities to the rest of the segment; yet, even under the previous arrangements, whose value was being commonly espoused, these assets were little more than a token.

Thus, while the status of *moja boswa* is described indigenously in terms of material obligation, an explanation for the norms governing this final stage of the process must be sought elsewhere. We have argued previously[13] that the primacy of the eldest son *at this moment* is concerned more with the transmission of the segment headship than it is with the creation of an objective resource-management capability. It is when a man dies and authority over the segment is transferred across the generations that constraints on the disintegration of the unit are at their least compelling; for it is at precisely this point that the *common* interests of its members in property and position, articulated by their late father, now disappear, and the authority of his heir is as likely to be resented as accepted. At the same time, the unity of the segment, and its eventual elaboration into a higher-order structural unit, are fundamental features of the indigenous theory of social order. According to this theory, the division and elaboration of the hierarchy of coresidential politico-administrative units are closely linked to the growth, fragmentation, and reproduction of households and segments. As the household reaches the end of its cycle, it is believed that men will fight over property and position and that, though the unit will divide, its members will continue to live within the same higher-order grouping. This process of division, which is inscribed in the logic of the constitutive order, is held to underlie the formation of local segments, which usually comprise households with agnatically related heads. Similarly, as segments grow, they too will divide in the wake of agnatic conflict to form new wards, and so on. This process of spatially and structurally contained fission—in terms of which the unity of the segment is critical—is seen by Tswana as the very basis of social order. That it is a circular notion and a simplification is, of course, neither here nor there; it is enough that this indigenous theory of structual elaboration underpins the value attributed to the intergenerational unity of the segment. Under these conditions, then, the extra share of *boswa* serves as a token both of the transfer of legitimacy and of the continuity of the grouping at the moment of structural crisis.

In this sense, the devolution process—and the four primary characteristics of it that we have isolated—constitutes a mechanism for articulating property relations into an enduring structural order. The stress placed on inter vivos division and the primacy of the *moja boswa* are not perceived as conflicting principles; on the contrary, they are valued by Tswana as related devices that regulate inter- and intragenerational relations in such a way as to keep agnatic strife within established limits and ensure the perpetuation of the (agnatically derived) politicoresidential hierarchy that gives form to the community. Moreover, this indigenous perception does not contradict the view that rivalry between agnates is ubiquitous or that the agnatic domain is the proper locus of competitive enterprise. It merely reflects the conventional observation that, if such rivalry were not contained within the hierarchy, or if it resulted in its dissolution, the very foundations of the political order—and the essential values realized in and through it—would be destroyed. In this respect, too, the distributional nature of the system is seen to create a series of lateral ties binding the segment to other such units, thereby mediating potential lines of fission. In other words, the intricate network of linkages generated by the devolution process serves ostensibly to incorporate lower-order units into a wider social hierarchy. At the same time, however, this process is held to draw individuals and houses into inevitable conflicts of interest, the categories inscribed in the Tswana system of rank and relationship providing a set of rhetorical indices for the negotiation of access to control over goods and resources.

The fact that the transmission of property, together with its social implications, is conceived in this way is hardly surprising; it represents an expression—in terms of an order of material objects and of their appropriation and alienation —of the fundamental relations and principles upon which the Tswana sociocultural system is predicated. This will become increasingly clear as we proceed. However, it is necessary first to examine the manifest points of tension generated by the devolutionary process and the manner in which they configure indigenous experience, for it is this configuration that underlies the characteristic form and content of property disputes.

Property Relations and Fields of Tension

Tswana not only simultaneously maintain the ideal of agnatic unity and recognize its endemic tensions; they also perceive the property content of kinship relations in dualistic terms.

On the one hand, the smooth distribution of assets is held to discourage familial disputes. Thus the progressive, even-handed division of an estate according to established norms is not only a correlate of good intergenerational relations; it also facilitates conflict-free intragenerational ones. On the other hand, property is thought to be the principal channel of conflict, especially, as Tswana themselves point out, when access to material value is closely linked to the devolution of an office or a prized status. Outside the matrilateral domain—quintessentially the mother-child tie, linked sib-lingship, and the special bond between maternal uncles and their uterine nephews—*all* familial and close kinship relations are assumed to be potential loci of conflict. However, three fields of tension are indigenously identified: intergenerational, interhouse, and intrahouse.

Intergenerational Tensions

When it arises, intergenerational tension typically takes one of two forms: first, tension between father and son, which tends to occur either when the father delays the normal process of devolution and/or fails to act evenhandedly; second, tension between a paternal uncle and his brother's children, which is commonly associated with guardianship and the refusal to transfer assets.

Whatever his motives may in fact be, a father who delays the allocation of his assets usually justifies his behavior on the ground that his son or sons lack managerial skills. There may, of course, be sound reasons behind his actions, but such delays inevitably lead to a sense of grievance on the part of the children. Similarly, a man may survive beyond the typical span and retain an active interest in his property long after his offspring reach adulthood. In this situation, the tensions generated by the deferral of devolution are often exacerbated by another consideration: the fact that long-lived males generally contract plural marriages and so create additional houses. When this occurs, older children will receive a smaller proportion of their father's estate, a possibility of which they are acutely aware. Hence, intergenerational strains are overlain by conflicting interhouse interests.[14] As a result, mature sons tend to press for an early distribution, while their father may seek to avoid it. Case 21, which exemplifies the disagreements produced by delayed allocations and alleged inequities, also demonstrates the manner in which intergenerational tensions are expressed in mutual accusations of paternal neglect and filial mismanagement. It indicates, moreover, that the chiefly *kgotla* entertains the possibility that either or both may occur and must be negatively sanctioned when they do, for the ideals of filial rectitude and paternal responsibility to allocate property early and fairly are equally valued; indeed, they are held to be broadly reciprocal.

CASE 21:   KGASANE AND SENWELO[15]

Kgasane, of the Mosadimogolo *kgotla,* was a member of the Ntwane age-regiment [formed in 1892]. He is reputed to have built up a considerable herd of cattle as a youth, largely by selling arms during the Anglo-Boer War, but he entered a union for the first time only when he was already in his forties. This union produced a son, Senwelo (b. 1918), and later a daughter. While the two children were still young, their mother died, and Kgasane left Mosadimogolo to live with a second woman, Morekwe, on the western fringe of the village. Informants say that he neglected Senwelo and his sister, allowing their homestead to fall into ruins. Both were brought up primarily by maternal kinsmen.

Until the end of the Second World War, Senwelo spent most of his time away as a migrant laborer, finally settling down at Mochudi in about 1949. Soon thereafter, in response to complaints of neglect, Kgasane gave his eldest son a number of cattle to manage. The herd was composed of some of Kgasane's own stock, beasts that had been earmarked for Senwelo and others that had been set aside for Senwelo's mother's house. Under normal circumstances, Kgasane, who was over seventy by now, would have left these animals entirely under Senwelo's management and would also have transferred them to his ownership while he himself was still alive. The old man remained vigorous, however, and wished to retain overriding control of the herd. As a result, he repeatedly gave instructions concerning its husbandry. But Senwelo, who remained mindful of his father's early neglect and continued preference for the second house, ignored Kgasane's orders, even to the extent of selling beasts on his own initiative.

In 1958 Kgasane complained to the chief's *kgotla* that Senwelo was wasting his cattle. The latter admitted that he had disregarded his father, but he justified this on the grounds of paternal neglect and favoritism for the second house (a fact that was notorious at Mochudi). Reproved by the chief for allowing the homestead of his first wife to fall into ruins, Kgasane made no attempt to demand the cattle back. The matter ended with the chief carefully identifying, within the herd held by Senwelo, those animals that the son himself had acquired, those that were *tshwaiso* beasts, those that were house cattle, and those that still belonged to Kgasane. Of the last category, eight head were set aside as *bogadi* for Senwelo's mother, which was still outstanding. Senwelo was then warned to do nothing with the residue that might be contrary to his father's wishes.

It seems that Senwelo disregarded the chief's orders, for, in 1961, Kgasane returned to the *kgotla,* complaining again that Senwelo was selling his beasts without permission. By now, Kgasane was at least ninety; but he still had not transferred ownership of the animals he had given to Senwelo to manage. The chief repeated his warning to Senwelo to do as his father instructed and, specifically, to give him a beast that could be sold to maintain the homestead of the first house.[16] Kgasane died a few years later without having made over to Senwelo the stock under his control. Senwelo has nonetheless retained these cattle and has not been challenged about this by members of the second house.

Tension between paternal uncles and their nephews is also associated indigenously with the devolution process, although informants point out that the conflicts of interest dividing them may extend far beyond it. The logic of this tension is held to derive from the rules regulating guardianship: if a man dies leaving the distribution of his estate incomplete, particularly if his sons are still immature, discretionary control over the property and its eventual division passes to the senior surviving brother of the deceased. There is, moreover, no fixed age at which the heirs may be said to have reached maturity. Unless there exist strong, perhaps exceptional, bonds of trust and confidence within an agnatic segment, disputes tend to arise as the children reach adulthood and either agitate for the transfer of their inheritance and/or accuse their guardians of misappropriating their rightful assets. Indeed, the temptations facing guardians in this regard are widely recognized. Nevertheless, the extent to which such accusations have any basis in fact is difficult to assess, since most agnatic conflict is attributed to avuncular interference and much of it never reaches the courts. The standard Tswana explanation has it that, in protecting and furthering the interests of their own children, brothers do not hesitate to erode the interests of their nephews and to sow seeds of dissension among them. Where the brothers are of different houses, this becomes even more acute, since, as we have demonstrated, their relative status (and that of their descendants) is especially open to competitive negotiation. In short, the expectation that nephews and their paternal uncles will fight over property and status is a recurrent theme in everyday life; whether it is a self-fulfilling prophecy or an accurate generalization after the fact, dispute-settlement agencies have to hear such disagreements with great regularity.

One variant of this type of intergenerational conflict may manifest itself when an unmarried mother dies young. When this happens, her children are usually affiliated to her own natal segment, and their maternal uncles assume guardianship. The matrilateral bond is then often transformed; at least in content, it may become a (quasi) agnatic one, and the avuncular relationship may become as strained as it frequently is in the agnatic context. In fact, the emergent definition of relations appears to follow broadly the same pattern as that observed in the case of all multiple links (chap. 2): when the bond is affectively close and conflict-free, its matrilateral component is stressed; but, once it becomes tense, it acquires a patrilateral definition. As case 22 shows, an avaricious uncle may exploit the ambiguities involved in order to further his own personal ends.

CASE 22:   SEEPI AND MOTSISI[17]

Mma-M, of the Ratsheola *kgotla* at Mochudi, bore a son, Motsisi, while she was living as an unmarried woman in the homestead of her younger brother, Seepi. While the child was still young, she went away alone to work in Johannesburg, where she died. Following this, the sum of £87/10s was remitted and placed by the chief in the care of her senior agnates. When Motsisi grew up, he asked Seepi for this money and also demanded that he be allowed to dismantle and remove the house his mother had occupied. Seepi denied both requests, saying that he knew nothing of the money and that the house, which was situated within his homestead, had devolved upon him when Mma-M died. Motsisi took his grievance to the chief.[18]

When the dispute was heard, it emerged that, over the years, Seepi and other members of the segment had used the cash, of which none now remained. Some of it had gone toward the costs of Seepi's own marriage, some had been spent on the purchase of cattle, and some had been handed over in compensation for a successful pregnancy claim against Motsisi. Nevertheless, Seepi argued that the money had not been directly in his care; the bank book had been given by the chief to another member of the segment. He claimed, moreover, that the money had been required to meet the expenses of Motsisi's education, marriage, and duty to defray the pregnancy claim. In short, as his maternal uncle, Seepi had, he asserted, looked after the interests of the youth; as his "father" (i.e., senior agnate), he had exercised guardianship and control over the inheritance to meet Motsisi's obligations.

The chief found that Seepi had "eaten" Motsisi's inheritance and ordered him to return the R175 (about $202; £87/10s under the new currency). He also said that the complainant should be allowed to take away and rebuild his mother's house. Motsisi's claim that his uncle should be responsible for the money rested on the view that Seepi was his jural "father," Mma-M having died unmarried. In finding as he did, the chief accepted his line of argument. This construction was called into question only by Seepi's skillful manipulation, throughout the course of the relationship, of the ambiguity of his position as Motsisi's closest agnate and his mother's brother.

Even when the sons of a deceased man are all mature at the time of his demise, disputes may still ensue if the devolution process has been delayed. Despite the stated norms to the contrary, some men retain ownership over most of their cattle throughout their lives, while others fail to make allocations in all appropriate directions under the *tshwaiso* arrangement. In such cases, whether or not instructions are given preceding death, the distribution of the estate may occasion acute disagreements. Over 60 percent of property disputes between close kin that reach the chief's *kgotla* revolve around the allocation of assets undivided when a man dies.

Intrahouse Conflict

Intrahouse disputes, which occur with comparatively less frequency than either intergenerational or interhouse ones, rarely derive from inequities of property distribution. For, even if a father favors a particular son among a set of full siblings, it is difficult for him to allocate a significantly larger proportion to that child without incurring negative sanctions; a mother and her kin will generally seek to ensure that the respective interests of each member of the house are protected. In the event that favoritism is exercised, moreover, the indignation of the other children is usually directed not at the favored sibling but at the father; hence intrahouse tension is seldom a corollary of the division of the estate itself.

Disputes may arise, however, when a son (usually the eldest) is vested with managerial rights over assets that either have yet to be divided[19] or have been allocated to his widowed mother, his sisters, or his immature brothers. In much the same way as a paternal uncle, in his capacity as guardian, is frequently held to "eat up," or refuse to hand over, the inheritance of his charges, an older brother may be accused of furthering his own interests (and, if he has entered a union, those of his own children) at the expense of the other members of the house. Case 23 provides a typical example of this situation.

CASE 23:   A MOTHER AND HER SON[20]

Johanna entered a union with a member of the Mabodisa *kgotla* before the Second World War and a son, Makgatse, was born to them. Shortly after his birth, however, the father died. *Bogadi* cattle were presented in respect of Johanna, who had also brought some *serotwana* beasts with her to her marital house. While Makgatse was a child, his late father's stock and the *serotwana* animals were looked after by a paternal uncle, but he himself was put in charge of them early in the 1950s.

Some time after this, Johanna returned to live in her natal ward, but, at first, Makgatse continued to plough for her and see to her maintenance. He gradually ceased to do this, however, and failed to give his mother the proceeds when he sold the offspring of the *serotwana* beasts. Eventually, Johanna complained of his neglect to the ward *kgotla*.

When the case was heard, Johanna complained that Makgatse had retained her *serotwana* cattle but did not support her or give her the benefit of her property. The son admitted that he still held the animals but insisted that he ploughed for his mother and otherwise saw to her maintenance. The headman ordered that the defendant's herd be brought together, and it was found that the issue of the original *serotwana* cows amounted to twenty-four head. Makgatse was instructed to hand these over to Johanna. He then appealed to the chief, who upheld the decision of the ward *kgotla*.

That intrahouse tension resulting from the alleged mismanagement or expropriation of the assets of some of its members by others is usually confined to the determinacies of property-holding is explained by the fact that the relations involved are *not* potential loci of competition over seniority and, hence, over office and/or status; for full siblings are ranked according to age, a rule which, save under exceptional circumstances (see chap. 2, n. 14), effectively precludes negotiation.[21] Intrahouse relations thus contrast sharply with interhouse (and, therefore, half-sibling) relations, which are readily open to rivalry over the definition of rank; indeed, we have repeatedly stressed that manipulative rivalry of this kind characterizes Tswana sociopolitical processes at all levels of the hierarchy. As this contrast once again confirms, the house represents the only potentially solidary unit of political action in the society; since only one male member can compete for any representative office, it is typically held to be in the others' direct interest to support him.[22] Hence, situations of purely interpersonal hostility apart, the members of the unit may be expected to express a unity of interest in opposition to other like groupings, at least for much of the duration of the developmental cycle. Under these conditions, internal dispute, when it occurs, rarely extends beyond the short-term exigencies of property management.

Interhouse Conflict

Tswana themselves see interhouse relations as constituting the most pervasive field of tension, since the interests of these units in property and rank are held to be inherently divergent. In the past, when polygyny was widely practiced, disputes between cowives and between spouses appear also to have been attributed to divergent house interests. Today monogamy—or, more precisely, serial monogamy (Comaroff and Roberts 1977b)—precludes hostility between wives, although a living one may fall into disagreement with her partner over his relative treatment of her offspring. Moreover, the matrilateral kin of each of the houses tend to watch over the affairs of their respective sister's children and, in so doing, may come into conflict with their father and/or his other affines.

Much present-day interhouse tension derives purely from rival property interests. Apart from anything else, one set of full siblings (or their matrilateral kin) may simply resent the existence of another and its entitlement to a share in the estate. Resentment of this kind is frequently expressed in covert complaints that the rival siblings are actively seeking to obtain more than their due proportion. The majority of serious interhouse disputes over material assets arise, however, during the period between the death of the father and the final distribution of his heritable wealth, particularly when some of his children are still immature. Such disputes typically take one of three forms. First, the eldest son, along with his senior surviving agnates, may have the responsibility of effecting the division of an incompletely devolved estate. This often leads to allegations against him, made by junior half-brothers and sisters and their maternal uncles, of self-interest and of bias in favor of his own house. Second, while all of a dead man's property may have been allotted or earmarked, it may continue to remain together as one physically undifferentiated holding under the temporary control of the *moja boswa*. In this case, the senior heir will usually be said, sooner or later, to be delaying the process of distribution. The situation is inevitably exacerbated if, under the guidance of his mother's brothers, he hands over the shares of his uterine siblings while retaining those of the other children, ostensibly because they are still too young to be given theirs. Third, when the *moja boswa* does maintain rightful guardianship over the inheritance of the younger children, he may be accused of managing it, or disposing of some of it, to his personal advantage or to that of his house. Although similar accusations may also be made by siblings, the indigenous predisposition to anticipate interhouse rivalry makes accusations all the more likely to occur between, or on behalf of, members of the different units. Tswana suggest, moreover, that hostility between any two half-siblings will invariably coalesce their respective uterine sibling groups and range them against each other. An example of interhouse dispute hinging entirely upon property relations is provided by the case of Ranko's cattle (case 19).

At the risk of laboring an earlier point, we reiterate that interhouse tension is not confined to matters of property. Inasmuch as the Tswana community is ordered into a hierarchy of progressively more inclusive politicoadministrative units, each with an agnatic core and a territorial base, access to authority at all levels depends on the reckoning of agnatic rank, and, since this reckoning derives ostensibly from the relative status of wives, its competitive negotiation always proceeds in terms of interhouse relations. Thus conflict between sets of uterine siblings over heritable wealth may be overlain by rivalry over rank. Where such rivalry has broader implications—e.g., when seniority in a given household also provides access to an office—the negotiation of property rights within it may represent the idiom for political competition of larger scale. In this situation, the entitlement of the *moja boswa* to an extra share of the residue of his father's estate may have limited material value in itself, but the status that this token symbolizes is highly prized. Indeed, it could involve control over such resources as land allocation, dispute-settlement agencies, and public communication at a higher politicoadministrative level. Competition, then, may proceed on the basis of who should be *moja boswa*—i.e., in terms of heritable property rights—but its object is not restricted to this question.

Now this consideration in turn reintroduces the problem of marriage and *its* relation to property distribution and interhouse linkages. Thus far, in discussing devolution, we have held constant the negotiability of conjugal bonds. In general terms, however, the ambiguities surrounding the definition of unions do not greatly affect the division of estates. When a union endures for more than a year or two and produces children, the man will usually begin to allocate his assets along the lines described above—unless, of course, he specifically intends to repudiate the bond. The fact that marriage is seen as the outcome of a relationship over time is clearly consonant with the processual nature of devolution arrangements. It is only when a crisis arises that the process is aborted. In the case of divorce, the question posed by premature dissolution is easily resolved: the woman receives a property award and has no further interest in the estate, while her children, whose house persists, continue progressively to be given their shares. If separation occurs, or the union is dissolved after being defined as a casual relationship, the man may try to recover some of the assets that have already been divided, often by claiming that they had never been formally allocated. In fact, individual strategies vary in this respect; some, especially the wealthy, may not be anxious to precipitate a public dispute and may simply leave matters as they stand. The fact that such ad hoc arrangements may be made means that the devolution process does not, of itself, reduce the potential manipulability of marriage. Conversely, however, the ambiguity associated with the definition of marriage may be invoked during the later phases of the devolution cycle, particularly in the context of interhouse conflict; for when such conflict involves rivalry over rank, the status of conjugal relations may be called into question. In the polygamous past, the relative position of cowives was readily open to redefinition, since the rules governing it were, de facto, anything but unequivocal (see Comaroff and Roberts 1977b). With the spread of serial monogamy, though, the norms regulating the rank of houses have become simplified; chronological order of marriage is now held to dictate it entirely. Hence, the only way in which junior sons can assert their seniority is by arguing that their father's earlier union or unions were casual ones. This is not to say that every junior house engages in such efforts; nonetheless, the jural nature of Tswana marriage does admit the potentiality, and this may be exploited when property and status become the object of interhouse political competition.

The Management of Property Interests and Relations

In describing property devolution among the Tswana, we focused initially on formal arrangements, stressing their processual and distributive nature, their relationship to the ascription of status, and their implications for structural continuity. The isolation of the three fields of tension in turn served to demonstrate that these arrangements are not necessarily expected to preclude conflict. On the contrary, property-centered rivalries within the primary kinship universe are a ubiquitous feature of community life, a fact reflected in the frequency with which they develop into open disputes. In the legal context, however, such cases are not uniform in either modes of argument or the delivery of judgments. In some instances both the suits and the chiefly decisions are addressed specifically to the distribution of material rights; in others, this aspect is relegated to the realm of the circumstantial, while the wider issue of the designation and content of relationships appears to assume centrality (see chap. 4). In the latter situation, the litigation is carried on in the idiom of property rights, but its essence patently lies elsewhere.

The source of this variability in modes of argument and judgment has already been anticipated. As we have pointed out, rivalries between close kin may be confined to the determinacies of access to heritable wealth or be generalized to the negotiation of rank and status. In other words, they may concern conflict over either property *interests* or the management of property *relations*. This distinction may be obvious, but it is also crucial. Not only does it underlie the logic of the dispute-settlement process; it also comprehends the material basis of much of the politics of everyday interaction between kinsmen. In order to elaborate on this, however, it is necessary first to devote further consideration to indigenous theory associated with the property dimension of kinship.

It seems clear, especially from the actions of litigants and dispute-settlement agencies, that the connection between property relations and the designation of kinship bonds is viewed as both indexical and dialectical (see pp. 175 ff.). The apparent circularity suggested by such a view has to be understood in light of the fact that Tswana theory is reducible neither to vulgar materialism nor to simplistic jural determinism. The indigenous theory is exemplified by the relationship between filiation and devolution. The recognition of a father-son tie prescribes the mutual involvement of two men in the progressive transmission of movable assets from one generation to the next, with all the reciprocal obligations that this connotes. Conversely, a devolutionary transfer, the

moment it is agreed to have been made, defines that particular relationship as a father-son tie. Thus, whatever the biological link between these men, the setting-aside of, say,
tshwaiso beasts affirms its designation in paternal-filial terms,
and, unless it is later disputed, this designation will continue
to describe the bond. As a corollary of this, the absence of
such transfers may express an attempt to repudiate filiation,[23]
again notwithstanding physical paternity. There are occasional exceptions, of course. However, once an individual
acknowledges a youth as his child, and as long as he continues
to do so, he is committed to the corresponding property
relations. This means that a father who wishes to sever contact with a son to whom he has already allocated assets has
these alternatives: he may try to recover the assets, or he will
seek to transmit his *total* inheritance to this son in advance of
the normal progress of the devolutionary cycle. As case 3
indicates, the latter act represents the unequivocal termination of the tie.

The accepted designation of a kinship bond, in summary,
entails a commitment to a specific property relationship and
vice versa; the two are perceived as reciprocal, as transformations of each other.[24] This is clearly consistent with the
sociocultural constitution of the kinship universe as it is outlined in chapter 2. When parties to a relationship apply a
particular label to the tie between them, as we have explained, this label is taken to signal their acceptance of the
reciprocal obligations and expectations associated with that
tie. The very fact of *agreed* labeling implies either that the
appropriate normative content is manifest—and that those
involved intend that their relationship should have this
content—or that it will become manifest in the foreseeable
future. The converse, of course, is also true: where two men
behave, by mutual consent, in the fashion expected of, say, a
mother's brother and his sister's son, the bond will, a fortiori,
be designated by the relevant vernacular term. At the same
time, however, the classification of social ties is not always
the subject of such consensus; the case histories underline
this problem, and we shall shortly return to it once again.

In a society in which the structural exigencies of the marriage system generate a universe of multiple ties with contradictory normative corollaries—insupportable, as this is, in

the behavioral context—it is not surprising that the definition (and, equally, the revision and redefinition) of particular social relations is perceived indigenously to be the object of transaction and that the management of such relations involves their meaningful construal as an *intrinsic* feature of interaction. All of this in turn throws light on the contrast between indigenous Tswana theory about these matters and the analytical perspectives of the jural approach. At least in its cruder forms, the latter implies that the ascriptive definition of a bond—whether derived from biology or its social analogue—determines its content *in advance* of interaction. Among the Tswana, what we commonly refer to as the jural (ascriptive) dimension of a relationship represents the translation, at a given point in time, of its manifest substance into culturally inscribed and normatively encoded labels. It is in this sense, then, that relational form and content are dialectically connected; given the (structurally predicated) tendency of the Tswana to negotiate and redefine relations, it could hardly be otherwise.

On the basis of these summary remarks, we may now return to the distinction between disputes over specific material interests and those that concern property relations at large. The first occur within the context of mutually accepted role relationships, in particular where a perceived disjunction develops between the (agreed) definition of a bond and its normatively legitimized material content; here, as we noted above, the nature of the bond itself is not called into question by any of the litigants. In terms of the taxonomy elaborated in chapter 4, such cases are of type 2; that is, disagreement is expressly restricted to the subject of rights in a designated value. Thus, in the course of the devolutionary process, tensions frequently emerge over the control of assets without the parties disputing that, for example, they are half-siblings and hence are all the legitimate offspring of a particular man, or that a given son among them is the *moja boswa* and is thereby entitled to an extra share of the unallocated balance of the estate. As cases 17, 19, 21, and 23 demonstrate, hostilities may break out over the timing of transfers, the exact size of individual shares, or, more often, allegations of mismanagement and misappropriation; but conflict in these circumstances is always limited to the protection of personal and/or house interests,[25] and its resolution tends to be treated in a matter-of-fact fashion by the dispute-settlement agencies. As the model in chapter 4 would suggest, the determinacy of the issues at hand means that the normative and procedural bases of the dispute process are comparatively unambiguous and straightforward.

The same model also indicates, however, that suits involving property *relations* are rather more complex; these usually fall at the polarity of the most generalized form of conflict (type 4; see pp. 116 ff., above), for here it is the nature of the relationship itself—its definition, substance, and, perhaps, its implications for rank and seniority—that is the ultimate object of contest. An example is again provided by the question of paternity. A youth may complain that his genitor is denying him his heritable rights only to hear the older man rejoin that they are not related as father and son. This denial may be rationalized in one of three ways: by the claim that the youth has so violated the relationship as to abrogate any further rights flowing from it (see case 3); by the assertion that the union between the youth's parents was a casual one; or by the contention, more rare now than in the past, that he was the offspring of a leviratic arrangement and hence is the (jural) child of another man. A similar example is afforded by case 24, except that here it was the children raised together in a domestic unit who contested the definition of relationships and statuses within it and, therefore, their respective property rights in the estate.

CASE 24:   MOSU'S CATTLE AND SEGOLO'S STATUS[26]

Mosu's first wife bore him a daughter, Matshabi, but no sons. Later he entered a union with another woman, from the Transvaal, who already had a child, Segolo, by another man. Segolo came with his mother when she settled with Mosu, who then treated him as a son. Thus, he earmarked some beasts for Segolo under the *tshwaiso* arrangement, even though there appears to have been no *dilo tsa patlo* or *bogadi* transferred in respect of the mother. When the older man died, the unallocated balance of his estate was divided by Matshabi's son, Mpho. None of these beasts was given to Segolo, although he was allowed to take away those that he had obtained by way of *tshwaiso* and cattle that had been allocated to the house of his mother. Segolo then came to the chief to complain about this.

In the *kgotla* hearing he began by asserting: "I am Matshabi's brother, the son of Mosu." He went on to present witnesses to the fact that he had received *tshwaiso* allocations but no *boswa* from Mosu's estate. Matshabi answered this by asserting that Segolo was not one of Mosu's children and, by definition, not her brother. In judgment, the chief stated that, since Segolo had been brought with his mother into the domestic group and had clearly been recognized by Mosu, he was one of the latter's children and should therefore receive *boswa*. Ten beasts were set aside for him.

Segolo thus sought a property order reflecting his claim to be Mosu's son and Matshabi's half-brother, a suit that she opposed by repudiating their bond and his legitimate membership in her father's descent grouping. By implication, the equivocalities surrounding the question of affiliation were invoked to justify both arguments. Matshabi, of course, had no control over the earlier transfers (the *tshwaiso* and house cattle) by means of which Mosu had in fact sealed his acceptance of Segolo as his child. In making his decision, the chief upheld precisely this: because Mosu had so clearly signified his acceptance of a father-son bond (which Segolo's behavior had done nothing to disconfirm), the complainant should continue to enjoy the rights emanating from it. Matshabi's attempts to revise the status of the relevant relationships and to win the appropriate property order failed as a consequence.

If we draw together our descriptions of the marriage and devolution processes, it becomes clear that the ambiguities associated with conjugal status and the affiliation of children are closely linked to the negotiation of property relations. Indeed, these ambiguities afford many possibilities for their management. Take the case where a woman bears a child, and two beasts are subsequently transferred from members of the genitor's descent group to the senior agnates of the mother. These may be construed as *bogadi,* signifying an affirmation of the creation of a marriage; they may be held to constitute *marebana,* representing compensation for the woman's pregnancy; they may also be presented to her agnates to affiliate the child to the man's descent group without affirming any further relationship to the woman. Further still, the transaction may imply that the woman and her child have remained members of her agnatic unit and that the beasts should thus be subject to the control of its members. Yet again, cattle may pass in a fiduciary capacity, as when they are cared for under some emergency by a dutiful "mother's brother"; if this individual happens also to be a close agnate, material rights and social relations may become even more confused and open to exploitation. Case 25 illustrates some of these complexities with particular clarity.

In disputes of this type, then, property rights may constitute only one of the elements of the contested relationship—although this one element may, of course, provide the primary motivation for the suit in the first place. During the legal process, moreover, it often assumes a metonymic value in the context of debates of more general scope. Thus, where litigants and/or agencies wish to affirm, discontinue, or redefine a disputed bond, they will seek (or make) property orders that reflect their different constructions of its content. The courts, for their part, are often faced with the problem of adjudicating between such rival constructions. Again, while they may make independent decisions and impose their own definitions, their judgments tend to flow largely from the attribution of fault, since this is held to be an index of the relative veracity of claims.

The final case included in this context serves to exemplify and synthesize many of the analytical themes with which we have been concerned in this and the previous chapters. Not only does it illuminate the nature of property relations and the status of social ties; it also raises questions of greater generality concerning constraints on social management.

CASE 25:   MODISE AND LESOKA[27]

Kubukwena, an immigrant from the nearby Kwena chiefdom, asked Rapolo (a member of the Phuting *kgotla*) for his daughter, Polena, as a fourth wife (see diagram). It seems that this request was granted, because, sometime before 1920, Polena went to live in a homestead prepared by Kubukwena; but no *bogadi* was presented. Polena bore two daughters, Phana and Mabure. Phana never married, but she gave birth to a son, Mojamorago, and two daughters, Sepo and Kerekeng. Mabure did marry, after both Kubukwena and Rapolo were dead. *Bogadi* cattle were presented for her, but these were claimed by Lesoka, the son of Polena's younger unmarried sister. Lesoka also took four beasts, which were paid as compensa-

MODISE VS. LESOKA: DRAMATIS PERSONAE

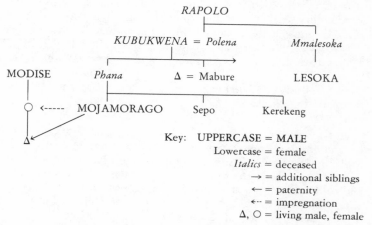

Key: UPPERCASE = MALE
Lowercase = female
Italics = deceased
→ = additional siblings
← = paternity
←·· = impregnation
Δ, O = living male, female

tion when Sepo was later made pregnant by a man named Teko, the son of Sefako Pilane. Lesoka justified this action on the grounds that Kubukwena had failed to present *bogadi* for Polena, and his claims were not resisted at the time by surviving male descendants of Kubukwena.

Some years after these events, when Mojamorago was a young man, he made one of Modise's daughters pregnant. When this pregnancy was noticed, and the girl named Mojamorago as being responsible, Modise visited Lesoka to inform him of what had happened. Before the birth, Lesoka returned this visit and told Modise that Mojamorago accepted responsibility and would enter a union with the girl. Modise put up no objection to this proposal. Later, when the baby was born, Modise reported the birth to Lesoka. Some months later, seeing that Mojamorago showed no sign of settling down with the girl, Modise again visited Lesoka and demanded instead the four head of cattle payable as compensation for pregnancy of an unmarried woman. But Lesoka repeated his promise that Mojamorago would marry. Still no union was established. Modise made further informal requests to Lesoka for the payment of compensation, but without success. Eventually, Lesoka told Modise that, because Mojamorago was a member of Kubukwena's agnatic grouping, Kubukwena's sons should pay for the pregnancy. Modise then approached members of this group, but they too refused to take responsibility for the pregnancy.

Having failed to settle his claim through these informal approaches, Modise then took his complaint to Sekapa Mariri, headman of the Phuting *kgotla,* to which Lesoka belonged. Sekapa also tried informally to persuade Lesoka to pay the compensation demands, but his efforts were unsuccessful. Lesoka again denied responsibility, on the ground that Mojamorago was a member of Kubukwena's descent group. He also said that, because of this, the dispute was not one that could be properly handled formally by his own ward *kgotla.* Accordingly, Sekapa reported the matter to the chief.

The following speeches were recorded when the dispute was heard by the chief:

MODISE: I am suing Lesoka for seduction. Lesoka's child impregnated my daughter. She had a child by him. After my daughter told me that Lesoka's son had impregnated her, I went to Lesoka and told him about the pregnancy. After the baby was born, I went and told Lesoka that the baby had been born.

Lesoka came to me before the birth of the child and told me that he had asked his son about the matter. He said his son admitted paternity, and Lesoka told me that his son intended to marry my daughter. I told him that, if his son intended to marry my daughter, then I had no objection. I waited for a very long time, but there was no sign of preparations being made for marriage. Eventually, I decided that it was wise for me to ask Lesoka to pay damages for seduction if the son no longer wished to marry my daughter. I repeatedly went to Lesoka's place to ask him to pay the damages, but each demand was met with a promise to marry. The promise to marry was never fulfilled.

For a very long time I tried to persuade Lesoka to pay me, but he failed. Eventually I was forced to hand the matter to his headman, Sekapa, so that he could deal with it. When the matter was supposed to be heard by the headman, the headman told me that Lesoka had said that he did not want the matter to be heard in Phuting *kgotla* nor indeed in the Mabodisa *kgotla.* Rather, he wanted the matter to be decided by the chief's *kgotla.*

Lesoka now repudiates liability for damages for seduction. He says the child is Kubukwena's and therefore that it is only fair that Kubukwena should pay. The matter was reported to Kubukwena's children, that is to say, Rasekhurutshe, Shadi, Samotho, and Rasekei. They refused to pay as well, on the ground that the illegitimate child was not their responsibility.

When I realized that Lesoka was reluctant to pay and also unwilling to pay, I resolved to bring the matter to the chief's *kgotla.*

SEKAPA MARIRI (headman, Phuting *kgotla*): Modise reported the matter to me. He told me that Lesoka was refusing to pay damages for seduction. I talked to Lesoka, trying to persuade him to pay damages to Modise. He told me that the boy who impregnated Modise's daughter was not his son but Kubukwena's son. Lesoka told me that his case was such that it could not properly be handled by the Phuting *kgotla* or the Mabodisa. Only the chief's *kgotla* could manage it.

JOHANAH MOREMI (daughter of Kubukwena by his first wife): The boy who impregnated Modise's daughter is Lesoka's son and not Kubukwena's son [i.e., descendant]. The reason I say that is because I took part in arranging the marriage of Mabure, Kubukwena's daughter. *Bogadi* was paid for her. Lesoka took the *bogadi* cattle paid for Mabure. Lesoka argued that Kubukwena had not been formally married to his aunt [i.e., Polena, his mother's sister]. After that incident Lesoka went to my father's enclosure and took cattle belonging to Mojamorago [that is to say, the boy who impregnated Modise's daughter]. He took those cattle without consulting anybody. Lesoka also took the cattle paid for the seduction of Mojamorago's sister. He took them from Sefako Pilane. Mojamorago is Lesoka's son on the following grounds: Lesoka took the cattle paid for Mojamorago's aunt as *bogadi*. When Mabure got married, he took Mojamorago's cattle. He [also] got seduction damages from Sefako. They were damages for the seduction of Mojamorago's sister. Lesoka took all the cattle mentioned above in his capacity as father. Now he is faced with a responsibility that he has to shoulder in the same capacity as father, and he wants to avoid it.

SAMOTHO MOLWANE (daughter of Kubukwena by his second wife): Mojamorago is my younger sister's son. Her name is Phana. After Mojamorago impregnated Modise's daughter, Lesoka was informed of the matter. He was made aware that Mojamorago had impregnated Modise's daughter, but Lesoka did not tell anybody.

Lesoka took the cattle paid for the *bogadi* of Mabure, who is Mojamorago's mother's sister. Lesoka also took the cattle for the seduction of the other sister of Mojamorago's from Sefako. All the time Lesoka treated Mojamorago as his son, but, now that Mojamorago is in trouble, he [Lesoka] no longer wants to continue as a father. Lesoka should pay Modise the damages on behalf of Mojamorago because all the cattle are with him.

RASEKHURUTSHE LESEJANE (an agnate of Kubukwena): I can testify that Mojamorago's cattle are with Lesoka. Even the cattle paid for Mabure's *bogadi* are with Lesoka. Mabure is Mojamorago's mother's sister. Further, Lesoka took the cattle for the seduction of Mojamorago's younger sister from Sefako. Lesoka should be held responsible for what Mojamorago has done because he has always acted as the latter's father, because he is keeping Mojamorago's cattle. Lesoka was not supposed to take Mojamorago's cattle.

LESOKA: Modise came to me and told me that Mojamorago had impregnated his daughter. I asked the boy, and he admitted responsibility. I then told Modise that Mojamorago had admitted responsibility and that he had indicated that he wanted to marry the girl.

I am quite aware that Modise wants me to pay damages on behalf of Mojamorago, and I refuse to be held liable on behalf of Mojamorago. In 1963, Mojamorago's mother, that is to say Phana, came to me in the company of Modise. Modise then told us that Mojamorago had impregnated his daughter. I received his complaint and promised to ask the boy in question [Mojamorago]. After Mojamorago came, I told him that Modise had lodged a complaint to the effect that he had impregnated Modise's daughter. Mojamorago replied that Modise's complaint was true, and he explained that he intended to marry the girl. I relayed this story to Mojamorago's mother, and she pointed out that Mojamorago had already told her the same story.

Some time later, Modise came to me and demanded that I should pay seduction damages on behalf of Mojamorago. I refused to pay damages on behalf of Mojamorago because he is not my son. He was not even to be my charge. I had to pay seduction damages for him. Mojamorago is my aunt's son (that is, my mother's sister's son).

After Mojamorago impregnated Modise's daughter, I did not tell any of Kubukwena's children, that is, Johanah and Samotho. It was only Phana who knew about it.

It is true that I took the *bogadi* cattle paid for Mabure, and I also took Mojamorago's cattle, as well as cattle paid as seduction damages for the younger sister of Mojamorago.

I was given cattle paid for Mabure's *bogadi* by Phana so that I could look after them. Those cattle rightfully belong to Mojamorago. He should use them for paying seduction damages after consulting his MZ Mabure.

The cattle that were paid by Sefako as seduction damages for Mojamorago's younger sister are also in my possession. They are among my cattle, but I never told any of Kubukwena's children that I had received any seduction damages for Mojamorago's younger sister, called Sepo.

CHIEF (Linchwe Kgafela): Modise, I have listened carefully to the case between you and Lesoka, concerning seduction damages. Lesoka, you must admit that Modise came to you and told you that Mojamorago had impregnated his daughter. You do not deny his allegations. Above all, you promised Modise that Mojamorago would marry his daughter. You failed to fulfill your promise about marriage. You refused to meet the demand by Modise for the payment of seduction damages. You have made schemes by which you can disclaim liability on behalf of Mojamorago on the alleged ground that he is not your son. Clearly, the evidence that has been adduced from this *kgotla* is consistent with one fact, that Mojamorago is your son because you took the *bogadi* cattle paid for his sister. You also took the cattle paid for the seduction of his younger sister. This *kgotla* believes that Mojamorago is your charge and that you are therefore liable on his behalf.

Lesoka, this *kgotla* finds against you. You must pay Modise four head of cattle, since you have Mojamorago's cattle. You will also pay an extra beast for wasting Modise's daughter's time by promising marriage and then breaking your promise. She probably would have been offered marriage by somebody else had she not pinned her hopes on you. In all, you will have to pay five head of cattle. This *kgotla* orders that you should, by October 14, 1965, have paid the five head of cattle.

Several points emerge from case 25, and, in making them, we seek also to illustrate and summarize the discussion thus far. The dispute began with a straightforward and un-contested claim concerning a material interest: Modise's en-titlement to a compensatory *marebana* payment for the im-pregnation of his daughter, an entitlement he was prepared to waive if her former lover would agree to enter an enduring union. At first, Lesoka did not deny Modise's construction of the relevant events and relations. By the very fact that he agreed to discuss the matter in his role as Mojamorago's "father" (i.e., agnatic guardian) he tacitly acknowledged some responsibility for expediting Modise's claim, the veracity of which he never questioned. Clearly, at this stage he believed that the youth could be persuaded to settle down with the pregnant girl, thereby resolving the problem with no cost to anyone. Indeed, this would have had the added benefit to Lesoka of reasserting his "fatherhood" of Mojamorago and, by extension, his rights in the *bogadi* and *marebana* cattle he had earlier appropriated in an agnatic capacity. When it became obvious that this was not to be, and that he was about to be held personally liable for paying the fine arising out of the recalcitrant Mojamorago's actions, Lesoka responded by transforming the dispute into one over property relations.

Lesoka tried to effect this transformation by redefining the status of earlier unions in such a way as to repudiate his guardianship over Mojamorago and to deny the latter's membership in his agnatic segment. The precise forms this transformation took, as the transcript of the case demonstrates, varied over time to meet circumstantial contingencies. Long before the dispute first arose, he had been able to assert that, because no *bogadi* had been presented by Kubukwena for Polena, their children and remoter offspring belonged *not* to their genitor's descent grouping but to Polena's and, therefore, his own. This strategy had been profitable because it had enabled Lesoka to gain control over Mabure's bridewealth and the *marebana* paid for Sepo's pregnancy; this he had done, quite explicitly, in his role as the head of their agnatic segment. It was only much later, when he was confronted with the fact that Mojamorago was *also* his charge, that the cost of all this became apparent. Nevertheless, despite having consistently justified his construction of the relevant field of relations by insisting that Kubukwena and Polena had been involved merely in a casual union, Lesoka sought to revise this when confronted with Modise's demands. He now offered that they had in fact been validly married and that, consequently, Mojamorago was the agnatic descendant of Kubukwena and not his responsibility. (It follows also that Phana's union with his genitor had also not been a marriage, but this was never contested at any stage.) Of course, as we would by now expect, these manipulations all derived from the fact that the status of the union in question was inherently ambiguous and open to contrasting interpretations, each of which had very different implications for property relations.

It is significant that, at the outset, Modise appeared quite amenable to accepting this radically revised construction, for he immediately approached Kubukwena's agnates in an effort to exact compensation. It was only when this failed that he finally decided to sue Lesoka in terms of the latter's earlier admission of (agnatic) responsibility. But the sequence of Modise's actions indicates that he never simply dismissed the *possibility* of a revised version of the configuration of relations and statuses that informed the dispute. What perhaps persuaded him to make Lesoka the object of his complaint was the fact that Kubukwena's agnatic descendants reacted forcefully and in concert, while Lesoka appeared to enjoy markedly less support. In any event, by adopting this strategy, Modise placed a complex dispute, involving a ramifying set of property relations, before the ward court and then the chief.

A related point should also be noted here, since it again refers back to our earlier remarks. When he came before the settlement agencies, Lesoka was largely unsupported by his own agnates. For structural reasons that have already been spelled out, enduring segmentary divisions do not necessarily, or even usually, form the basis of factional alignments in such processes. Thus, in this dispute, the initiative remained firmly and exclusively with Lesoka, who sought to configure (and later transform) a wide set of linkages surrounding himself entirely on his own account and without reference to his other close kin—and this in spite of the fact that his control over Mabure's *bogadi* and Sepo's *marebana* might have been expected to benefit his agnatic segment, albeit indirectly. However, this shared interest was not sufficient to elicit their solidarity in supporting the defendant. Kubukwena's agnatic descendants did, by contrast, display conspicuous unity. This was predicated on their perception that they had a substantial common cause in opposing Lesoka, in repudiating his claim, and hence in supporting Modise. It is significant, then, that the backing enjoyed by the complainant came more from this source than from his own close kin. But the transiency of their coincident interest, and of its expression in collective action, is underlined by the fact that this agnatic segment does not seem to have had a history of common enterprise; they had certainly not combined to fight Lesoka, as they well might have, when he first appropriated the *bogadi* and *marebana* cattle. In short, structurally defined alliances and oppositions do not generate an enduring pattern of support or collective activity, nor do they prevent an individual from constructing a meaningful set of relations around himself.

Quite the reverse: their absence reinforces the individuation of the social field and places the onus squarely upon actors to contrive that field on their own behalf.

The absence of structurally defined alliances and the concomitant onus placed on the individual to construct a field of relations for himself is, in turn, reflected in the readiness with which Tswana themselves accept the notion that the definition of social linkages may be reconstrued and transformed. As we have already noted, a good example is provided by Modise's response to Lesoka's various assertions about the nature of his relationship with Mojamorago. It is widely assumed, moreover, that such efforts to contrive a social field will usually be strategically motivated—an assumption that is sometimes made explicit. Thus, as Johanah Moremi's statement shows, none of the participants in the case entertained any doubt about the intentions lying behind the defendant's characterization of events and relationships. In his final speech the chief summed it all up by telling Lesoka: "You have made schemes by which you disclaim liability."

Let us return briefly to these "schemes." During the latter part of the hearing in the chief's *kgotla,* when he realized the strength of his opposition and that his suit was about to be rejected, Lesoka revised his argument. He reasserted that Kubukwena and Polena had been properly married, but he offered a different interpretation of the events surrounding the crucial *bogadi* transfer in respect of Mabure. These cattle, he stated, had actually been presented to Phana. She accepted them as the senior child of Kubukwena, who had no sons. She then handed them on to Lesoka, as her (classificatory) mother's brother, to look after in a fiduciary capacity; indeed, this was favor that a good mother's brother might be expected to do for his sister's child.

The precise motivation behind this amended version of the facts is not entirely clear, but it did place Lesoka's behavior toward Phana and her children (Mojamorago among them) in a more favorable light, and it legitimized his original acquisition of the *bogadi* cattle, which he had taken "so that [he] could look after them." Perhaps he still felt that, by claiming to be a mother's brother—a privileged bond, after all—he retained a residual chance of escaping liability and thus being able to keep the animals for the foreseeable future, albeit only in a fiduciary capacity. If nothing else, this version added another dimension, and greater credibility, to his denial—in spite of the fact that he was holding the incriminating beasts —that he was Mojamorago's senior agnate. His possession of the cattle had been mercilessly exploited by rival witnesses in repudiating his defense; the amended argument at least offered some explanation for, and counter to, such circumstantial evidence.

Lesoka's claim to be Phana's maternal kinsman had already been implicit in his earlier assertion that Mojamorago was the agnatic descendant of Kubukwena, but, in the course of justifying his holding of Mabure's bridewealth, he now made it explicit. This interpretation of course represented a radical shift from the one he had stressed before the dispute occurred, according to which Phana and her children were members of his agnatic segment. These various claims, and their revision over time, illustrate yet again our earlier statements concerning the ex post facto labeling of matrilateral and agnatic bonds, their mutability for purposes of the management of careers in everyday life, and the dialectical relationship between the definition of such bonds and their imputed substance.

Finally, just as his case illuminates the close connection between the management of property relations and the construal of conjugal status, Lesoka's predicament demonstrates also that individuals do not engage in such activities as totally unconstrained actors. While it is true that the social universe of the Tswana is perceived to be highly negotiable, its members find, at the beginning of their adult lives, that they are located in a field of relations that imply normatively defined expectations—a field partly constituted by the actions of their predecessors. Now, every attempt to manipulate this set of social linkages also *creates* new constraints, whatever its effects may be in freeing the actor from existing ones. These constraints are not merely a function of the pragmatic fact that managerial activities may be opposed by others who perceive them as threatening their own interests, although such limitations do constantly make themselves felt. Rather, they represent the *intrinsic* corollaries of career management over time. Thus Lesoka's appropriation of his mother's sister's daughter's bridewealth, which afforded him access to a substantial resource, had to be justified by a particular definition of all the relationships and statuses that were relevant to that exchange. Lesoka did not have just one alternative in this, however. He could, for example, have asserted fiduciary control as a mother's brother from the very start. But his potentially more profitable construction, which he did not immediately eschew when challenged with Moja-morago's guilt, ultimately caused him to face the conse-quences of his earlier actions. Had he not claimed at the earlier time to be the recipient of Mabure's *bogadi* as her senior agnate, the outcome might have been considerably dif-ferent. The reaction of Kubukwena's descendants could not have taken the form it did, for their opposition was a direct response to the implications of Lesoka's own previous stra-tegic choices. On the other hand, had he placed himself in the role of mother's brother earlier on, other constraints would have flowed from that strategy.

The general principle is clear. From an individual stand-point, constraints and liabilities are the *cumulative* manifest consequence of social management itself. Every action and decision in this respect, whether undertaken by intent or default, structures a person's social field by generating con-tingent expectations and obligations. Hence, the negotiation of that field becomes more difficult—or, possibly, more expensive—as life takes its course. Indeed, with the passage of time, individuals tend progressively to be "locked" into or-dered sets of role relationships, partly of their own con-trivance, as alliances and oppositions are defined with ever greater clarity and they are left with less and less room in which to maneuver; in the process, of course, the network of social ties surrounding them gradually loses its ambiguity. This pattern, according to which constraint slowly increases and ambiguity is correspondingly reduced, is related to the processual character of both conjugality and devolution. Marriage, as we have noted, is the outcome of a relationship over time, just as devolution represents the progressive movement of control over property and position across gen-erations. Both are characterized by the individual's increasing loss of initiative in the negotiation of his social universe. In chapter 2 the systemic properties of this process were spelled out: the final phases of the marriage and devolutionary cycles, which may be closely articulated, represent the points at which the managerial enterprises of one generation reach their finality and are reckoned up, as social and political initiative is transmitted to the next. The transmission of *bogadi* and *boswa* are frequently the symbolic moments of this transmission; at least transiently, the endemic ambiguity of the manifest universe is removed and reduced to order.

In this chapter and the preceding one we have sought to elucidate the character of conjugal and property relations as they relate to processes of social management and dispute. We have suggested that the phenomenal nature of these relations and processes—and, moreover, the ideology and order of values in terms of which they are experienced by Tswana—are comprehensible only when they are referred to the logic of the sociocultural system at large. But there still remains the question we posed at the outset: What explains the dualism in the Tswana conception of their world, according to which social life is described as rule-governed yet highly negotiable, normatively regulated yet pragmatically individualistic? And how does this conception systematically configure the outcome of disputes? It is with these problems in mind that we begin our analytical synthesis.

7

Our insistence that the nature of the dispute process is fully comprehensible only when it is located within the *total* fabric of the sociocultural system is not novel. Indeed, this assumption has underpinned much of legal anthropology. However, the relationship between the dispute process and the system of which it is a part may be envisioned, in theoretical and methodological terms, in a number of fundamentally different ways. In our concluding chapter we shall contrast our own position in this regard with those of other approaches, but here we shall extend and integrate our analysis by seeking to account, first, for the form and content of Tswana dispute processes and, second, for the relationship between norm and outcome. In doing so, we shall consider further the apparent ideological paradox expressed in the indigenous view that everyday life—and the disputes that occur in its course—is at once rule-governed yet characterized by the individualistic pursuit of utility, for which purpose rules may be deployed as resources. It is in this dualism, we argue, that the meaningful construction of the Tswana dispute process is expressed.

The Logic of Dispute

Given their ideology of pragmatism and the conviction that the onus of career management falls on the individual, it is not surprising that Tswana display a proclivity for litigation and an abiding interest in it. In this context, the *kgotla* represents a public arena in which personal ambitions and competing efforts to contrive relations and rights can be expressed and legitimized. Moreover, the *tsheko* (case) is a moment in the flow of everyday life in which intersecting biographies are crystallized and acted out and the implicit subtleties of particular relationships are laid bare. In an endemically fluid universe, such moments are of critical importance to the participants, and to third parties they are a potentially valuable source of information. All this, however, raises two problems concerning the systemic nature of processes of conflict and confrontation. These problems may be put as questions of form and substance. First, who are likely to engage in such confrontations, and over what types of issues are they likely to do so? Second, what patterns the content of the disputes that arise in the day-to-day affairs of any community?

Schapera (1963a:168 f.) has offered the most detailed available data on the incidence of litigation involving different categories of kin and affines among the Tswana in general. Apart from cases of conflict between royals over succession and inheritance,[1] he considers 477 disputes, the distribution of which may be summarized as follows: 250 (52.4 percent) were between husbands and wives, most of them concerning the state of their relationship, its termination, or the rights and liabilities arising out of it; 80 (16.8 percent) involved affines; and 147 (30.8 percent) arrayed kinsmen against each other. In short, 69.2 percent arose from the establishment of unions and the relationships generated by them—a fact that would appear consistent with our characterization of the negotiability of conjugality and affinity (chap. 5). The 147 disputes between close kinsmen also reveal some salient patterns: 128 (85 percent) involved agnates, especially brothers and half-brothers (48 cases), fathers and sons (27), and father's brothers and brothers' sons (27); 17 were between mothers and sons, and only 2 were between mother's brothers and sisters' sons, both of which involved rather special circumstances.[2] Schapera goes on to mention (p. 169) that, among ordinary members of chiefdoms, the "vast majority" of cases between kin "were concerned mainly with inheritance or ownership of property, parental or quasi-parental rights and duties, and questions of personal status"; some of these also entailed access to formal offices in the administrative hierarchy. This distribution conforms broadly to our own data collected among the Tshidi and Kgatla, with one qualification: the linkages denoted in *any* such statistical data must be understood to refer to the definitions *recognized* between the parties at the time of litigation. Many, as we might expect, would in fact be multiple bonds, and it should not be inferred that the figures cited above, and confirmed by our own material, imply static or unchanging relationships; in fact, it is sometimes through litigation that their definition is transformed (see, e.g., cases 3 and 25).

While Schapera's figures must, then, be regarded with caution, they would appear to lend strong support to our assertion that the negotiation of property and marriage-type relations is the stuff of social management and of the contrivance of individual careers in community life. Indeed, in choosing to examine dispute processes with reference to these aspects of the lived-in universe, we have sought specifically to demonstrate the relationship between the construction of the sociocultural system and the quality of everyday interaction and confrontation. The demonstration may be taken a step further, however, for the statistical data cited above also illuminate in greater detail the logic underlying conflict between related persons. Inasmuch as the constitutive order generates the two primary and opposed domains and a residual class of remote kin and strangers, each corresponding to a set of basic social values, it shapes the manner in which cases between various categories of people tend (or tend not) to surface. Moreover, because it also establishes the social value of marriage and affinity as perceived by the Tswana, the same is true of the nature of actions between couples and affines as well. In order to amplify this, since it is already anticipated in the earlier chapters, we first examine disputes involving close kin and then those between affines and spouses.[3]

As we already know, relational labels *index* the substance of linkages with reference to normatively recognized expectations derived from the conception of the house and its sociocultural elaboration (see chap. 2). This fact, in turn, explains why, in the first place, very few cases arise within the matrilateral domain, between linked siblings,[4] or between men and those regarded as their maternal kin. If, on the one hand, litigation occurs between multiply linked parties, it is highly unlikely that they will be stressing the matrilateral component of the bond at the time, although it is possible, as we have pointed out, that the dispute itself will mark a change in the designation of a relationship whose content has been in the process of renegotiation. Where, on the other hand, only a single-stranded (matrilateral) link exists, there is little in its *intrinsic* nature that may give rise to conflict (cf. Schapera 1963a:171). Quite to the contrary, this domain is prescriptively associated with moral solidarity and social complementarity; as Tswana see matters, it represents an individual's primary source of support, so that he would be foolhardy to jeopardize or abuse it by precipitating hostilities. (Significantly, in the very few instances of such "abuse" that informants could recount, the actions of the perpetrator were usually described as being symptomatic of mental disturbance.) Nevertheless, there are rare occasions, generally attributed by Tswana to personal eccentricity or irrational intransigence, on which such cases arise. They are viewed as anomalous and particularly unfortunate; patently, they transgress the boundaries of the domains and introduce confusion into the value order by challenging the moral unity of the matrilateral universe. What is more, they generally evoke homilies to this effect from the settlement agencies. A statement made by the late Tshidi chief Kebalepile, in a case involving a young man and his MB, illustrates this:

> Rre-L, I say to you it is unnatural for a man to bring his *malome* [MB] to the *kgotla* with a complaint. This case should not come before me. Cases like this must not happen. Men live peacefully with their mother's people [*ba ga etsho mogolo*] or we ask where they come from. How can a man fight with his *malome?* We Barolong do not know such things.

It is beyond coincidence that, on the very few occasions when we have observed such cases, they have invariably taken one of two forms: (1) one or both of the parties assert that the behavior that led to the suit represented a temporary aberration and that the intention behind their bringing it is to restore the appropriate relationship; or (2) they seek to repudiate and sever the existing bond entirely. It also follows that, in situations of the first kind, the hearing will focus on a specific event, such as the violation of a piece of property; in the second, it will be addressed to the general character and history of the bond, with particular actions being adduced as symptoms of hostility rather than its primary cause. In short, the relationship should be made to conform to its normative definition or be redefined or terminated. That this is so, of course, is a corollary of the indexical nature of the labeling of kinship linkages.

One fact, however, remains unexplained. Why it is that disputes sometimes take place between mothers and sons? It is clear that such disputes arise relatively infrequently; in Schapera's sample of cases between kin and affines, they represent only 3.5 percent of the total, an average of two suits in five years in each of the large chiefdoms. Nonetheless, they do occur. Unfortunately, Schapera does not detail the circumstances surrounding them, but our own data suggest that, except where a widow claims to have been neglected by her son (case 22), such cases typically surface under one of two conditions: (1) where children claim that a widowed mother is meddling in their property interests (in two such instances, significantly, it was alleged that she had behaved "like an interfering *father*"); and (2) where a mother displays material favoritism toward one child, thereby souring relations with the others. In both situations, conflict is ostensibly caused when the maternal bond is infused with a particular kind of property relation, most often when the mother is placed, or places herself, in a quasi-paternal role with respect to her children's affairs. This tends to happen especially when households are headed by widows or other females, a pattern becoming more common in recent years (Comaroff and Roberts 1977b). Like the other suits involving linkages in the matrilateral domain, these are regarded as unfortunate anomalies and are generally explained by invoking social change and the fact that women are sometimes compelled to act for and like men by force of modern circumstance. This rationalization reflects the cultural basis of indigenous attempts to account for transformations—brought about primarily by the exigencies of proletarianization within the southern African political economy—that have increasingly been impinging on Tswana life. In terms of established categories, the intergenerational transmission of heritable wealth and the management of property relations are largely a male preserve; they belong securely in the agnatic domain.

Mothers are envisaged as being involved in this process essentially as the partisans of the houses they produce. When this gender opposition is transgressed, particular women are thus seen as having to assume *male* roles; in this way, sex and gender are differentiated in order to sustain existing normative expectations. This explanation, however, is becoming more difficult for Tswana to sustain, and there are indications that the sociocultural construction of the division of labor is undergoing reevaluation in some chiefdoms.

In stark contrast to matrilaterality, agnation is expected, in the normal course of things, to be fraught with antagonism; few Tswana would express surprise at Schapera's finding (1963a) that 85 percent of cases between kin involved parties who designated their relationship primarily in agnatic terms.[5] Both this statistical incidence and, more generally, the taken-for-granted association of agnation with enmity and rivalry are clearly sited in the logic of a system that ranks the agnatic domain in structural opposition to its matrilateral counterpart, and locates status and property relations within it (chap. 2). It is in this sense that the Tswana display what is often referred to as a "patrilineal bias," despite the absence of large-scale corporations or segmentary lineages as these are typically defined (see Fortes 1953). Any activity that involves access to, or control over, human or material resources, position, or wealth *necessitates* the negotiation of agnatic linkages. This, after all, is the politicosocial corollary of the ideology of ascription and of its deployment in the distribution of rank and authority at *all* levels within the administrative hierarchy. As we have seen, moreover, the nature of the Tswana world ensures that persons are inexorably drawn into such managerial processes, whether or not they enter them by their own volition.

However, disputes between agnates are not all of a kind. In chapter 6 we described the three fields of tension that manifest themselves in the context of everyday life. The fact that there are three such fields flows from the way the house reproduces itself and is integrated into the social order; so, too, does the form and substance of the disputes that arise in each of these fields.

The first field of tension, situated in intrahouse relations, is the predictable product of the developmental cycle of the unit. As we have already noted, disputes within it rarely, if ever, involve linked siblings or brothers and their unlinked sisters (see n. 4). Once more, the prescriptive complementarity of the B/Z bond places it above negotiation and dispute. In fact, in our own experience, linked siblings who do not enjoy amicable relations will seldom admit it. If anything, they tend to avoid each other, rationalizing this behavior by referring to unfortunate and temporary circumstantial factors. On the other hand, open conflict between brothers does occur, but it is generally confined to that point in the cycle when the house fragments and one or more of the sons set up new households. It will be recalled that the divergence between brothers' interests is a necessary condition of social reproduction and elaboration and is intimately connected to the symbolic and material dimensions of devolutionary arrangements. These arrangements foreshadow the division of the house by allocating property to each of its members while they are still children, ideally leaving only a small undistributed balance to be transferred at the death of the father. *Within* the unit, of course, the right to the largest share of *boswa* is not subject to argument, since it always passes to the eldest as a token of the transmission of status. The fact that disputes between full brothers do not involve property relations per se is entailed in the structural constitution of the house and encoded in the rules of rank, which make this unit coalesce in opposition to other groupings for a number of political and economic purposes. Nonetheless, while a set of full brothers may not be able to contest their standing in relation to one another, conflict over their material interests is especially likely to occur if the division of an estate remains incomplete when their father dies or if one of them assumes guardianship over the property of his younger siblings.

It should be stressed, further, that property interests and relations symbolize the major complementarities and oppositions both within the house and beyond its boundaries. For example, the unity of linked B/Z pairs is marked by the fusion of their material interests, a fusion metonymically expressed in the purely notional use of a sister's bridewealth for her brother's marriage. Similarly, while matrilateral bonds are associated with a series of nonnegotiable ritualized exchanges, the reckoning of agnatic rank is entailed in highly negotiable property relations. If we extend this observation to brotherly ties, and draw these various strands together, a pattern becomes clear.

During the early part of the developmental cycle, full siblings are located in a house whose interests are necessarily bound up together in opposition to the interests of their half-siblings. Before the unit fragments, the material equality of the children is expressed in the expectation that, the undistributed balance apart, they will receive roughly the same inheritance; this equality itself marks the fact that the houses that will be reproduced in the next generation will be like and opposed units within the social order. The fusion of interests will continue as these children mature, and the division of the estate, while set in motion by premortem allocations, is never fully complete until they are all adults. When they have all reached adulthood and have received their portions before the death of their father, the fragmentation of the house will probably proceed without dispute. (As we noted in chapter 6, disagreement over the equity of shares is infrequent.) Quite simply, each member will take his property at the appropriate moment and establish himself independently.

In contrast, when a father dies before all the sons of any unit are old enough to assume control over their own affairs, and especially if the division of his estate is still to be finalized, a contradiction arises in intrahouse relations; for under these conditions guardianship over the wealth of the younger children will have been vested in their older brother,[6] who has by then left the house and entered the competitive context of the agnatic domain. In order for these younger children to initiate their own careers, they must eventually obtain control over that wealth; it is the sine qua non of their independence. By the time they attempt to do so, however, the guardian of their property is no longer a party to the unity of interest that defined the natal grouping and so is no longer subject to the structural and material constraints it imposed. From his standpoint, his junior brothers are already the object of agnatic rivalry. From the systemic perspective, this pattern may be a function of the reproduction of houses and the cyclical divergence of material interests that marks the movement of the B/B bond into the political context of the agnatic domain; but in the pragmatic experience of those involved, it expresses itself as a direct opposition of interests: while younger siblings *must* appropriate their inheritance in order to obtain their independence, the oldest always finds it against his interest, and that of his offspring, to hand it over. It follows, too, that, if all the brothers are already adults when their father dies but the division of the estate is not complete, their interests will already have diverged by the time the remaining wealth is to be distributed. In such circumstances, disputes over allocations may be expected to occur with great frequency.

In fact, given the existing ideology of agnation, Tswana regard it as entirely predictable that men who have gained control over property, or have the opportunity to do so, should avoid relinquishing it until and unless it becomes absolutely necessary. Furthermore, because older brothers are often long established in their careers before they are confronted with such demands, they may well succeed both in expropriating some of the heritable stock meant for another and in delaying the final transmission of the remainder for a considerable time. The absence of a sharply defined age at which youths attain their majority—itself an implication of the processual devolutionary arrangements—provides the rhetorical terms used in justifying such actions and in counterargument against accusations of expropriating or withholding inheritances. Sometimes, of course, a guardian will be put under pressure to transmit the portions due to his siblings and may yield to it without open confrontation; as we pointed out in chapter 4, decisions to enter formal proceedings depend on a number of situational factors. In sum, the fact that intrahouse disputes take the form that they do follows from contradictions that manifest themselves when the social fragmentation of the unit occurs unevenly.[7] Just as the timing and scope of brotherly conflict are contained by a set of structural exigencies, so its substance derives ultimately from the sociocultural underpinnings of house formation and transformation.

The two other fields of tension may be understood by extending the same analytical perspective a step further. Interhouse tension, perhaps the most common locus of disputes,[8] derives from the entailed association of property relations and rank, which characterizes the constitution of the agnatic domain outside the house itself (see chaps. 2 and 6).

We have already examined interhouse relations so extensively that little more need be said about them here. To summarize briefly: since access to *all* resources and positions in the politicoadministrative hierarchy is predicated on the reckoning of agnatic standing, houses are inexorably arrayed against each other as soon as a member of one of them lays claim to a rank. Whether the objective is a segment elderhood, a headmanship, the chiefship, or merely the everyday assertion of seniority over others within a field of multiple linkages, the manipulation of agnatic relations and of the relative standing of houses is a corollary of most managerial enterprise. This manipulation, we emphasize, is not a matter of personal volition; it inheres in the logic of the rules and in the fluid character of the social field. Of course, not all agnatic rivalries end in public confrontation; individuals may transform their close kin into clients in such a way (i.e., "eating" them by creating indebtedness through a lengthy and often subtle series of transactions) that open dispute is not a viable recourse for the subordinated party or an attractive proposition for the superordinate one. Indeed, as in case 25, a man may successfully ensure that another is effectively *prevented* from utilizing the settlement agencies in the course of their rivalry. On the other hand, this is the field within which disputes are most often *provoked* in order to obtain recognition for a transformation of status relations (see chap. 4).

It is beyond the scope of this discussion to account for the range of conditions under which agnatic competition is likely to develop into cases that reach the *kgotla*. It is clear, however, that, when such disputes do occur, they are rarely restricted to property interests. Only when an older half-brother's guardianship of assets leads to allegations of malpractice—but when none of those involved seeks to renegotiate rank—will suits be restricted in this fashion. Much more commonly, it is the disputants' relationship itself, in both its social and material dimensions, that is called into question. Such confrontations may concern access to the position of *moja boswa* during the devolutionary cycle, or they may occur subsequently, when relations within the parental household (and sometimes beyond) are contrived in order to legitimize the appropriation of statuses within the hierarchy. Whatever the precise context in which dispute surfaces,

however, and despite the Tswana proclivity to interpret it
with reference to pragmatic individualism, the nature of
interhouse conflict is entailed in the construction of the agnatic domain. The frequency, form, and substance of such
conflict are founded on the prescriptive differentiation of this
domain and the manner in which it orders politicoadministrative arrangements among the Tswana. Furthermore, for reasons that will by now be obvious, interhouse
relations represent a paradigm for the politics of agnation at
large: any competition for influence or position among patrilateral kin is, in essence, a rivalry between houses produced
by a shared ancestor and reproduced across the generations,
and particular units, whether or not they take the initiative in
such processes, are ultimately drawn into their purview (see
chap. 2).

Within the third field of tension, intergenerational relations, the major loci of dispute—the F/S and FB/BS bonds
—combine the sociocultural elements that give form to the
intrahouse and interhouse fields. Tension between father
and son is expressed primarily in two modes of disagreement.
The first mode arises out of allegations that the parent is
favoring one house over another. It is closely associated with
rivalries over interests (and perhaps over rank as well) between sets of full siblings; indeed, as participants tend to view
these matters, such cases are often construed as manifestations of interhouse antagonism, the father typically being accused of yielding to pressures on behalf of the favored unit
and being "eaten," as a result, by its protagonists. There is
some justification for this view; since conflict of this kind
derives ultimately from the structured opposition of half-
brothers, it *is* in fact a transformation of interhouse dispute.
In contrast, the second mode of disagreement has its roots in
the deferral of the devolutionary process, an act that delays the
fragmentation of houses and prevents their members from
establishing independent careers. Under these conditions the
complaints against the father are similar to those made against
a guardian who withholds heritable property longer than his
charges believe to be justifiable. Such delays, as we noted
earlier, may also imply the threat that the father will enter
additional unions and so diminish the portions of his estate
that his offspring would hope to receive.

At the same time, Tswana hold that father-son disputes are lamentable and to be avoided. This follows from the fact that the developmental cycle of houses allows the senior generation to keep control over their affairs for the duration of their active lives and yet devolve property and the initiative for social management to their children at the precise moment the latter become mature enough to begin their own careers. This cyclical view has its constitutive basis in the logic of social reproduction; its normative expression in the established conception of the devolutionary process is described in chapter 6. When, however, the realization of this process is blocked—as, for example, when a father enjoys above-average longevity—a sufficient condition for dispute is generated; for the values subsumed in filial respect and dependency, on the one hand, and paternal responsibility, on the other, are brought into situational contradiction. What is more, since neither of these values has logical preeminence, such cases can never be resolved by the mechanical application of a particular norm. We shall later consider the principles underlying the outcome of confrontations of this kind. The point here is that the form of father-son dispute does not arise out of randomly antisocial behavior on the part of either of the parties, though it may be exacerbated by it; rather, it is the product of a discontinuity of values, inherent in the construction of the social process, that surfaces when practical contingency violates the "natural" order of things.

Conflict between paternal uncles and their brother's children, like interhouse confrontations, may be restricted to questions of property interest arising out of guardianship or may extend to argument over rank and relations. The latter typically occurs when a yFB contests the validity of the union (or unions) that produced his nephews in order to establish his own seniority and that of his children over them; conversely, a similar assertion may be made about the marriage (or marriages) of an oFB in order to subvert the standing of his children vis-à-vis their patrilateral cousins. In describing patterns of dispute, Tswana often characterize FB/BS cases as the quintessence of agnatic conflict; they appear to view confrontations over guardianship and those involving status as expressions of the same essential opposition of interests that impels these parties into antagonistic rivalry (even though

Schapera's data suggest that their incidence is no greater than that of F/S actions).[9] This perception derives, perhaps, from the fact that the FB/BS bond combines, within the context of a single relationship, the elements that shape *all three* fields of tension: as a guardian, the FB may perpetuate parental control over his brother's children after the death of their father, thereby deferring the fragmentation of their house; as their father's (full) sibling, moreover, his motives for doing this are located in the divergence of his interests from those of the father (and, by extension, the father's offspring), so that the usual conditions for brotherly expropriation may also be manifest in this bond; and, as the progenitor and protagonist of patrilaterally linked houses, which are necessarily opposed to the houses of his brother's children, his relations with the latter are typically sucked into the nexus of interhouse rivalries as well. As this implies, the FB/BS tie represents the sociocultural fusion of the three fields. That it is a frequent locus of dispute over both interests and relations is therefore entirely predictable; so, too, is the fact, that, in indigenous imagery, it represents the standardized embodiment of agnatic conflict. In this sense, it is the exact inversion of the MB/ZS bond.

In summary, then, the form and substance of disputes between close kin follow a series of predictable lines, notwithstanding their apparent diversity. The relative absence of matrilateral conflict, like the tendency of agnatic rivalries to occur within three ordered fields, is the corollary of a sociocultural system that brings persons of specifiable categories into endemically competitive relations over particular values and precludes or restricts the scope of confrontations between others. Moreover, as we demonstrated in chapter 5, the frequency and content of disputes arising out of conjugality and affinity are integral to this systemic pattern. Given Tswana marriage rules, many such cases involve agnates and, therefore, are frequently overlain by interhouse or intergenerational conflict; in fact, a disagreement over the status of a particular union may be symptomatic of, and provide the rhetorical focus for, more generalized antagonisms.[10] All this, however, simply underlines the fact that marriage—whether with kin or nonkin and whether one's own or those of persons over whom one exercises control—is both a medium and a context in which persons may strive to act upon a field of ambiguous and often hostile relations. From the actor's perspective, as we saw earlier, it affords the opportunity to transform rivalries into complementarities, to "eat" real or prospective opponents, to recruit support external to the *losika* as a long-term means of dealing with agnates, to appropriate resources, or to establish mutually gainful relations for their own sake. But these goals are themselves the surface expression of a constitutive order that shapes both the sociocultural basis of interest and the values to which social activity is meaningfully addressed.

These features of the sociocultural order are intimately related to the structured individuation of the lived-in universe that, in turn, underlies the nature of marital relationships among the Tswana. As we showed in chapter 5, marriage is always a state of becoming, its maturation being intimately connected to the realization of affinal alliances. Under such conditions, the status of unions, like the rights embodied in them, is never established at their genesis, and it necessarily remains implicit and negotiable while they last. Indeed, this is reflected in the semantics of everyday terminological usage (see above, p. 134), just as it is socially contained in the absence of collective or public involvement in conjugal formation. At the same time, precisely because of the fluid, contradictory, and managerial quality of the social field, in which alliances readily lapse or give way to rivalries when other relationships impinge on them (see case 25), the prospect that any union will endure is not great; nor do Tswana expect that it should be otherwise. In short, the ubiquity of disputes over marriage and affinity, their cultural ambiguity and social negotiability, is also inscribed in the construction of the Tswana world and the processes generated by its internal contradictions (see chap. 2).

Because the status of unions is designated neither a priori nor in a series of clearly demarcated processual steps, a contradiction may arise when a union is prematurely terminated; for there is nothing *intrinsic* to conjugal formation that could mechanically determine its definition or the consequent devolution of reciprocal rights and liabilities. Nonetheless, a human and material product requires to be divided, and, if the parties concerned cannot effect this on their own account, there must be some terms of reference on which to proceed. Among the Sotho, it appears that the issue to be addressed in such circumstances is "how much" of a marriage exists (Murray 1976:104). The Tswana do not formulate matters in exactly this way, but the social and semantic parameters are similar. The continuum of unions described in chapter 5 comprises a number of status categories, each of which encodes a set of rights accruing to the respective spouses on the dissolution of their bond. Therefore, if they disagree over the mode of termination, they must place different constructions upon their union; they have no other choice. Hence, the object of dispute necessarily turns on the question of classification, and, since each of the available categories on the continuum has a set of normative attributes, disputants will rarely argue over a particular incident or obligation. Instead, they will seek to construe the relationship in its totality with respect to such a set.

Tswana themselves may ascribe the frequency of disputes and their own "litigiousness" to the ubiquitous pursuit of utility. Nevertheless, it would be ingenuous, as Hamnett has pointed out (see above, p. 16) and we have repeatedly stressed, to explain conflict processes purely in terms of pragmatic individualism. The form and substance of disputes, and Tswana ideology with respect to them, are *alike* surface realizations of the system in which they are encompassed. To invoke the one in accounting for the other would therefore be tautological. Hence, in synthesizing the analytical strands developed in chapters 2, 5, and 6, we have sought throughout to sustain our initial programmatic assertion by locating dispute within the total logic of this system. We do not mean to imply, however, that social processes, or their ideological dimension, are always contained in and by a structure of which they are merely the determined expressions. Quite the opposite is true: the constitutive order and the lived-in universe exist in a dialectical relationship, and it is in this that the historicity of any system resides. As this suggests, the processes that occur in everyday life have the capacity to transform its constitution, such transformations being ultimately reflected by changes made in the normative repertoire (see chap. 3). Thus, although we have located our analysis in the contemporary Tswana context, we do not envisage the Tswana sociocultural formation as being in any sense ossified in the "ethnographic present."[11]

In accounting thus far for the form and content of dispute, moreover, we have concentrated on conflict involving close kin and affines, not only because such conflict represents a high statistical proportion of cases but also, and more significantly, because it is crucial for comprehending the normative basis of everyday life and the confrontations that occur within it.

In order to take our analysis further, however, it is necessary to examine the systemic connection, in the context of dispute, between actions involving close relatives and those involving distant kin and unrelated persons—cases which, since they are not intrinsically the product of fluidities and contradictions in the social field, are more restricted and specific in character. Consequently, we now return to the model outlined in chapter 4. This, we suggest, provides a crucial insight into the relationship between modes of dispute, the meaning of rules, and the determination of processes.

Rules, Regularities, and Outcomes

The model of dispute processes outlined in chapter 4 is founded on two manifest dimensions of confrontation: litigant intentions and litigant relations. Each may be represented as a continuum, the first lying between the poles of value orientation and relational orientation, the second between determinate and generalized social linkages (see pp. 113 ff.). These dimensions cross-cut each other to yield four modes of dispute, which, in turn, constitute a linear progression with respect to their procedural and substantive character. To reiterate, the four ideal types are: (1) disputes in which an action over a specific value arises between persons involved in a determinate relationship; (2) disputes in which confrontation over such a value occurs in the context of a generalized bond; (3) disputes in which determinately linked persons contest the nature of their relationship; and (4) disputes in which the definition and quality of a generalized bond itself becomes the object of conflict. In exemplifying these types, we demonstrated that there is a consistent variation in the direction of (1) to (4). This variation is expressed in the following ways: in increased procedural flexibility; in the declining significance of circumstantial factors in debate and decision, with inversely greater emphasis being given to the prior history of the relationship between the litigants and interactions surrounding it; and in the generalization of the object of dispute and a growing tendency for there to be rival efforts to impose a paradigm of argument upon it. This linear progression, then, is marked by an ostensible movement from circumscription to ambiguity. At one extreme, the parties appearing before the settlement agencies appear to be closely constrained by the plight in which particular events or actions have placed them. At the other, not only may they contest the object of dispute, but the onus is entirely on them to construct its terms of reference. In the former situation, furthermore, the agencies deal precisely and predictably with the suits brought before them. These, as a Tswana chief put it, in English, are "open-and-shut cases; everybody knows the result, the defendant as well, before they come to the *kgotla."* This may exaggerate matters somewhat, but the gist is clear. In the latter situation, by contrast, part of the problem, from the judicial perspective, may be to establish what the dispute is actually about and to reduce it to an issue (or series of issues) that may be adjudicated upon. Indeed, the chiefly tendency to invoke norms in just such circumstances (chap. 3) is a function of this process of reduction.

In theory, the category of dispute into which any case will fall depends entirely on the manner in which it is constructed by the litigants and presented to the dispute-settlement agencies.[12] In practice, however, the parties concerned never enjoy a total freedom of choice; there are always factors, both subjective and objective, that constrain their activities. The first of these factors, as we noted in chapter 4, flows from the personal predicament in which a prospective litigant finds himself at the onset of a dispute. Whether he simply seeks compensation for the alleged violation of, say, a piece of property or exploits the situation for more wide-ranging purposes may depend as much on his financial state as on his political ambitions and his location in a field of social linkages. What he does will also be influenced by the identity of his opponent and the quality of the relationship between them. The degree to which he actually retains the initiative to make such choices is, of course, distinctly variable. As Lesoka found, in case 25, the consequences of earlier managerial activities sometimes combine to rob an individual of all room for maneuver. In addition, extrinsic limits, again in varying measure, may be imposed by the nature of the incident that precipitated the action, especially if it involves determinately linked disputants. Thus, for example, the chance trampling of a field of corn by cattle (case 5) does not allow much scope for anything but a case of type 1, although, as case 7 indicates, defendants often demonstrate considerable ingenuity in transforming to their own advantage a suit over an apparently specific incident. All these constraining factors, however, are ultimately subsumed in the two axial dimensions of the model. And, once a particular dispute is established within one of the four categories, its substantive character will take the form associated with that category, with all that that implies for the content and quality of the discourse entered into by the participants.

This model, we submit, provides a critical analytical link between the nature of dispute processes and the sociocultural system in which they are located. On the one hand, it establishes the modalities of everyday confrontation and their respective rhetorical and substantive correlates; on the other, its parameters are firmly grounded in the logic of that system. Clearly, the fact that the dimensions of the model are subsumed in relations and intentions is intimately connected to the construction of the Tswana universe. The contrast between generalized and determinate relations is in fact a representation of the distinction between the linkages contained in the *losika* and those that fall outside this shifting and ambiguous field of primary kin. It is therefore understandable why cases of types 2 and 4 tend to be more marked by the deployment of procedural flexibility and competitive rhetoric than are those of types 1 and 3. The former are always situated in a more complex and enigmatical social context, which inevitably bears on the discourse in one form or another. In addition, the difference between value-oriented and relationally oriented intentions corresponds to that between rivalries over interests and those concerned with the definition of relations. Again, it is a property of the individuation and fluidity of the social order that linkages between persons are always at least potentially negotiable. In confrontation, then, litigants face a choice: they *must* either accept and perpetuate, or contest and seek to alter, the nature of their bond with reference to an available set of normatively inscribed categories.

One or the other of these two possibilities *necessarily* becomes manifest in the dispute process; this is what distinguishes cases of types 1 and 2 from those of types 3 and 4, and it underlies the contrast of substance between them. The two dimensions that shape the different modes of confrontation, in other words, are not merely rooted in the fabric of the sociocultural order. In describing the systemic connections between, first, conflict involving close kin and conflict involving determinately linked persons and, second, rivalries over interests and relations, they also illuminate the manner in which Tswana experience the regularities underlying diverse kinds of dispute in their lived-in world.

Because cases of types 1 and 2 are closely circumscribed by the determinacy of context-specific situations and because they concern rights and access to value *within* normatively acknowledged relations, they can be argued and decided with reference, tacit or express, to the rules—embodied in *mekgwa le melao*—that inform those relations. On relatively rare occasions contradictory norms may be adduced. When this happens, the settlement agencies must decide to give priority to one norm (as, for example, in case 1) and hand down a judgment accordingly. (Sometimes, as we have seen, chiefs take the opportunity to establish the general precedence of these *mekgwa,* thereby transforming the repertoire in the process.) Such decisions, however, merely reinforce the more general implication that disputes of types 1 and 2 appear to the Tswana as unequivocally norm-governed. Indeed, any attempt on the part of defendants to repudiate decisions or to act intransigently in these cases casts doubt on their own integrity and reputation. Such behavior may also provoke negative moral sanctions and further action on the part of the agencies for what amounts to contempt. Thus, while cases of types 1 and 2 differ somewhat in their procedural forms, both are *experienced* by Tswana as highly predictable and rule-determined; these are the "open-and-shut" cases of which the chief spoke.[13] What is more, because their rhetorical and social construction restricts disagreement over paradigms of argument or the object of dispute and emphasizes the circumstantial, the indigenous perception is both self-validating and consistently reinforced. Such confrontations do appear to be regulated, in their intrinsic nature, by *mekgwa le melao,* and they are regularly settled.

Cases of types 3 and 4 take a markedly different course. Because they involve persons engaged in the negotiation of relations, they take two forms: either one party seeks to transform a social linkage while the other does not, the latter therefore arguing that the dispute ought properly to concern a specific incident or interest within the context of an existing bond; or both may engage in the effort to impose a definition on that bond, but in different ways. Whichever form they take, disputes of these kinds hinge on the interpretation, and the reduction to order, of a range of events. Rhetorically, they demand a construal of the history of interaction between the litigants and, frequently, of their interactions with those around them as well (see, for example, cases 8 and 9). These events and interactions, like the field of relations within which they occur, are inherently ambiguous; indeed, they must be meaningfully constructed before they acquire social currency, not least in debate before the settlement agencies, where such matters necessarily require explication.

As we saw earlier, *mekgwa le melao* constitute the repertoire of concepts and precepts with reference to which such constructions may be expressed. In fact, from the indigenous perspective, this repertoire is their exclusive source; involvement in public discourse presupposes the acceptance of its limits in establishing the range of meanings that may be imposed on social action (see J. L. Comaroff 1975). This explains, for instance, why Chief Kebalepile uttered his homily in dismissing the suit brought by a young man against his mother's brother, a suit he termed "unnatural" (p. 219), or why men who alienate their matrilateral kin may sometimes find their mental stability called into doubt; save in exceptional circumstances, everyday conflict between matrilaterally linked kin cannot be otherwise meaningfully rationalized within the existing limits of *mekgwa le melao.* Of course, the normative repertoire may be put to novel use by a skillful speaker—typically by exploiting its incoherencies or by combining its component elements in hitherto unforeseen ways (see case 1)—and it does change over time (see chap. 3; see also below); but, at any historical moment, it represents the manifest budget of terms that can be brought to bear in the process of interpretation and evaluation.

Now, because cases of types 3 and 4 involve the construal of relations with reference to categories inscribed in *mekgwa le melao,* litigants must engage in what appears to be normative manipulation in the construction of their suits and countersuits; for, whether or not they are explicit in their invocations, both must select and configure one or more norms in order to assign meaning to relevant events. Moreover, since they find themselves in an adversary situation, each must assert the contextual precedence of the norms on which his case depends (see below). Even where the parties do *not* contest the normative referents of a dispute but differ over the facts within an agreed paradigm of argument, they are putting the same rules to rival interpretative uses. Either way, *mekgwa le melao* are being strategically appropriated and manipulated by individuals in the cause of their competing constructions of reality.

The lengths to which litigants go to contrive effective rhetorical positions may differ greatly. Some appear to respond passively to the predicament in which they find themselves and offer ingenuous and highly situational arguments; others seek advice and work hard to arrive at the most persuasive of the available alternatives. Nonetheless, whether the strategic decisions are implicit or explicit, effective or ingenuous, the structure of argument in disputes of types 3 and 4 in itself engenders the rivalrous deployment of the repertoire. Obviously, furthermore, the precise terms in which this deployment is expressed will vary between types 3 and 4, since each has its own special context. For reasons already spelled out, cases of type 4, which follow the lines described in the preceding section, tend to be more frequent and complex; but the emphasis on the strategic appropriation of *mekgwa le melao* is common to both.

The manner in which *mekgwa le melao* are deployed in cases of types 3 and 4, in turn, takes us back to a point made in chapter 3, namely, that the norms embodied in the repertoire are not, by and large, hierarchically valued in the abstract by Tswana. Rather, they obtain their priority, in relation to one another, in the circumstantial context of debate and dispute.

Thus, few Tswana would contemplate, in purely formal terms, the problem of whether a particular *mokgwa* is more important than another; by virtue of the cultural constitution of their repertoire, the question makes little sense. This explains why litigants who adopt different paradigms of argument are compelled to assert the preeminence of the *mekgwa* on which they base their claims. It also explains why the outcome of cases of these types can never be decided by the application of a single rule or set of rules; it is beyond their intrinsic nature to do so. That these things are so is reflected in the assumptions disputants make in formulating their suits; they appear to take it for granted that the successful contrivance of a relationship depends on the construal of as much of its history and contemporary character as possible in relation to the widest available set of normative referents. This is especially evident, for example, in the arguments offered by Molefe and Madubu (cases 8 and 9) for the purpose of contesting the status of their union. Each attempted to account for a considerable flow of events and incidents in such a way as to make them conform to, or diverge from, the total range of normative elements relevant to the constitution of a marriage.[14] As this implies, too, Tswana have it that rhetorical skill, which is recognized to be distinctly variable, lies in the ability to construct a consonance between a range of normative referents and the broadest possible sweep of events.

It is not surprising, therefore, that cases of types 3 and 4 are thought indigenously to reflect the self-interested managerial activities of individuals or that they are seen to be characterized by a pragmatic and manipulative deployment of *mekgwa le melao*. Unlike cases of types 1 and 2, their outcomes cannot be predicted in advance by straightforward inference from a set of rules that might in the abstract appear to apply to the facts of the dispute; for the applicability of the rules may be as much the subject of debate as are the facts. Perhaps this is why Gluckman and Krige found it so difficult to foretell decisions in not totally dissimilar legal contexts (above, p. 10). It is a difficulty the Tswana themselves share. Because of their construction, such cases *are* unpredictable, and that is why, perhaps, they often call forth great public interest. For they depend on a number of factors extrinsic to the normative repertoire. Important among these is the exact manner in which the biographies of the parties intersect at the moment of dispute—a consideration that subsumes their relative support in the matter at hand, the implications of prior managerial activities, the ways in which their previous actions toward each other have been presented to and understood by those around them, and so on. They also include the relative success of the two parties or their partisans in exploiting the procedural flexibilities of the dispute process (cf. Motshegare Ramalepa's activities on behalf of Madubu in case 8). But the significance of rhetorical factors is very great. It is contingent on the Tswana concept of veracity, which derives from the assumption that social reality exists primarily in the manner in which it is constructed (see chap. 2). There is no concrete set of social facts "out there" against which the truth value of words or propositions can readily be measured; veracity subsists, rather, in the extent to which events and interactions are persuasively construed and coherently interpreted. Hence, while it sometimes happens that adjudicators seek to minimize the disadvantage of inarticulate litigants by interpolating pointed questions, able speakers often win (or influence) cases that, to the observer, may seem relatively weak. For their part, the agencies seek to test the coherence and relative fault of the disputants by evaluating the degree to which they can account for their own and their opponent's actions within the terms of the argument they establish and by the weight of support given to their suits by their respective witnesses. Nonetheless, it is not possible, outside the particular context of disputes, to designate a set of "objective" factors that will uniformly predict their course or outcomes; indeed, this is, as we have emphasized, inimical to their very form.

The contrast between types 1 and 2 on the one hand, and 3 and 4 on the other, then, is clearly expressed in the relationship between rule and outcome. In the former, *mekgwa le melao* are perceived, in a self-validating fashion, actually to *determine* decisions in a mechanical manner. In the latter, it is recognized that they cannot do this; but it does not follow that disputes of these types do not appear to be norm-governed. Quite to the contrary, the normative repertoire does regulate debate and decision because it must be deployed to select relevant events and impose order upon them. Here, however, "norm-governed" does not refer to the determination of outcomes but to the meaningful constitution of argument and adjudication; moreover, because judgment depends on an agency's evaluating suits within an agreed paradigm of argument, on finding for one or the other of two competing paradigms, or on introducing an independent one, decisions alway *appear* to be situated in the requirements of *mekgwa le melao*. Again the perception is self-validating: the normative order is experienced as giving predictability to everyday life, despite its ubiquitous negotiability.

If we draw all this together, the apparent dualism in Tswana ideology becomes explicable. For it is clear that this dualism reflects the substance of everyday experience; quite simply, the normative repertoire is consistently seen both to regulate dispute processes and to be the object of strategic negotiation. This is because, far from being all of a kind, these processes embrace a range of forms, each characterized by systematically different modes of argument and terms of reference. At one extreme, cases between persons involved in mutually acknowledged relations are perceived as highly specific and rule-determined; as such, they are formulated, presented, and judged within ostensibly narrow normative confines. At the other extreme, the rivalrous deployment of *mekgwa le melao* and contention over the priority and/or construal of particular precepts are a function of the meaningful constitution of the discourse itself. Indeed, because the rules embodied in the repertoire are not relatively valued in the abstract, litigants who adopt different paradigms of argument *must* assert, implicitly or otherwise, the precedence of their respective normative referents. As this represents itself to Tswana, complainants and defendants are typically cast as adversaries whose usual objectives are to increase gains and reduce losses. At the same time, suits and judgments are always finally situated and rationalized in terms of *mekgwa le melao;* consequently, the dispute process regularly sustains its norm-governed appearance, despite the recognized unpredictability of outcomes in these cases.

It is not, however, merely within the context of confrontation that interaction is seen indigenously to be rule-governed and yet negotiable, normatively constrained and yet pragmatically individualistic. For Tswana, the dispute process represents everyday life in a microcosm. As we remarked in chapter 1, this process appears, in Tswana characterizations of their own world, to bear a metonymic relationship to the social process at large; in describing, for example, the chiefship, administrative arrangements, or the politics of succession, the dimensions they stress are the ostensibly legal ones. It is not surprising, therefore, that the dualism in Tswana conceptions of the dispute process instantiates the ideological character of the encompassing universe itself. The latter, too, is seen to be both regulated by *mekgwa le melao* and yet pervaded by competitive individualism. Nor does it need to be reiterated that this dualism derives from the fact that the form and content of disputes—like the model we have elaborated to account for their logic—is securely grounded in the constitution of that universe. It is also subsumed in the assumption that acknowledged social relations must correspond to a set of defining normative criteria. These establish the appropriate behavioral proprieties associated with any relationship; and, as long as the relationship is reciprocally sustained, any disagreements that arise ought to be resolvable with reference to the relevant precepts. But, simultaneously, the social field immediately surrounding any person is recognized to be ambiguous and potentially hostile. It is thus inherent in the quality of everyday life that individuals will be drawn into the contrivance and management of the linkages that affect them most closely. The mutual acknowledgment of many of these linkages is, as a result, expected to be transient. Moreover, while their negotiation must be expressed in terms of *mekgwa le melao,* outcomes cannot be prescribed by normative reckoning. The dualism in Tswana ideology, then, in its application both to the exigencies of the dispute process and to the encompassing nature of the lived-in universe, is not really paradoxical. Its experiential terms are given in the construction of the sociocultural system.

This account of the logic of Tswana dispute processes— which, we suggest, may have applications beyond the confines of the Tswana world—addresses a series of substantive issues that have long pervaded legal anthropology. First, it

illuminates the problem of normative determination, indicating why a priori assumptions cannot be made about the
manner or extent to which conflict and confrontation are
resolved by the application of rules. It follows, too, that any
debate that casts a rule-centered approach against utilitarian-
ism or interactionism as competing explanatory paradigms is
theoretically ill-founded, just as it is misguided to reduce
everyday life, in any ethnographic context, to a battle between custom and interest. Every sociocultural system, we
submit, constitutes (1) a set of normative terms within which
interaction may proceed and be rendered meaningful, (2) the
values and utilities to which such interaction may be addressed, and (3) the ideology in which they are expressed. It
is, therefore, in the totality of relations between these elements of a lived-in order that the logic of dispute—and, indeed, the logic of all social processes—must ultimately reside. The attribution of analytical priority to either norm or
utility, then, inevitably reduces the nature of social experience and its systemic construction to a shadow of its intrinsic
complexity.

As this implies, the opposed perspectives of the "rule-
centered" and "processual" paradigms in legal anthropology
have tended to err by stressing the analytical preeminence of
one or the other dimension of dispute processes. The rule-
centered paradigm has typically stressed the normative and
institutional aspect of social order and the resolution of dis-
cord; the processual paradigm stresses the inherent nature of
social conflict and the negotiation of rules and reciprocities in
the pursuit of interest. As our model demonstrates, the limitations of these two emphases may be transcended, for the
dimensions of conflict they address are properly embraced
within a single explanatory approach—provided that due
recognition is given to the *total* range of modes of dispute and
the systematic diversities of form and content characteristic
of them.

Finally, it is apposite to observe that Fallers's continuum
of "legalism" (see above, p. 15), which was intended as a basis
for comparing different systems, may be broadly applied to
the linear progression of types of dispute *within* the Tswana
universe. At one end of this progression, cases have an outward appearance corresponding closely to our own folk

model of a quintessentially "legal" confrontation; at the other, they appear more diffuse and "political" in character. The fact that these modes of dispute represent the poles of a single continuum, however, underlines the danger of assuming clear distinctions between "the political" and "the legal" (cf. Abel 1973). Indeed, this is a distinction that Tswana would not readily make; among them, "political" cases are, in fact, largely indistinguishable from "law" cases. The arenas in which they occur, like the rhetorical forms they take, are identical. Quite simply, since the dominant mode of political management involves the negotiation of rank and relations, most of these cases are disputes of types 3 and 4. The more general point is that, by elaborating a model of processual forms that comprehends the order underlying diverse modes of confrontation, it also becomes possible to illuminate the articulation of what we might otherwise reify as "legal" and so differentiate it from the "political."

Conclusion

8

In chapter 7 we drew together our arguments concerning the nature of the normative order and the manner in which it is perceived and deployed by the Tswana. Relating this order to the total sociocultural context in which it is located, we explained the logic underlying dispute processes, with particular reference to marriage and property devolution. In doing so we sought to account both for systemic variations in the form and determination of these processes and for the ideological dualism that pervades Tswana life. Having thus established the analytical basis of our approach within the confines of the Tswana ethnography, we now consider some of its more general implications.

Most immediately, this analysis reaffirms existing doubts about the value of distinguishing "the legal" as a discrete field of inquiry. The notion that "law" ought properly to be a separate and privileged area of anthropological investigation has a long and respectable history; it was well entrenched even before Radcliffe-Brown accorded it a central place in his proposed "social physiology." But recently there has been a growing reaction to this position (see chap. 1), based partly on the empirical objection that most small-scale societies lack institutional arrangements or processes that can be preclusively designated as "legal." The implication is that a narrowly defined, judicially oriented anthropology of law is viable at best in a relatively few, highly centralized, systems. Perhaps it was this consideration that persuaded Fallers (1969) to propose his continuum of "legalism" and to treat law as a variable for purposes of comparative analysis. Such solutions, however, merely displace the problem by an appeal to taxonomy; for, by implication, the "legalistic"

243

societies remain amenable to law-centered analysis, while the rest require another approach to illuminate their more diffuse processes of conflict resolution. But this agenda makes the established paradigms of legal anthropology still more sharply opposed than they are at present. Indeed, it may reify the two approaches into "regional theories" in much the same way as has allegedly occurred with alliance and descent theory in studies of kinship systems. Even more important, it leaves unanswered the substantive criticisms that have been leveled at the assumptions underlying these paradigms (see chap. 1).

All of this has been brought into clear focus by the Tswana ethnography. With their governmental hierarchy, judicial dispute-settlement agencies, and elaborate repertoire of rules and procedures, the Tswana ought presumably to be as good subjects as any African people for rule-centered analysis. Nevertheless, we have demonstrated that this tradition—in spite of the fact that Schapera's classic studies are firmly grounded in it—does not, and cannot, comprehend the essence of Tswana dispute processes. Nor, on the other hand, can utilitarian individualist approaches provide an adequate explanation. Within these chiefdoms, disputes range between what are ostensibly norm-governed "legal" cases and others that appear to be interest-motivated "political" confrontations (chaps. 4, 7). The point, however, is not simply that these different modes coexist in one context (see Gulliver 1979:19) but that they are *systematically* related. They are, together, transformations of a single logic, whose varying realizations are expressed in the articulation of the relations and intentions that shape any particular action. As we have stressed, therefore, the Tswana data demand an analytical approach that can account for such diversities of form and determination. We would argue, furthermore, that the same thing is true in other sociocultural contexts, including our own.

If our account underscores the dangers of both taxonomic reductionism and the analytical application of Western folk models to other "legal" cultures, it does so not merely in negative terms, for a number of constructive implications flow from it. For instance, the "resource-oriented" approach of Tswana litigants and judges to their norms stands in sharp contrast to the assumed relationship between rule and out-come—derived from a naive view of Anglo-American legal systems—that has frequently been carried over into studies of small-scale societies. As we have shown, it is simply mis-guided to seek predictive regularity in Tswana disputes on the basis of jural determinist assumptions. This demonstra-tion not only reiterates the familiar admonition that con-ventional (Western) folk wisdom may not export well in the guise of analytical concepts; more significantly, it also suggests that the systematic variations embraced within the logic of Tswana dispute processes may find an analogue in other cases. The same thing might be said of patterns of norm invocation (chap. 3) with respect to norms whose applicabil-ity is rejected by settlement agencies in one or a series of cases. In Western legal systems such norms are perceived to be "wrong" and may lose their validity. Among the Tswana, they merely retreat back into the generality of *mekgwa le melao,* insulated from a particular outcome through the use of differential speech forms; they thus remain capable of being invoked again, on a later occasion, without any implication that there has been a loss of validity. As a result, the status accorded to legal norms in one culture cannot be taken for granted in others, as has often been the case. At the same time, however, the association between patterns of norma-tive utterance and the construction of paradigms of argu-ment, which we have demonstrated in the Tswana case, may turn out to have some application beyond their world.[1]

The general point may also be extended to the analysis of African systems of marriage and property devolution. We pointed out in chapters 5 and 6 that legal concepts have been freely employed with respect to both. Sometimes the deriva-tion of these concepts has been deliberate, but often they have been appropriated unself-consciously and without theoretical reflection. So far as conjugal formation is con-cerned, this ethnocentric analytical tendency has frequently placed a considerable strain on the data, as is becoming in-creasingly apparent from recent African studies (see Roberts 1977; J. L. Comaroff 1980). In the Tswana context the asso-ciation between compliance with formal procedures and va-lidity, certainly assumed in our own folk system, cannot be safely made. Nonetheless, the jural approach to the study of marriage continues to be widely applied in other small-scale societies, and the suspicion remains that its justification lies more in the preconceptions of anthropologists than in anything suggested by the data themselves.[2]

Similarly, the common-law category of inheritance, concerned solely with the passage of property on death, has been widely utilized in the analysis of non-Western systems. This was certainly the case in Schapera's earlier accounts of Tswana devolution (1938). Yet, as we have shown, important intergenerational transfers occur on other occasions, and elaborate efforts are made to dissociate devolution from death. Thus, an exclusive focus on the latter, or any fragmented treatment of the different stages in the overall process, must result not only in a distorted characterization but also in the excision of the transmission of material objects from the total context that gives it meaning. Again, we would argue that, in any society, the a priori imposition of such analytical limits serves to conceal the involvement of devolutionary arrangements in the reproduction of the social order and the manner in which they impinge on relations in the lived-in universe. This may be particularly evident among the Tswana, where status and property relations are dialectically entailed in each other; once more, however, the Tswana are hardly unique in this regard.

In summary, our account, instead of merely restating the allegations of conceptual ethnocentrism so often leveled at the existing paradigms of legal anthropology, suggests a variety of ways in which the analysis of the Tswana system can illuminate our understanding of arrangements in other societies. But, as we have repeatedly emphasized, this requires the elaboration of an approach that can account both for the *total* logic of dispute processes and for its systemic contextualization. It is precisely this kind of approach that we have attempted to develop here.

At the beginning of this account, we argued that the relative lack of theoretical development in legal anthropology is to be explained partly as the result of the parallel and largely independent development of two major analytical traditions. Before the 1920s, the comparative study of law was the focus of great scholarly optimism, since it promised to illuminate matters of central concern to social scientists: in the terms of that period, how societies held together, managed conflict, and accommodated change. There is no denying that there have been considerable achievements, especially in the context of individual ethnographies. This has been particularly marked, we would suggest, precisely when efforts have been made to confront questions in such a way as to transcend the limits of the rival paradigms, as Gluckman, for example, sometimes succeeded in doing. Nonetheless, as paradigmatic differences developed and hardened, so too did a concomitant series of tacit conceptual oppositions: thus an emphasis on norms and institutional arrangements became the analytical priority of the one orthodoxy, just as social action and process did for the other. As a result, the relationship between rule and process has rarely been subjected to examination in other than restricted functional or transactional terms. Most legal anthropologists laid the problem aside, relegating it to the realms of a taken-for-granted contrast between the "ideal" and the "real." With hindsight it is easy to observe that this contrast frequently obscured the logic of dispute and, in particular, the articulation of rule and process. We have attempted to demonstrate that, among the Tswana, where the social field is recognized to be fluid and negotiable, *mekgwa le melao* represent a symbolic grammar in terms of which reality is continually constructed and managed in the course of everyday interaction and confrontation. Far from constituting an "ideal" order, as distinct from the "real" world, the culturally inscribed normative repertoire is constantly appropriated by Tswana in the contrivance of social activity, just as the latter provides the context in which the value of specific *mekgwa* may be realized or transformed. In short, notwithstanding the classical opposition drawn between them, norm and reality exist in a *necessary* dialectical relationship, a relationship that gives form to the manner in which Tswana experience and navigate their universe. As this implies, changes in the repertoire occur when transformations in the sociocultural system impinge on indigenous consciousness; and, when they do, they have consequences for future social processes. Viewed from this perspective, one major and troublesome problem of jurisprudence may be seen to be illusory. We refer to the "gap" problem—so called because apparent disparities between rules and behavior are allegedly incapable of elucidation—which ceases to exist once rules and behavior are seen to be generated from the same systemic source.

This brings us to our final comment. In order to illuminate the nature of dispute and the relationship between rule and process, we have elaborated a model to account for diverse modes of confrontation and have attempted to locate this within the logic of a sociocultural system. In doing so, we have avoided teleological assumptions concerning both the contribution of dispute settlement to the maintenance of order and the mechanical determination of processual outcomes by structural exigencies. We have also avoided a conception of society as either a moral universe, in the Durkheimian sense, or a field of endemic conflict and antagonism, in the tradition of, say, the Manchester School. Moreover, just as we have not reduced the dispute process to an institutional adjunct of social structure, so we have not sought to explain it in terms of a series of functional requirements. Rather, we have tried to show that the constitution of the sociocultural system, precisely because it gives form to the opposed domains of moral complementarity and social rivalry, shapes an order of manifest linkages and values. These, in turn, configure the relations and interests that are negotiated in the context of dispute and, therefore, the form and content of processes of confrontation.

In the course of demonstrating this, however, we have not simply had to depart from previous efforts to account for the relationship between conflict and the social order; more fundamentally, we have found it necessary to formulate a particular analytical conception of the sociocultural system itself. For, in order to elucidate the nature of this system, it has proved crucial to distinguish, and establish the connection, between the surface forms of the lived-in world and the principles of its constitution and, at another level, to examine the dialectic between the phenomenology of everyday life and the structures that give it meaning.

In methodological terms, there is something of an analytical mutuality—perhaps even a circularity—in all this. On the one hand, the logic of dispute is ultimately situated in the encompassing system and can be comprehended only as such.

But, on the other, it is in the context of confrontation—when persons negotiate their social universe and enter discourse about it—that the character of that system is revealed. Because this is true, the dispute process may provide an essential key to the disclosure of the sociocultural order at large. As we stated at the outset, the argument for perpetuating a discrete anthropology of law, if this implies the continued reification of "the legal," is not compelling. But there is no gainsaying the theoretical insights into the subtle complexities of other cultures afforded by the analysis of dispute.

Notes

Chapter One

1. At this stage we use "legal anthropology" in the conventional sense, but merely for convenience; our substantive reservations with regard to it will become apparent later.

2. For a recent (general) theoretical essay that bears on this, see Crick 1976. Any number of relevant writings could be cited, however, since the issue ultimately concerns the very nature of comparative sociology.

3. A conspicuous exception to this generalization is Laura Nader. In an overview of the field (1965) she notes the discontinuity of interest dividing those who study "conflict resolution" from those who are concerned with "legal procedure" and "judicial process." This distinction, as will become clear, corresponds broadly to our own. In a later essay, written with Yngvesson (1973), she explores it further, although in less explicit terms.

4. It is to be found, for example, in Hobbes's *Leviathan* (1651).

5. The very label that was applied to studies in this area—i.e., "primitive law"—also confirms this.

6. It is important to emphasize that Schapera's purpose was to produce a handbook that could be put to practical use by the colonial government and its personnel in the administration of the Tswana and their courts, and it should be recalled that, as he put it himself, he was concerned with the "letter" rather than the "spirit" of Tswana law (1938:x). But his practical objective does not in itself explain why the Tswana material needed to be cast in a framework derived from another system.

7. Judging from Pospisil's own case data and from accounts of similar Papuan communities, it is difficult to escape the conclusion that this characterization owes more to his preconceived ideas about the nature of law than to the realities of the Kapauku

dispute-settlement process. Pospisil has strongly reproached scholars who have been less inclined to force similar figures from other societies into a judicial mold. An example is his criticism (1972) of Gulliver's treatment of Ndendeuli "notables" in *Neighbours and Networks* (1971).

8. Nader and Yngvesson (1973:889) list some examples of writings that, by their criteria, would fall within this paradigm: Hoebel 1940, 1954, Gluckman 1955a, 1955b, Bohannan 1969, Pospisil 1958b, 1969, Schapera 1938, 1969, and Richardson 1940. For more complete historical reviews of the field, however, see Moore 1970 and Nader 1965.

9. This debate, which drew considerable attention, persisted from the late 1950s until at least 1969. Representative defenses of the authors' positions are included in the second editions of Bohannan's *Justice and Judgment among the Tiv* (1968) and Gluckman's *The Judicial Process among the Barotse of Northern Rhodesia (Zambia)* (1967), although each made other statements as well (see, e.g., Bohannan 1969). Moore (1969, 1970) has summarized the debate and, perhaps most welcome of all, Nader (1969:5) announced its final resolution in her review of the Wenner-Gren Conference on Law in Culture and Society. Along with many of the participants in that conference, we believe that the debate was predicated on a false problem in the first place; consequently, we do not rehearse the arguments.

10. Nader and Yngvesson (1973:896–97) make the same point, in relation to the work of Barton (1919), Pospisil (1965), and others, when they ask for the *grounds* on which the inventories of rules collected by these writers are designated as "law." The implication is clear: the onus is on the fieldworker to establish that a given set of precepts fulfills a range of *stipulated* criteria, a task that has yet to be successfully accomplished.

11. Hamnett (1977:8), in an effort to defend Gluckman's view of the specificity of law, argues that the "indigenous character" of the Bantu stem *-lao* "is fully established in the literature": simply, it means "law." Hamnett, however, disregards Schapera's cautionary observation (1938:36; 1943a:4) that the terminological and conceptual boundaries of this and related terms may *not* be clear among the Tswana (see also chap. 3, below).

12. Gluckman's assertion has received varying responses; cf. Moore's acceptance of it (1970) with the more critical views of March (1956), Ayoub (1961), Douglas (1956), and Bohannan (e.g., 1969).

13. It might seem curious that we place these ethnographic studies of Turner and Colson in a different paradigmatic category

from Gluckman's work on law, especially in the light of their common intellectual association in the "Manchester School." (In fact, Turner [1957:xxxii–xxxiii] has explicitly stressed the assumptions they shared, as did Gluckman on many occasions.) This dualism in respect of Gluckman's position in the history of ideas, however, has also been noted by Kuper (1973:184): "[Gluckman's] own major research in this period . . . was at a tangent to the work he inspired. This was his study of Lozi law." It is unquestionable that much of the modern British work that has elaborated the "processual" approach was given impetus, and developed, by Gluckman's programmatic and *general* analytical writings. Yet, within the specific confines of legal anthropology, his own studies certainly did essay a much narrower approach. It is beyond our present scope, unfortunately, to explore further this aspect of Gluckman's intellectual biography, important though it clearly is for a full understanding of the development of legal anthropology.

14. Roberts (1976:675) also lists these examples with similar comment, and adds those of Berndt (1962), Young (1971), and Koch (1974).

15. In the light of our earlier reference to the comparability of the "formalist-substantivist" debate in economic anthropology, it is salutary to note Sahlins's comment (1972:xii) that there can be "no ground for the happy academic conclusion that 'the answer lies somewhere in between.' "

16. The recent tendency to view political and legal processes in terms of the construction and management of meaning echoes a more general orientation in anthropological theory according to which man is seen as a "meaning-maker" and the discipline itself is seen as a semantic inquiry.

17. Seasonal variations in rainfall are, however, considerable. For example, 739 mm. fell in 1974–75, but only 297 mm. fell in 1972–73 (Republic of Botswana, *Statistical Abstracts,* 1975:3).

18. For a recent breakdown of patterns of rural income and its distribution in Botswana, see Republic of Botswana, *Rural Incomes Distribution Survey, 1974–75.* J. L. Comaroff (1981) discusses Botswana government policy with respect to rural development and demonstrates why it has led to distinctly variable patterns of economic transformation.

19. The district used to be known as the "Barolong Farms." For an account of its origins and history, see Schapera 1943b and J. L. Comaroff 1977, 1981; both also record further details concerning its unusual residential, economic, and political arrangements.

20. This community was not always as productive as it is now, however. The rise in outputs began in the 1960s and was caused by

a complex combination of factors, discussed in J. L. Comaroff 1977, 1981.

21. Following established usage, and in order to avoid confusion, we shall refer throughout to the South African Tshidi-Rolong as the "Tshidi," to the grouping across the border as the "Botswana Rolong," and to both together simply as the "Rolong." A word on relevant Tswana prefixes and suffixes is also in order: *mo-* indicates the personal singular (thus, e.g., "Mokgatla" = a Kgatla individual); *ba-* is its plural form ("Batswana" = Tswana people); *se-* denotes language ("Serolong" = the Rolong language); and *-ng* transforms a noun into its locative ("Kgatleng" = the Kgatla territory).

22. We found South African census figures—and statistics on the black areas in general—to be grossly unreliable. As a result, the data quoted here are based on calculations made from field surveys.

23. For accounts of Tshidi history, see Molema 1966 and Matthews 1945.

24. A brief account of the transformations brought about among the South African Tswana communities by the introduction of the "homeland" is given in J. L. Comaroff 1976 (see also J. L. Comaroff 1974). More detailed descriptions of Bophuthatswana, its constitution and its operation as a system of local government, are to be found in Jeppe 1974 and Butler et al. 1977.

25. Schapera (1952) has described the heterogeneous "ethnic" composition of Tswana chiefdoms in some detail. Immigrant groupings, which make up the majority of the population in many of these chiefdoms, were usually fitted into the existing hierarchical politicoadministrative structure either as wards or subwards. Chiefly policy varied, however, with respect to leadership arrangements.

26. See Schapera 1938:104 ff. Male and female regiments, formed after initiation every five years or so, were also summoned for purposes of defense and public work.

27. We discuss the hierarchy, for different purposes, in chapters 2 and 3. "Sections," which are made up of a number of (related) wards under the jurisdiction of the most senior of the headmen, are not found in all chiefdoms. Even where they do exist, they appear to have become less important in recent times as politicoadministrative units. This is so even in the case of the Kgatla, where the section organization was recognized during the colonial period by the establishment of "native courts" corresponding to the original section jurisdiction at Mochudi.

28. We do not detail the formal procedures followed by these agencies; they have been thoroughly dealt with by Schapera, and they also become clear from the cases included in several of the later chapters.

29. Strictly, the translation should be "Tswana customs and laws," since *mekgwa* (sing. *mokgwa*) is generally taken to refer to "customs," and *melao* (sing. *molao*) to "laws." The phrase *mekgwa le melao* is used interchangeably with *melao le mekgwa*. The semantics of the component terms are considered in chapter 3, where we discuss the normative repertoire in detail.

30. In almost all contemporary accounts of Western legal systems the relationship between rule and outcome is seen as problematic, but even in the most sophisticated discussions, such as those of Levi (1949), Hart (1961), and Dworkin (1967), the differentiated character of legal rules is either insisted on or taken for granted.

31. A fact to which the published ethnographies testify. See Schapera 1938; Roberts 1972a.

Chapter Two

1. Kuper, who notes Radcliffe-Brown's observations, mentions some of the better known of these efforts (Kuper 1975a:71). Sheddick's contradictory remark about the Southern Sotho (1953:28) is perhaps the best example: "Descent follows the patrilineal system and is at the same time cognative [*sic*]."

2. We do not mean to imply that Kuper is himself unaware of this. On the contrary, he devotes considerable attention in his essay to the structural implications of the marriage system.

3. While the practice of polygyny has decreased markedly, it has given way to a pattern of serial monogamy. We have described this elsewhere (Comaroff and Roberts 1977b) and have pointed out that the transformation has made little difference to the way the politicoresidential hierarchy is conceived.

4. This fact has prompted Schapera (e.g., 1938:12 f.; 1953:40 f.) to refer to these units as "family groups." In terming them "local agnatic segments" we do not differ with him on their composition. We seek merely to stress the fact that their ideology and core membership derive from the agnatic principle. It is true, however, that they are *not* nesting units in a segmentary patrilineal system.

5. It should also be noted that, where an immigrant household settles with a segment to which it is not agnatically related, it will gradually grow into a segment in its own right. With the further passage of time it may proliferate into two or more such segments and emerge as an independent ward. Hence, when viewed processually, the agnatic ideology will eventually apply to the composition and incorporation of these units as well. This pattern is of relevance, too, in understanding the remaining features of the politicoadministrative structure.

6. When segments act together, most usually to consider disputes or to make arrangements for such occasions as funerals, they generally do so only with respect to the concerns of a *domiciled* member. Once an individual moves away permanently, he is usually excluded from the activities of the group, which in turn treats his affairs as beyond its (formal) sphere of interest.

7. Since 1970, land affairs in Botswana have been vested in local land boards. As a result, formal chiefly authority in this area has diminished, although some chiefs wield considerable power in the land boards (see J. L. Comaroff 1977, 1981; Roberts 1981).

8. Indeed, Gluckman (1963:22), on examining the Tswana literature in the light of his efforts to establish that such rules are always negotiable, felt it necessary to concede that theirs "do not produce the same doubt over who is the main heir."

9. J. L. Comaroff (1978) has rehearsed these problems in arguing that the concept of an "ascriptive political system" is a contradiction in terms. In the same essay he offers a lengthy treatment of the Tshidi theory of ascription and achievement, with special reference to the process of succession and competition surrounding the chiefship.

10. For example, severe illness. Alleged incompetence, unless regarded as evidence of serious malpractice or debilitation, is not usually given as sufficient grounds, at least in formal terms.

11. The example, like the one recorded on pp. 42 f., above, is a case that occurred in Mafikeng; it is reproduced in part from J. L. Comaroff 1974. More detailed data, drawn from the history of the Tshidi chiefship, are presented elsewhere (J. L. Comaroff 1978), where their implications for approaches to the analysis of succession are also considered.

12. It follows that, if the unit concerned is the chiefdom at large (which will be the case in rivalries over the chiefship), this field may potentially include the entire royal descent group, although the qualification noted below in the text, which excludes men with living older full siblings, also applies here.

13. Because age determines intrahouse rank and was (until recently) *publicly* inscribed in affiliation to chronologically ordered age-regiments, a man cannot usually contest the seniority of his elder brother. The only way he *might* do so—and it endangers his own credibility—is by asserting that his sibling is either criminally incompetent or insane. Of course, with respect to the *next* generation, a younger brother might dispute the status of his oBs by calling into question the union that had produced the house concerned.

14. These facts explain why 80 percent of all successions to the

Tshidi chiefship appear anomalous (see above, p. 36); that this is so is a corollary of the ascriptive justification of the present office-holder, translated into genealogical terms with reference to the prescriptive rules. A future incumbent might rationalize his status, and reconstitute the genealogy, in such a way that a different per-centage of previous holders would become recognized as having been chiefs. The so-called "anomalous" cases, then, are the expres-sion of a particular methodological perspective, one that misunder-stands the logic of the system.

15. Besele had been the last incumbent but two. Any of his sons could conceivably have claimed the chiefship by asserting that they had been raised by him in the name of Kebalepile, his full brother, who lacked a recognized heir at the time—providing they could establish, as Lotlamoreng was now seeking to do, that Kebalepile *had* been Montshiwa's heir. (There were other possibilities, but this was a convenient one.) For Besele's successors in office, Badirile and then Bakolopang, had had a very different version of the genealogy accepted. According to this, their mother had been the *seantlo* for Montshiwa's (alleged) childless principal wife; their house thus ranked first, while that of Kebalepile and Besele had occupied a position of relative juniority. So, too, had the house of Lotlamoreng, who was construed as a (jural) son of Montshiwa by an independent wife ranked even lower. Lotlamoreng's claim, it should be added, was mounted against Bakolopang; hence this genealogical configuration.

16. This interdependence is to be stressed: intradescent group formations emerge, or are negotiated, in their own right and thereby motivate competition over status. Evidence for this is to be found in J. L. Comaroff 1973.

17. We should like to express our gratitude to Marshall Sahlins for helping to clarify this point.

18. Schapera (1949:104 f.), who notes the "remarkably few" marriage prohibitions among Tswana, suggests that unions between men and their *half*-brother's daughters are not permitted among Rolong and Kgatla. There may, however, be some ambiguity con-cerning this, for in a survey conducted in Mafikeng in 1970, which included some Kgatla families, informants were divided in their responses to the relevant question. It should be added that those who counted themselves as devout Christians tended to answer that such marriages are prohibited, and they gave instances of childless ones to "prove" that they bring evil. Others, however, were not unanimous on the issue. A few offered rather more fortunate examples of marriages between half-siblings and between men and the children of half-brothers.

19. As we have noted, the ascriptive rules stress the *political* unity of the house, in opposition to similar units, *within* a generation. This, however, does not contradict the indigenous view that the (intrahouse) bond between brothers gradually develops into a potentially conflictive one, especially in relation to the next generation (see chap. 6).

20. Ambivalent, that is, because a father's commitment to any one house may be undermined by his relationship to others (see chap. 6).

21. Limitations of space preclude a full analysis of Tswana kinship terminology, important though it is. For summary accounts of this terminology, see van Warmelo 1931, Schapera 1953, and Kuper 1975a.

22. Traditionally, there was an established procedure by which a man convicted in the chief's court of a serious crime—including sorcery and homicide—could try to escape from the *kgotla* and reach the *segotlo* of the chief's mother (the "mother of the people"). If he succeeded, he was granted sanctuary and, it is said, pardoned.

23. We use standard kinship abbreviations, according to which each relationship is denoted by its first letter (e.g., B = brother; S = son; C = child; etc.); a sister is represented by the letter Z.

24. Where guardianship is vested in a father himself, a transformation of the same principle applies. As we shall point out in chapter 6, there is an established norm that says he should ensure that the devolution of his property is completed, save for a small balance unallocated during his lifetime. In other words, the interests of the house should here too be transferred to its members by the time the later stages of the developmental cycle are reached.

25. While it is not apposite here to enter general theoretical discussion concerning exogamy, it does seem significant—and suggestive—that the range of exogamic proscriptions corresponds exactly to the social field within which elemental structures and values are reproduced. Marriage within the boundaries of this field would, of course, confuse the constitutive categories and oppositions upon which the sociocultural system is founded.

26. Several aspects of this analysis of the marriage system are worked out in Comaroff and Comaroff 1981. There, however, the structure of choice is described in slightly different terms, since the discussion is addressed to other issues. The essential principles nevertheless remain identical.

27. This is clearly a male-centered conception of marriage and affinity. However, it reflects the indigenous notions with which we are presently concerned: men marry (*nyala*), women are married (*nyalwa*), a view that, at this level, is affirmed by most Tswana of

either gender. This is not to say that women may not actively engage in managing the conjugal and affinal relations to which they are party; it means merely that such efforts are rationalized and expressed in terms of the cultural paradigm described here.

28. Given the overall frequency of agnatic marriage and the social implications that flow from it, it is virtually unknown for a FBD union to be that alone; in almost all such cases (we know personally of no exceptions), the bond between partners is multiple. Informants, moreover, appear to confirm this, which is to be expected in the light of the conception of the *losika*. (The same, of course, need not necessarily be true of matrilateral marriage; it may easily occur between partners who are not linked in any other way.)

29. This will also be the case when a marriage is to a woman from the neutral universe beyond the two domains.

30. Informants will, when questioned, state FZD and MZD marriages as third and fourth preferences, but it again appears that partners are rarely selected *because* they stand in these relationships to a wife-taker. Generally such ties, where they exist between a husband and wife, are (unstressed) components of a multiple bond.

31. It also follows that when this happens, and as long as the concomitant state of relations persists, a marriage in the next generation will be construed as a matrilateral one (see below).

32. At the systemic level, of course, it is relational categories that we are primarily concerned with. But the management of close genealogical ties follows from these same principles. Thus, for example, a Tshidi chief had a warm, mutually supportive relationship with one of his multiply linked ("real") MBs and a competitive one with another. He referred to the first man, in every possible context, as *malome* (MB) and to the second as *rrangwane* (FyB). The closeness of kinship bonds per se does not necessarily limit the negotiability of their definition. Quite to the contrary: the closer the relationship between two persons, the more likely it is to be a multiple one, thereby potentiating its negotiation in the terms we have described.

33. The conflation and confusion of relationships that flow from patrilateral parallel cousin unions explain to some extent, perhaps, why both alliance and descent theory have remained notably silent on FBD marriage systems (see Bourdieu 1977). Here kinship and affinity are not rigidly opposed or separated, despite Fortes's claim (1962:2) that this dichotomy must exist in "every social system." In short, the boundaries between wife-giving and wife-taking groupings, as units of alliance, are always distinctly ambiguous.

34. A qualification should be made here. When such claims are successful, an individual may then go on to seek higher position,

again by redefining rank relations; but, if he chooses to do so, he will proceed by construing relative statuses in a progressive sequence. His first effort will be to assert his seniority within a segment, thereby claiming to be its elder and configuring a set of immediate relations around himself. Once this position is achieved, he proceeds to stress the seniority of that segment vis-à-vis other units; by doing this, he seeks to define a yet wider range of ties by extension from the first; and so on. The process, therefore, is one of gradual elimination of ambiguity from ever wider fields of sociopolitical linkages.

35. A gift ostensibly presented at the successful completion of negotiations to arrange a marriage (see chap. 5).

36. This text is reproduced from J. L. Comaroff 1980, an essay that contains a more detailed analysis of affinity than is possible here.

37. At funerary rites, one of the most important public activities is the *tatolo,* held after the burial, at which the genealogy of the deceased is enunciated. This usually draws great interest and close attention, for it is here that his career is summarized and the state of his field of relations, encoded in the appropriate terms, is spelled out.

Chapter Three

1. In an unpublished report to the Bechuanaland Protectorate Administration. Quoted in Schapera 1943a:4.

2. Of course, many disputes involve disagreement over the facts at issue. This, however, tends to take place in the context of an *agreed* normative paradigm. Among the Tswana, argument occurs usually over *either* facts *or* norms, rarely over both simultaneously (see below for examples).

3. Most commentators hold that, in Western societies, the capacity of innovation in the law to produce social change is very limited (Aubert 1966:99).

4. This description of *mekgwa le melao* has implications not merely for the comparative study of "customary law" but, more generally, for recent debate on the nature of African systems of thought, of which normative orders are patently an integral part. Some time ago, Worsley (1957, reprinted 1970:300) noted the tendency, particularly in structural functionalist analyses, to stress the unity of belief and ideology in non-Western cultures. Especially with the revival of the intellectualist position, most commonly associated with the writings of Horton (e.g., 1967), the predilection for seeking logical coherence at the experiential level in such non-Western

systems has continued to be manifest, despite the efforts of some authors (e.g., Lukes 1970; Hollis 1970; Gellner 1970) to underline the hazards. J. Comaroff (1980) has considered the complexity of the problem with respect to Tshidi cosmology and the management of misfortune. On the one hand, as she demonstrates, actors' everyday experience of their universe is replete with contradiction and ambiguity; indeed, the repertoire of (invoked) beliefs has an apparently *anti*systemic quality. Yet, on the other, this antisystemic quality is itself predicated on a discoverable semantic structure. While this is not a wholly novel observation, she goes on to suggest that a central problem in the analysis of "thought systems" lies in accounting for the relationship between that structure and the nature of everyday experience. This, of course, parallels our statements in chapter 2 regarding the articulation of the constitutive and lived-in levels of the Tswana sociocultural order.

5. Elsewhere (Comaroff and Roberts 1977a) we have considered the answers offered in the existing literature. We sought to show that all these answers are based on factors extrinsic to the process of legal argument—e.g., the structure of dispute-settlement agencies—and that none of them bears empirical scrutiny. We took care, however, not to dismiss the possibility that extrinsic factors might eventually prove important, but we suggested, as we do here, that the intrinsic form of legal argument provides an explanation that, for purposes of comparative study, might profitably be synthesized with (or subsumed in) structural considerations.

6. The degree to which "the rules" are insulated from the arguments in which they are invoked is illustrated by the fact that people in *kgotla* seldom attend closely to the parts of a speech concerning direct exposition of rules but begin to listen carefully when the speech moves on to the actions of the persons involved in the case. A noticeable feature of the records kept in the Tswana chiefly courts is that sections of speeches delivered in the formal code are seldom recorded. This puzzled us at first, since it was clear from listening to disputes that *both* codes were often used. When we discussed this matter with clerks, they would say, simply, "Yes, of course, so-and-so said a few words about marriage, but we never record these statements." The implication was that the rules themselves are not contentious.

7. The texts reproduced here are translations of contemporary verbatim transcripts taken in Setswana by a court clerk in Mochudi. For reasons of space we have had to edit them, but we have attempted to retain the fullest possible version.

8. At the time of this dispute, Mmatlhong was about eighty years old, being a member of the *Kuka* age-regiment (formed in 1901).

9. *Serotwana* is a mode of devolution, analogous to dowry, practiced by the Kgatla. It is discussed further in chapter 6.

10. Since the Kgatla did not arrive in their present territory until 1871, it seems unlikely that this site ever had been cultivated.

11. Although the main actors in this case lived in different intracapital wards, they occupied adjoining sites alongside their lands between November and June.

12. *Monna* (lit. "man") is generally used to address a man who is either junior to the speaker or a familiar age-mate.

13. The utterance of these two obscenities constitutes an almost stereotyped sequence of abuse; however, except when exchanged between youthful members of the same age-regiment, they are taken very seriously and often lead to fighting.

14. This recalls a statement made by Raditladi at the segment meeting; "Modisana" refers to Raditladi's agnatic segment. Mmusi and Mmamotalala, mentioned in the previous sentence, were members of the ward into which Kwetse had married. (All others are included in the genealogy.)

15. Raphiri was married to Mmatlhong's daughter. The fact that he had accepted Mogorosi's warning was strong evidence for the latter's claim, for, by the *serotwana* arrangement according to which the field had been transmitted, it would have been inherited by Raphiri's wife on Mmatlhong's death. Hence he would have had a direct interest in rebutting Mogorosi's warning if he had thought that the transfer had not taken place. Mogobye was the husband of the daughter of Raditladi's brother, Phopi.

16. Tswana distinguish sharply between cleared ploughing fields and bushland, which is usually held to be commonage under the ownership of the chief. This distinction became a crucial factor in the final judgment.

17. This refers to the earlier meetings of the agnatic segment, at which the first conciliatory efforts were made.

18. Nkonyane was the oldest living sibling of Mogorosi. He was, however, Mogorosi's half-brother, having been born into a senior house. As such, he had succeeded to his father's position as head of the segment.

19. In order to clarify our use of terms, we reiterate that, by "explicit reference," we mean a normative statement that may be understood without reference to the facts or context of a particular case; an "implicit reference" is one in which facts are adduced in such a way as to be comprehensible only in terms of an accepted (but unstated) norm. Moreover, explicit invocations may be direct ("It is the law that . . .") or indirect (e.g., "I ask whether it is proper that . .") in their formulation and phrasing.

20. Indeed, Mooki's wife stated in evidence that he had said that he was not actually dividing his estate. He simply wished to give Namayapela his portion in order to terminate the relationship.

21. He could do so because the disputants did not differ over the normative bases of the three aspects of the argument taken separately; rather, they disagreed on the norms at issue in the dispute *as a whole.*

22. Cases among the Tswana vary widely in the extent to which the disputants are interrupted and questioned by intervening third parties. When this does occur, it appears to follow the same general principles as those observed in the discourse of litigants and judges. In most cases, the questioning proceeds on the basis of the facts as described and interpreted by the disputants. Only when a questioner attempts to impugn the paradigm of one of the disputants are norms likely to be expressly invoked.

Chapter Four

1. By 1969–70, the attempt to reach a mediated settlement, prior to a formal hearing at the chief's *kgotla,* had become a regular administrative procedure among the Tshidi. When disputants presented themselves to the tribal secretary for a date to be set for their hearing, they were asked to outline their cases to him, and he tried—sometimes successfully—to resolve the matter. The Tshidi tend to describe such outcomes as informal settlements effected at the chief's *kgotla.*

2. A disputant may also attempt to establish a supporter in the guise of neutral mediator in order to appear to be seeking a settlement; it is regarded as morally creditable to be seen to be engaging in at least some settlement-directed efforts.

3. Where appropriate, names of participants in the various cases have been abbreviated and/or altered to protect their identities.

4. Transient (determinate) relationships are those in which the link between the parties ends when the relevant exchange or transaction has been completed; for example, the one supplies a good or a service to the other in return for immediate payment. Delictual relations also fall into this category. An enduring determinate relationship among Tswana is exemplified by the sharing of a common boundary between agricultural holdings by two otherwise unrelated (noncoresident) men. We employ the term "determinate" with some reservations; however, we are not aware of another usage that would connote exactly what we intend here. "Contractual" has too limited and specific a meaning, while "single-

stranded" (or "simplex") is too general and refers primarily to form rather than content.

5. The tendency to construct arguments, in disputes over relationships, by focusing on a particular right or object is extremely widespread among Sotho-Tswana.

6. We do not argue that litigants' goals and relations are the *only* factors that inform the course of dispute processes; we merely suggest that they constitute the two primary dimensions in which most circumstantial and social considerations are subsumed and expressed among Tswana. Kuper (1971:23 f.), for example, has discussed the significance of the relationship of the court to the parties. He asserts that this factor, in conjunction with that of litigants' relations (as identified by Gluckman, 1955a:21 and passim), influences the chosen mode of settlement. While we did not find the relationship of the parties to the court to be an independently significant factor and hence do not deal with it here, the point might indeed be important for purposes of comparative analysis.

7. We reiterate that an individual's agricultural holdings outside his village of domicile may border on those of unrelated members of other wards.

8. A variant of this situation occurs when either disputant recruits a third party to accompany him to discuss the incident with the other. Under these conditions the third party may act as a mediator in order to expedite a settlement.

9. Had he done so, of course, the dispute would have been transformed into one of type (4) (see below).

10. Among the South African Tshidi, the right to allocate land lying outside the village has become somewhat ill-defined in recent years. In theory such land is divided by the chief among the ward headmen, who then distribute it. But this arrangement in turn depends on the rule that every citizen must be domiciled in a (village-based) ward, an arrangement that is becoming gradually more difficult for local authorities to sustain (J. L. Comaroff 1976). As a result, agnatic segments established permanently outside Mafikeng have tended to gain some autonomy with respect to landholding and distribution, and patterns "on the ground" are diverging increasingly further from the ideal. Rre-L's segment was effectively domiciled outside the capital. He was the only member who still retained a homestead in the village.

11. The areas of the Tshidi chiefdom outside the capital are grouped into "provinces" comprising one or more villages and agricultural holdings (see chap. 1). Each has a headman whose homestead is in the central village of the province. Some provincial headmen, however, also hold offices (as ward or section headmen)

in Mafikeng. In these circumstances they either move regularly between their two residences or appoint a representative to act in their stead at one of them. As we pointed out earlier, the Tshidi, unlike most Tswana, have *five* levels in their hierarchy of agencies; where they are active, the *kgotla*s of the section headmen fall between those of the ward and the chief.

12. I.e., the headman had become an indebted client of Rre-S.

13. Motshegare's approach to this whole quarrel must have been colored by the fact that his own daughter had been promised marriage by a Masiana man who then deserted her after the birth of a child. The dispute over that incident had dragged on for several years and remained a source of tension during the period in question.

14. Typically, those related to chiefly legislative pronouncements (cf. Schapera 1943a).

Chapter Five

1. The vernacular term varies from chiefdom to chiefdom, as does the content of the gift. For convenience, we refer to it throughout as *dilo tsa patlo*.

2. There is evidence that this tendency is not new. As case 25 indicates, some unions were established with little formality as long ago as 1920, and it is possible that this is also true of "marriages" established before then.

3. Schapera suggests otherwise: *patlo* must occur, he states, for a marriage to be regarded as "proper" (1938:131–32), and, "no matter what other ceremonies have been observed, no form of cohabitation . . . is ever considered a true marriage until these [*bogadi*] animals have been given . . . ; if it [*bogadi*] is still outstanding, the couple are held to be living in concubinage" (1940b:73). As the cases below will demonstrate, the definition of unions turns out to be rather more complex than this.

4. Schapera (1938, 1940b) recognizes that arrangements for the actual transfer of bridewealth vary between the different Tswana chiefdoms. He is nevertheless consistent in associating the payment of *bogadi* (or the promise of payment) with the jural validity of a marriage. In a survey conducted in February, 1973, however, Roberts found that, of thirty-one couples living together in open and continuous cohabitation in the Rampedi ward in Mochudi, four had not obtained the agreement of their kin and no prestations had passed between the two groupings. Moreover, in ten cases (32 percent) no *bogadi* had been transferred. In twenty-one cases (68 percent) both *dilo tsa patlo* and *bogadi* had been presented, while, in

another six (19 percent), only the former had passed. These figures are included only to give a broad idea of incidences; in the absence of contextual material to indicate the timing and circumstances of the transfers, they are of limited use.

5. As Adam Kuper (personal communication) has reminded us, it is often argued that "the point of delaying payment may be precisely that the debt *is* the relationship, balanced by the continued claim of the wife's people on the children. The payment of *bogadi* ends this at the moment when a new series of debt relationships is being established, with a different balance of claims, perhaps with the same people." This is consistent with the view that the *creation* of a debt, and not necessarily its defrayal, may define a marriage. Significantly, however, Kgatla and Rolong informants tend themselves to offer a different interpretation: the deferral of *bogadi* transfers leaves room for maneuver and the possibility of repudiating one set of ties in the course of creating another. Defrayal, on the other hand, closes options and generates constraints. In other words, the significance of deferred payment, as it is experienced from *within* the system, lies in the micropolitics of career management. We shall consider this further in the latter half of the chapter.

6. This case history is compiled from reports of the dispute given to Roberts by Motshegare Ramalepa, Segonyane Dithare, Amos Kgamanyane Pilane, and other Kgatla informants and from records of the hearing before the Tlagadi *kgotla* and the chief's *kgotla* (Case No. 51 of 1962). The original records were translated by Passevil Phumaphi.

7. Such a union enjoys approval among the Kgatla, who often state a man should first seek a wife among his (real or classificatory) mother's brother's daughters.

8. This would have been a perfectly acceptable sororatic arrangement had Madubu's senior kinsmen agreed to it (see Schapera 1938).

9. This amount, if correct, would have constituted a generous provision. Through this assertion, Molefe suggests that Madubu may be at fault as a poor home manager.

10. I.e., Mmaseteba, Mankge's third wife.

11. He alludes here to a dispute that arose following the birth of children to Madubu's younger sister.

12. The speaker refers to the fact that Sebopelo, the Masiana headman, and other senior members of the Masiana *kgotla* were absent from the initial discussion of Madubu's future. The implication is that the meeting was improperly conducted.

13. One of Rankatsu's sons.

14. Motshegare refers to an undertaking Molefe had given when he had previously been ordered to maintain Madubu.

15. I.e., the children borne by Madubu's younger sister under the sororatic arrangement.

16. Two senior members of the Tlagadi ward who had allegedly been delegated by Motshegare to make the allotment.

17. All other aspects of the dispute—e.g., the status of the sororatic relationship and the affiliation of the children, the issue of neglect, and the residential rights of Madubu—were ultimately subsumed in this question.

18. Of course, her kinsmen denied that this was the case, and it is unlikely that these negotiations were formally conducted. It is significant, however, that Madubu claimed that they had been, for it emphasizes that circumstantial ambiguities surround many of the incidents associated with the marriage process and that litigants may exploit them in making their cases. Had the occurrence of *patlo* represented a nonnegotiable incident, Madubu could never have argued in the way she did. Presumably she hoped that the visit of Lekula to Mookane could be construed as *patlo* negotiations, and, had her kinsmen supported this view, it might have been difficult for Molefe to establish a contrary interpretation.

19. In fact, Letsebe had no option, given his actions at the meeting of the agnatic segment. Any other argument would have involved the tacit admission that he and his agnates had flouted an accepted procedural norm by terminating a marriage, an order only a chief can give. Since this norm touches directly on chiefly authority, Letsebe might have feared being fined yet again for contempt.

20. This is not to say that Tswana do not, or cannot, classify any ongoing relationships. For example, a small number are viewed as unlikely ever to become marriages; they are seen as being firmly situated at the informal end of the continuum. The emic stereotype of such relationships is provided by transient workers, visiting a chiefdom, who enter casual unions with no intention of sustaining them. Conversely, some bonds are indisputably seen as marriages, having lasted a long time. Most, however, occupy the middle ground between the two polarities for much of their duration, and it is these we concentrate on here. Ongoing casual relationships, in which the parties expressly preserve only a limited commitment throughout, fall outside the ambit of the present analysis—a reservation that should be borne in mind in the context of the general statements made here.

21. One obvious context in which the creation of new statuses may be expressed is kinship terminology. However, since the Tswana pattern of close-kin marriage generates a complex overlap of relational categories, the establishment of an affinal link often cannot be marked off exclusively in this way. In addition, the terms for affines (*bagwe/bagwagadi*) are used freely for addressing and

referring to a wide range of people—a fact that Tswana explain by saying, "It is because we all marry each other all the time."

22. In the past, the more frequent practice of the levirate and sororate made the status of many unions even more ambiguous and open to negotiation. Indeed, much political competition among the Tswana revolved around the effort to manipulate the relative seniority of houses, and this generally involved the successive redefinition of the rank and status of cowives (J. L. Comaroff 1978). Because the levirate and sororate are of decreasing importance in modern Tswana life (although they still figure in political rivalry and the retrospective definition of genealogical rank), we do not consider them in any detail here.

23. As we said earlier, this is less likely to be the case if *bogadi* has been presented, unless the status of the transfer itself is questioned (as it is, for example, by Lesoka in case 25). We reiterate, however, that early transfers, which may constrain competitive negotiation, occur quite rarely in many communities.

24. Again, Madubu's efforts to have her relationship with Molefe classified as a marriage demonstrably had its basis in material advantage (case 9).

25. Case No. 63 of 1968, heard in the chief's *kgotla* at Mochudi.

26. Some Rolong informants liken this to the situation in the past, when a *mmelegi* ("nurse," "helper"), usually a younger sister, accompanied a woman to her husband's homestead and was impregnated by him. In such circumstances, debate often followed as to whether the girl was a *mmelegi*, a *seantlo*, or an independent wife.

27. Case No. 4 of 1961, heard in the chief's *kgotla* at Mochudi.

28. We may speculate that by this time it would have become apparent to Tollo that the case was running against him. His admission that Motlakadibe was his wife may thus have been an attempt to solicit the leniency of the chief and to even matters up: by agreeing that a marriage existed, the defendant was also accusing Motlakadibe of adultery (of which she could not have been guilty were she not married) and, hence, was claiming an infringement of his rights *in uxorem* over her. Given the vigor of Thage's argument for the validity of the marriage, Tollo might have used this ploy as a second resort, which, in effect, balanced his neglect against her adultery and might have been anticipated to lessen the prospect of a costly property disposition.

29. The account of case 12 is drawn from discussions Roberts held with Kgatla informants at Mochudi during February 1973 and from the record of Case No. 83 of 1964, heard in the chief's *kgotla*.

30. This fact provides further evidence for our statement (p. 158) that, despite the stated norms, *exclusive* rights to sexual access

(and hence to compensation when these are violated) are ultimately contingent on the *presentation* of *bogadi*.

31. Case No. 24 of 1965.

32. Case No. 25 of 1966.

33. The normative precept, as we have noted, also conflicts with the tendency to award substantial property dispositions to the divorced woman. Here, however, Nkidi was awarded no property. There are several possible reasons for this somewhat exceptional outcome, the most likely of which is that Nkidi precipitated the dissolution of the marriage by returning of her own accord to her agnates. The latter did not petition the chief on her behalf, so that she was not the complainant in the case and hence not the party seeking compensation. Since no fault had accrued to Moakofi in the first instance, it is difficult to see how the chief could have made an award to Nkidi.

34. Case No. 45 of 1965.

35. The distinction between cases of divorce and those in which a casual union has become the object of dispute tends to be clearly made by the settlement agencies, which usually offer an explicit definition of the relationship under scrutiny.

36. Kuper (1975a:72) notes that, while Tswana tend to speak of the *losika* as if it were a bilateral stock (which it would be if all marriages were between kin), there is some ambiguity associated with the term. The Rolong appear to use it to connote a bilateral stock when they are discussing kinship in the abstract; but when informants talk of kinship relations in the behavioral context, the *losika* is almost invariably characterized as an ego-centered field (see also chap. 2).

37. A "multiple" relationship, it will be remembered, is one in which two people are linked by more than one relationship *category* (i.e., agnation, matrilaterality, etc.). It thus contrasts with Gluckman's notion of a "multiplex" bond, which may involve a single relationship category but always entails a multiplicity of role relationships.

38. Because the events and relationships described here are still of a highly sensitive nature to those concerned, we have not only changed the names of all relevant persons but have also not identified the community in which the case occurred. This particular case involves a royal career, but J. L. Comaroff (1980) provides another one, rather more detailed, which demonstrates that essentially similar processes occur among commoners too.

39. Because the period of fieldwork ended soon after the installation, we are unable to document subsequent events.

40. Limitations of space preclude a detailed descriptive analysis

of the relationship between affinity and the management of marriage. This question, and it is a complex one, is discussed more fully in the essays listed in the footnote on page 132. We should like to stress, however, that we do not suggest that the negotiability and ambiguity surrounding the conjugal bond are never removed. The final removal of such ambiguity, which is closely linked to the final payment of bridewealth and the structural "fixing" of unions, is analyzed in J. L. Comaroff 1980.

Chapter Six

1. Some of the ideas developed in this chapter were first discussed in Roberts and Comaroff 1979, and there is thus some overlap between the two. Since the earlier paper was addressed to property devolution among the Kgatla, our present examples and cases are drawn primarily from this ethnographic source; in any case, available records of comparable property disputes among the Rolong are unsatisfactorily brief. The Rolong and Kgatla share, however, a markedly similar devolution system. The differences between them, where relevant, will be noted in the text.

2. Although there has been little systematic investigation of processes of property devolution in England, it is well known that devolution there is sometimes associated with incidents other than death. The device of settlement is one of long standing, and, since the latter part of the nineteenth century, the introduction of death duties has involved lawyers in major exertions to dissociate the passage of property from the incident of death.

3. The *serotwana* practice appears to constitute an instance of dowry, pace Goody (1973), who seems to suggest that such marriage transfers do not occur in Africa, except in areas of Muslim influence.

4. Land is rarely, if ever, included in the unallocated balance; it is generally divided among the houses earlier in the developmental cycle.

5. Rolong rules are almost identical to those of the Kgatla, except that, among them, greater flexibility is shown with respect to the devolution of unallocated cattle to daughters. This may be linked to the fact that in Rolong society the practice of *serotwana* is not universal and that the practice of *tshwaiso* seems to be on the decline.

6. Case 17 was related by Amos Kgamanyane Pilane and Selogwe Pilane. Their account is confirmed by the transcript of the case in the chief's *kgotla* (No. 22 of 1957).

7. Many Kgatla told Roberts of this case, including Amos Kga-

manyane Pilane, Senwelo Sejoe, and Dikeme's son, Selogwe. Their accounts agree on the facts stated here.

8. Case 19 was related by Molelekwa Selemogwe and other Kgatla. The hearing in the chief's *kgotla* is recorded as Case No. 51 of 1963. The statements of Gouwe and Mothei are translations of the vernacular record.

9. Schapera (1938). Such case histories as are available also confirm this.

10. See Roberts 1971, 1972a.

11. We are grateful to Segonyane (Mankge's second son), Motshegare (headman of the ward in which Mankge lived), and Amos Kgamanyane Pilane for the details of the estate described in case 20.

12. The term *boswa* is not used to refer to any other part of the estate; it is reserved exclusively to describe the unallocated residue.

13. Roberts and Comaroff 1979; see also chap. 3, above. We outline merely the essence of the argument here.

14. Many Rolong informants suggest, moreover, that a man tends to favor the children of the woman to whom he is currently married, since she is in a position to influence him. This, of course, would have the effect of prejudicing the interests of their older half-siblings.

15. Case 21 was related by Amos Kgamanyane Pilane. See also Case No. 26 of 1958 and No. 13 of 1961.

16. It is to be noted that the chief did *not* order Kgasane to transfer the residue of the herd under Senwelo's management. This may be explained by the fact that his earlier judgment—which reproved the old man for his dilatory behavior and effectively divided the stock at issue—implied the recognized devolution of most of Kgasane's assets; hence the relatively small proportion left over, the control of which was not under dispute, could easily have been viewed as potential *boswa* and therefore still under the rightful ownership of the father.

17. Case 22 was related by Amos Kgamanyane Pilane. See also Case No. 8 of 1964 at the chief's *kgotla,* Mochudi.

18. Ratsheola *kgotla* is a subdivision of the large Kgosing section, which falls directly under the jurisdiction of the chief. As a result, the chief could be approached by Motsisi in the first instance, as a headman would be in other wards.

19. On some occasions among Rolong, large assets (e.g., tractors) are allocated jointly, and their management may lead to friction.

20. Case No. 18 of 1954, at the chief's *kgotla,* Mochudi.

21. This is the only ranking rule that is effectively nonnegotiable (see J. L. Comaroff 1978).

22. Tshidi informants often point this out, and historical evidence (J. L. Comaroff 1973) shows it to have a solid grounding in fact.

23. Whether or not filiation is publicly repudiated, the absence of devolutionary transfers in some cases certainly leaves the status of the relationship ambiguous and open to doubt, and it often leads to dispute.

24. The nature of the connection between property (and, more broadly, economic) relations and the kinship order has, of course, been the object of considerable theoretical debate, most vigorously entered by Fortes (e.g., 1969:200 ff.), Worsley (1956 passim), Leach (1961), and Tambiah (1965). While our own position will be seen to differ significantly from that of each of these writers, we do not intend to address the general issue here; at this stage we are concerned merely with outlining the indigenous viewpoint on the subject.

25. As our description of the fields of tension would suggest, this restricted form of dispute is particularly characteristic of cases involving intrahouse relations. Intergenerational and interhouse disagreement, in that order, are progressively less likely to be contained in this way. It should also be noted that, when parties to property disputes state their claims strictly in terms of control over interests, they are in fact implying their acceptance of an extant definition of the relationship between them. This is an implication that appears to be clearly understood both by litigants and by dispute-settlement agencies.

26. Case No. 9 of 1964 at the chief's *kgotla,* Mochudi.

27. Case No. 75 of 1965 at the chief's *kgotla,* Mochudi. Also related, among others, by Samotho Molwane.

Chapter Seven

1. Schapera (1963a:169) adds explicitly that the "configuration of kinship disputes" among commoners and royals is much the same.

2. One involved a MB who, in his capacity as a diviner, claimed doctoring fees from his ZS. In the second case the defendant was a ZS who had engaged in the verbal abuse of his MB; before the *kgotla* he asserted (unsuccessfully) that he had merely been indulging in a joking relationship with the older man.

3. We shall examine cases involving nonrelated persons and distant kin in the next section, where we discuss the relationship between different modes of dispute and rules and outcomes.

4. Schapera does not include a figure for this category for the Tswana at large, but we know of no cases involving linked siblings and of few between brothers and their (non-linked) full sisters.

5. Moreover, only a small proportion of agnatic rivalries actually end in *kgotla* cases; these rivalries are a constant feature of everyday interaction, and it is only under particular conditions (see chap. 4) that open confrontation is precipitated.

6. If guardianship has been vested in anyone else—especially a FB or a ¹/₂B—the disputes that arise out of it will occur in one of the other two fields of tension, i.e., intergenerational or interhouse relations. Under such conditions, conflict within the house is unlikely to surface at all; if anything, the interests of its members, whatever their respective ages, will converge, at least temporarily, against an outsider.

7. Guardians occasionally do volunteer to hand over the inheritance of their siblings without delay, but, as both Tswana believe and observation confirms, their failure to do so occurs with extraordinary regularity. When pressed for possible motives to explain voluntary relinquishment, informants frequently lighted on a transcendent interest, one whose greater utility for the guardian might take precedence. A hypothetical example, offered by a Rolong commoner, suggested that, if he wished to compete for an office, the older brother might seek to arrange a union for an acquiescent sibling in order to recruit the support of his prospective affines; in return for transferring this sibling's portion and helping to establish his independence, the older brother would expect considerable good will to accrue to him.

8. That this is so is not fully reflected in Schapera's figures (1963a), but that is because he includes brotherly and halfbrotherly disputes in a single category and also excludes from it rivalries that involve (royal) succession and the transmission of authority.

9. It should again be recalled that Schapera's data do not include royal-succession disputes (see n. 8). If they did, the proportion of FB/BS disputes would probably be considerably higher.

10. This is one of the reasons why, notwithstanding their utility as gross indicators, Schapera's figures ought to be treated with caution; for many cases ostensibly arising out of marriage and affinity are not necessarily about these matters alone, even though argument might revolve around the status of a particular union. Furthermore, most actions between spouses involve affines as well, and vice versa, so that the designation of a case as being about "marriage" or "affinity" may be less a reflection of its substance and motivation than of its rhetorical presentation.

11. Elsewhere (Comaroff and Roberts 1977b) we have considered the dialectics of legal change, with special reference to marriage. Moreover, J. L. Comaroff, in a paper entitled "Class and Culture in the Political Economy of an African Chiefdom," read at

Stanford University in 1979, has considered the systemic dialectics of the Tswana sociocultural order at large. This essay, currently being prepared for publication, is intended to foreshadow a lengthier study on the subject.

12. See chapter 4. The fact that the category of dispute depends on its construction and presentation by the litigants is itself a corollary of the existing arrangement, whereby virtually all cases are formulated by (or for) a complainant on his own account and are responded to by a defendant in the terms he chooses. The agencies rarely bring an action against anybody on their own initiative or seek to impose a priori limits on a debate presented to them.

13. This is not to suggest that judgments are utterly mechanical and uniform in cases of types 1 and 2. Apart from all else, the agencies may vary, even in ostensibly similar disputes, with respect to the fines and compensations they order and the degree to which they allow mitigating considerations to absolve a defendant of responsiblity. Chiefs, in particular, place differing weight on such factors as whether the conflict was brought about by chance or by malicious intent; whether or not the precipitating action was the first of its kind perpetrated by the individual concerned; the relative rectitude with which the parties behaved at the time of the events under dispute and in seeking a settlement thereafter; and so on. Nonetheless, from the perspective of both the litigants and the public at large, such considerations are expressed *within* the context of judgments made with reference to *mekgwa le melao*.

14. For another demonstration of this general rhetorical tendency, see case 25. This discussion further illuminates our use of the concept of "paradigms of argument" (see chap. 3). Once a litigant imposes a normative theme on a case, a set of interdependent *mekgwa* becomes relevant to his suit. (Indeed, it is this set that defines the case as, say, a "land dispute" or a "marriage dispute.") This normative theme then becomes the referential paradigm in terms of which his rhetoric is to be organized and evaluated.

Chapter Eight

1. Indeed, it has been a central assumption of our account that the examination of rhetorical and speech forms is fundamental to the analysis of the dispute process. On the whole, even in the very best legal ethnographies, this aspect has been largely ignored. Yet it is quite patently essential if one is to comprehend both the deployment of rules and the relationship between norm and process (see Bloch, ed., 1975).

2. It is also to be noted that the link between the allocation of conjugal rights and statuses and compliance with formal procedure is undergoing transformation in both North America and the British Commonwealth. A fundamental change of attitude has been revealed by some recent decisions in disputes over property between unmarried cohabitants and by such legislation as the British Columbia Family Relations Act (1972), which imposes maintenance obligations on the basis of cohabitation alone. Ironically, then, it appears that the jural approach to marriage is becoming less applicable in Western contexts; under these conditions, sociocultural models derived from Africa may become progressively more informative.

Bibliography

Abel, R. L.
  1973   A Comparative Theory of Dispute Institutions in Society.
         Law and Society Review 8:217–347.
Ardener, E. W.
  1971   The New Anthropology and Its Critics. *Man* (n.s.) 6:
         449–67.
Asad, T.
  1972   Market Model, Class Structure · and Consent: A Re-
         consideration of Swat Political Organisation. *Man* (n.s.)
         7:74–94.
Aubert, V.
  1966   Some Social Functions of Legislation. *Acta Sociologica*
         10:99–110. (Reprinted in V. Aubert, ed., *Sociology of
         Law*. Harmondsworth: Penguin, 1969.)
Ayoub, V.
  1961   Review: The Judicial Process in Two African Societies. In
         Community Political Systems, vol. 1, *International Yearbook
         of Political Behavior Research,* ed. M. Janowitz. Glencoe,
         Ill.: Free Press.
Bailey, F. G.
  1960   *Tribe, Caste and Nation: A Study of Political Activity and
         Political Change in Highland Orissa.* Manchester: Man-
         chester University Press.
Barkun, M.
  1968   *Law without Sanctions: Order in Primitive Societies and the
         World Community.* New Haven and London: Yale Uni-
         versity Press.
Barth, F.
  1959   *Political Leadership among Swat Pathans.* London School
         of Economics Monograph no. 19. London: Athlone
         Press.

1966   *Models of Social Organization.* Occasional Paper no. 23.
London: Royal Anthropological Institute.
1973   Descent and Marriage Reconsidered. In *The Character of Kinship*, ed. J. Goody. Cambridge, Eng.: At the University Press.
Barton, R. F.
1919   *Ifugao Law.* University of California Publications in American Archeology and Ethnology 15:1–186.
Beattie, J.
1957   Informal Judicial Activity in Bunyoro. *Journal of African Administration* 9:188–95.
Berndt, R. M.
1962   *Excess and Restraint: Social Control among a New Guinea Mountain People.* Chicago: University of Chicago Press.
Blau, P. M.
1964   *Exchange and Power in Social Life.* New York: Wiley.
Bloch, M. ed.
1975   *Political Language and Oratory in Traditional Society.* London and New York: Academic Press.
Bloch, M.
1977   The Past and the Present in the Present. *Man* (n.s.) 12:278–92.
Bohannan, P.
1957   *Justice and Judgment among the Tiv.* London: Oxford University Press for the International African Institute. (2d ed., with new preface, 1968.)
1969   Ethnography and Comparison in Legal Anthropology. In *Law in Culture and Society,* ed. L. Nader. Chicago: Aldine.
Botswana, Republic of
1975   *Statistical Abstracts, 1975.* Gaborone: Ministry of Finance and Development Planning, Central Statistics Office.
1976   *The Rural Incomes Distribution Survey in Botswana 1974–5.* Gaborone: Ministry of Finance and Development Planning, Central Statistics Office.
Bourdieu, P.
1977   *Outline of a Theory of Practice.* Cambridge, Eng.: At the University Press.
Brown, J. T.
1931   *Secwana Dictionary.* Tigerkloof: London Missionary Society.
Butler, J., Rotberg, R. I., Adams, J. eds.
1977   *The Black Homelands of South Africa: The Political and Economic Development of Bophuthatswana and KwaZulu.* Perspectives on Southern Africa, no. 21. Berkeley: University of California Press.

Casalis, J. E.
1859 Les Bassoutos. Paris: Meyrueis. (English translation: The
      Basutos. London: Nisbet, 1861.)
Cohen, A. P.
1975 The Management of Myths. Manchester: Manchester Uni-
      versity Press.
Cohen, A. P. and Comaroff, J. L.
1976 The Management of Meaning: On the Phenomenology of
      Political Transactions. In Transaction and Meaning, ed.
      B. Kapferer. Association of Social Anthropologists, Essays
      in Social Anthropology, no. 1. Philadelphia: Institute for
      the Study of Human Issues.
Colson, E.
1953 Social Control and Vengeance in Plateau Tonga Society.
      Africa 23:199–212.
Comaroff, J.
1974 Barolong Cosmology: A Study of Religious Pluralism in a
      Tswana Town. Ph.D. dissertation, University of London.
1980 Healing and the Cultural Order: The Case of the Baro-
      long boo Ratshidi. American Ethnologist 7:637–57.
Comaroff, J. L.
1973 Competition for Office and Political Processes among the
      Barolong Boo Ratshidi. Ph.D. dissertation, University of
      London.
1974 Chiefship in a South African Homeland: A Case Study of
      the Tshidi Chiefdom of Bophuthatswana. Journal of
      Southern African Studies 1:36–51.
1975 Talking Politics: Oratory and Authority in a Tswana
      Chiefdom. In Political Language and Oratory in Tradi-
      tional Society, ed. M. Bloch. London and New York:
      Academic Press.
1976 Tswana Transformations, 1953–75. Supplementary
      chapter in I. Schapera, The Tswana, rev. ed. London:
      International African Institute.
1977 The Structure of Agricultural Transformation in Barolong.
      Gaborone: Botswana Government Printer.
1978 Rules and Rulers: Political Processes in a Tswana Chief-
      dom. Man (n.s.) 13:1–20.
1980 Bridewealth and the Control of Ambiguity in a Tswana
      Chiefdom. In The Meaning of Marriage Payments, ed. J. L.
      Comaroff. London and New York: Academic Press.
1981 Class and Culture in a Peasant Economy: The Transforma-
      tion of Land Tenure in Barolong. In Land Reform in
      the Making, ed. R. P. Werbner. London: International

African Institute and School of Oriental and African Studies.

Comaroff, J. L. and Comaroff, J.
1981   The Management of Marriage in a Tswana Chiefdom. In *Essays on African Marriage in Southern Africa,* ed. E. J. Krige and J. L. Comaroff. Cape Town: Juta.

Comaroff, J. L. and Roberts, S. A.
1977a   The Invocation of Norms in Dispute Settlement: The Tswana Case. In *Social Anthropology and Law,* ed. I. Hamnett. Association of Social Anthropologists Monograph no. 14. London: Academic Press.
1977b   Marriage and Extra-marital Sexuality: The Dialectics of Legal Change among the Kgatla. *Journal of African Law* 21:97–123.

Crick, M.
1976   *Explorations in Language and Meaning: Towards a Semantic Anthropology.* London: Malaby Press.

Cunnison, I. G.
1959   *The Luapula Peoples of Northern Rhodesia: Custom and History in Tribal Politics.* Manchester: Manchester University Press.

Dahrendorf, R.
1959   *Class and Class Conflict in Industrial Society.* Stanford: Stanford University Press.

Douglas, M.
1956   L'homme primitif et la loi. *Zaire* 10:367–74.

Dworkin, R.
1967   The Model of Rules. *University of Chicago Law Review* 35:14–46.

Epstein, A. L., ed.
1967   *The Craft of Social Anthropology.* London: Social Science Paperbacks, in association with Tavistock.
1973   The Reasonable Man Revisited: Some Problems in the Anthropology of Law. *Law and Society Review* 7:643–66.

Evans-Pritchard, Sir E. E.
1940   *The Nuer.* Oxford: Clarendon Press.
1951   *Kinship and Marriage among the Nuer.* Oxford: Clarendon Press.

Fallers, L.
1969   *Law without Precedent.* Chicago: University of Chicago Press.

Firth, Sir R.
1951   *Elements of Social Organisation.* London: Watts.

Fortes, M.
1962   Introduction. In *Marriage in Tribal Societies,* ed. M. Fortes. Cambridge, Eng.: At the University Press.

1969 *Kinship and the Social Order: The Legacy of Lewis Henry Morgan.* Chicago: Aldine.

Fox, R.
1967 *Kinship and Marriage.* Harmondsworth: Penguin Books.

Geertz, C.
1973 *The Interpretation of Cultures.* New York: Basic Books.

Gellner, E.
1970 Concepts and Society. In *Rationality,* ed. B. R. Wilson. Oxford: Basil Blackwell.

Giddens, A.
1979 *Central Problems in Social Theory: Action, Structure, and Contradiction in Social Analysis.* Berkeley: University of California Press.

Gluckman, M.
1955a *The Judicial Process among the Barotse of Northern Rhodesia (Zambia).* Manchester: Manchester University Press. (2d ed., with two additional chapters, 1967.)

1955b *Custom and Conflict in Africa.* Glencoe, Ill: Free Press; Oxford: Blackwell.

1963 *Order and Rebellion in Tribal Africa.* London: Cohen & West.

1965 *The Ideas in Barotse Jurisprudence.* New Haven and London: Yale University Press.

Goldschmidt, W.
1967 *Sebei Law.* Berkeley: University of California Press.

Goody, J.
1966 Introduction. In *Succession to High Office,* ed. J. Goody. Cambridge, Eng.: At the University Press.

1973 Bridewealth and Dowry in Africa and Eurasia. In *Bridewealth and Dowry,* by J. Goody and S. J. Tambiah. Cambridge, Eng.: At the University Press.

Gulliver, P. H.
1963 *Social Control in an African Society.* London: Routledge & Kegan Paul.

1969a Dispute Settlement without Courts: The Ndendeuli of Southern Tanzania. In *Law in Culture and Society,* ed. L. Nader. Chicago: Aldine.

1969b Introduction: Case Studies of Law in Non-Western Societies. In *Law in Culture and Society,* ed. L. Nader. Chicago: Aldine.

1971 *Neighbours and Networks: The Idiom of Kinship in Social Action among the Ndendeuli of Tanzania.* Berkeley: University of California Press.

1977 On Mediators. In *Social Anthropology and Law,* ed. I. Hamnett. Association of Social Anthropologists Monograph no. 14. London: Academic Press.

1979   *Disputes and Negotiations: A Cross-cultural Perspective.*
        New York and London: Academic Press.
Hamnett, I.
1975   *Chieftainship and Legitimacy: An Anthropological Study of
        Executive Law in Lesotho.* London: Routledge & Kegan
        Paul.
1977   Introduction. In *Social Anthropology and Law,* ed. I. Ham-
        nett. Association of Social Anthropologists Monograph
        no. 14. London: Academic Press.
Hart. H. L. A.
1961   *The Concept of Law.* Oxford: Clarendon Press.
Hobbes, T.
1651   *Leviathan.* London: printed for A. Crooke. (Reprinted
        1929. Oxford: Clarendon Press.)
Hoebel, E. A.
1940   *The Political Organization and Law-Ways of the Comanche
        Indians.* Memoir of the American Anthropological Asso-
        ciation no. 54. *Contributions from the Laboratory of An-
        thropology,* vol. 4.
1954   *The Law of Primitive Man.* Cambridge, Mass.: Harvard
        University Press.
Hollis, M.
1970   The Limits of Rationality. In *Rationality,* ed. B. R. Wil-
        son. Oxford: Basil Blackwell.
Horton, R.
1967   African Traditional Thought and Western Science. *Africa*
        37:50–71, 155–87.
Jeppe, W. J. O.
1974   Local Government in Botswana. In *Local Government
        in Southern Africa,* ed. W. B. Vosloo, D. A. Kotze, and
        W. J. O. Jeppe. Pretoria and Cape Town: Academica.
Kapferer, B., ed.
1976   *Transaction and Meaning: Directions in the Anthropology of
        Exchange and Symbolic Behavior.* Association of Social
        Anthropologists, Essays in Social Anthropology, no. 1.
        Philadelphia: Institute for the Study of Human Issues.
Koch, K. F.
1974   *War and Peace in Jálémo: The Management of Conflict in
        Highland New Guinea.* Cambridge, Mass.: Harvard Uni-
        versity Press.
Krige, J. D.
1939   Some Aspects of Lovhedu Judicial Arrangements. *Bantu
        Studies* 13:113–29.
Kuper, A.
1970   The Kgalagari and the Jural Consequences of Marriage.
        Man (n.s.) 5:466–82.

1971   Council Structure and Decision-making. In *Councils in Action,* ed. A. Richards and A. Kuper. Cambridge, Eng.: At the University Press.

1973   *Anthropologists and Anthropology: The British School 1922–1972.* Harmondsworth: Penguin.

1975a The Social Structure of the Sotho-Speaking Peoples of Southern Africa. *Africa* 45:67–81, 139–49.

1975b Preferential Marriage and Polygyny among the Tswana. In *Studies in African Social Anthropology,* ed. M. Fortes and S. Patterson. London: Academic Press.

Leach, Sir E. R.

1955   Polyandry, Inheritance and the Definition of Marriage. *Man* 55:182–86.

1961   *Pul Eliya: A Village in Ceylon.* Cambridge, Eng.: At the University Press.

Levi, E. H.

1949   *An Introduction to Legal Reasoning.* Chicago: University of Chicago Press.

Lukes, S.

1970   Some Problems about Rationality. In *Rationality,* ed. B. R. Wilson. Oxford: Basil Blackwell.

Maine, Sir Henry S.

1861   *Ancient Law.* London: Murray. (Reprinted by J. M. Dent & Sons as no. 734 in Everyman's Library, 1965.)

Malinowski, B.

1926   *Crime and Custom in Savage Society.* London: Kegan Paul, Trench, Trubner.

1934   Introduction to H. I. Hogbin, *Law and Order in Polynesia.* New York: Harcourt, Brace.

March, J. G.

1956   Sociological Jurisprudence Revisited: A Review (More or Less) of Max Gluckman. *Stanford Law Review* 8:499–534.

Matthews. Z. K.

1940   Marriage Customs among the Barolong. *Africa* 13:1–24.

1945   A Short History of the Tshidi Barolong. *Fort Hare Papers* 1:9–28.

Mitchell, J. C.

1963   Marriage, Matriliny and Social Structure among the Yao of Southern Nyasaland. In *Family and Marriage,* ed. J. Mogey. Leiden: Brill.

Molema, S. M.

1966   *Montshiwa, Barolong Chief and Patriot.* Cape Town: Struik.

Moore, S. F.

1969   Introduction: Comparative Studies. In *Law in Culture and Society,* ed. L. Nader. Chicago: Aldine.

1970   Law and Anthropology. In *Biennial Review of Anthropology, 1969,* ed. B. J. Siegel. Stanford: Stanford University Press.

1978   *Law as Process.* London: Routledge & Kegan Paul.

Murphy, R. F.

1971   *The Dialectics of Social Life: Alarms and Excursions in Anthropological Theory.* New York: Basic Books.

Murphy, R. F., and Kasdan, L.

1959   The Structure of Parallel Cousin Marriage. *American Anthropologist* 61:17–29.

1967   Agnation and Endogamy: Some Further Considerations. *Southwestern Journal of Anthropology* 23:1–14.

Murray, C.

1976   Marital Strategy in Lesotho: The Redistribution of Migrant Earnings. *African Studies* 35:99–121.

Myburgh, A. C.

1974   Law and Justice. In *The Bantu-Speaking Peoples of Southern Africa,* ed. W. D. Hammond-Tooke. London: Routledge & Kegan Paul.

Nader, L.

1965   The Anthropological Study of Law. *American Anthropologist* (special pub. *The Ethnography of Law*) 67 no. 6, pt. 2:3–32.

1969   Introduction. In *Law in Culture and Society,* ed. L. Nader. Chicago: Aldine.

Nader, L., and Yngvesson, B.

1973   On Studying the Ethnography of Law and Its Consequences. In *Handbook of Social and Cultural Anthropology,* ed. J. J. Honigmann. Chicago: Rand McNally.

Needham, R.

1971   Remarks on the Analysis of Kinship and Marriage. In *Rethinking Kinship and Marriage,* ed. R. Needham. Association of Social Anthropologists Monograph no. 11. London: Tavistock.

Paton, G. W.

1964   *A Text-Book of Jurisprudence.* 3d ed., ed. D. P. Derham. Oxford: Clarendon Press.

Peters, E. L.

1980   Aspects of Bedouin Bridewealth among Camel Herders in Cyrenaica. In *The Meaning of Marriage Payments,* ed. J. L. Comaroff. London and New York: Academic Press.

Pospisil, L.

1958a   *Kapauku Papuans and Their Law.* Yale University Publications in Anthropology no. 54. New Haven: Yale University Press.

1958b Social Change and Primitive Law: Consequences of a Papuan Legal Case. *American Anthropologist* 60:832–37.

1965 A Formal Analysis of Substantive Law: Kapauku Papuan Laws of Inheritance. *American Anthropologist* 67 no. 6, pt. 2:166–85.

1969 Structural Change and Primitive Law: Consequences of a Papuan Legal Case. In *Law in Culture and Society,* ed. L. Nader. Chicago: Aldine.

1971 *Anthropology of Law: A Comparative Theory.* New York: Harper & Row.

1972 *The Ethnology of Law.* Addison-Wesley Modular Publications, Module 12, pp. 1–40. Reading, Mass.: Addison-Wesley.

Radcliffe-Brown, A. R.

1933 Primitive Law. In *The Encyclopedia of the Social Sciences,* vol. 9, pp. 202–6. New York: Macmillan.

1950 Introduction. In *African Systems of Kinship and Marriage,* ed. A. R. Radcliffe-Brown and D. Forde. London: Oxford University Press for the International African Institute.

1952 *Structure and Function in Primitive Society.* London: Cohen & West.

Richardson, J.

1940 *Law and Status among the Kiowa Indians.* American Ethnological Society Monograph no. 1. Seattle: University of Washington Press.

Roberts, S. A.

1970 *The Kgatla Law of Succession to Property.* Gaborone: Government Printer.

1971 The Settlement of Family Disputes in the Kgatla Customary Courts: Some New Approaches. *Journal of African Law* 15:50–76.

1972a *Tswana Family Law.* Restatements of African Law no. 5. London: Sweet & Maxwell.

1972b The Survival of the Traditional Tswana Courts in the National Legal System of Botswana. *Journal of African Law* 16:111–13.

1976 Law and the Study of Social Control in Small-Scale Societies. *Modern Law Review* 39:663–79.

1977 The Kgatla Marriage: Concepts of Validity. In *Law and the Family in Africa,* ed. S. A. Roberts. The Hague and Paris: Mouton.

1981 Arable Land Tenure and Administrative Change in the Kgatleng. In *Land Reform in the Making,* ed. R. P. Werbner. London: International African Institute and School of Oriental and African Studies.

Roberts, S. A., and Comaroff, J. L.
  1979 A Chief's Decision and the Devolution of Property in a Tswana Chiefdom. In *Politics in Leadership,* ed. P. Cohen and W. Shack. Oxford: Clarendon Press. (Festschrift for Professor I. Schapera.)
Rose, A. M.
  1956 The Use of Law to Induce Social Change. *Transactions of the Third World Congress of Sociology* 6:52–63. London: International Sociological Association.
Sahlins, M.
  1965 On the Sociology of Primitive Exchange. In *The Relevance of Models for Social Anthropology,* ed. M. Banton. Association of Social Anthropologists Monograph no. 1. London: Tavistock.
  1972 *Stone Age Economics.* Chicago: Aldine-Atherton.
  1976 *Culture and Practical Reason.* Chicago: University of Chicago Press.
Schapera, I.
  1933 Premarital Pregnancy and Native Opinion: A Note on Social Change. *Africa* 6:59–89.
  1938 *A Handbook of Tswana Law and Custom.* London: Oxford University Press for the International African Institute.
  1940a The Political Organization of the Ngwato in Bechuanaland Protectorate. In *African Political Systems,* ed. M. Fortes and E. E. Evans-Pritchard. London: Oxford University Press for the International African Institute.
  1940b *Married Life in an African Tribe.* London: Faber.
  1943a *Tribal Legislation among the Tswana of the Bechuanaland Protectorate.* Monographs on Social Anthropology no. 9. London: London School of Economics.
  1943b Report on the Land-Tenure System of the Barolong Farms in the Bechuanaland Protectorate. Unpublished ms., held by the Botswana National Archives, Gaborone.
  1949 The Tswana Conception of Incest. In *Social Structure: Studies Presented to A. R. Radcliffe-Brown,* ed. M. Fortes. Oxford: Clarendon Press.
  1950 Kinship and Marriage among the Tswana. In *African Systems of Kinship and Marriage,* ed. A. R. Radcliffe-Brown and D. Forde. London: Oxford University Press for the International African Institute.
  1952 *The Ethnic Composition of Tswana Tribes.* Monographs on Social Anthropology no. 11. London: London School of Economics.
  1953 *The Tswana.* Ethnographic Survey of Africa, Part III. London: International African Institute.
  1956 *Government and Politics in Tribal Societies.* London: Watts.

1957a Malinowski's Theories of Law. In *Man and Culture: An Evaluation of the Work of Bronislow Malinowski,* ed. R. Firth. London: Routledge & Kegan Paul.
1957b Marriage of Near Kin among the Tswana. *Africa* 27: 139–59.
1963a Kinship and Politics in Tswana History. *Journal of the Royal Anthropological Institute* 93:159–73.
1963b Agnatic Marriage in Tswana Royal Families. In *Studies in Kinship and Marriage,* ed. I. Schapera. Occasional Paper no. 16. London: Royal Anthropological Institute.
1966 Tswana Legal Maxims. *Africa* 36:121–34.
1969 Uniformity and Variation in Chief-Made Law: A Tswana Case Study. In *Law in Culture and Society,* ed. L. Nader. Chicago: Aldine.
1970 *Tribal Innovators: Tswana Chiefs and Social Change 1795–1940.* London School of Economics Monographs on Social Anthropology no. 43. London: Athlone Press.

Sheddick, V. G. J.
1953 *The Southern Sotho.* Ethnographic Survey of Africa, Part III. London: International African Institute.

Swartz, M. J., Turner, V. W., and Tuden, A.
1966 Introduction. In *Political Anthropology,* ed. M. J. Swartz, V. W. Turner, and A. Tuden. Chicago: Aldine.

Tambiah, S. J.
1965 Kinship Fact and Fiction in Relation to the Kandyan Sinhalese. *Journal of the Royal Anthropological Institute* 95:131–73.

Turner, V. W.
1957 *Schism and Continuity in an African Society: A Study of Ndembu Village Life.* Manchester: Manchester University Press.

Twining, W.
1964 *The Place of Customary Law in the National Legal Systems of East Africa.* Chicago: University of Chicago Law School.
1973 Law and Anthropology: A Case Study in Inter-Disciplinary Collaboration. *Law and Society Review* 7:561–83.

Vansina, J.
1964 *Le Royaume Kuba.* Annales—Science Humaines no. 49. Tervuren (Belgium): Musée Royale de l'Afrique Centrale.

van Velsen, J.
1969 Procedural Informality, Reconciliation, and False Comparisons. In *Ideas and Procedures in African Customary Law,* ed. M. Gluckman. London: Oxford University Press for the International African Institute.

Van Warmelo, N. J.
  1931 *Kinship Terminology of the South African Bantu.*
         Ethnological Publications no. 2. Pretoria: Government
         Printer.
Worsley, P. M.
  1956 The Kinship System of the Tallensi: A Revaluation. *Jour-
         nal of the Royal Anthropological Institute* 86:37–75.
  1957 *The Trumpet Shall Sound: A Study of "Cargo" Cults in
         Melanesia.* London: MacGibbon & Kee. (Republished by
         Paladin, 1970.)
Young, M.
  1971 *Fighting with Food: Leadership, Values and Social Control
         in a Massim Society.* Cambridge, Eng.: At the University
         Press.

Index

Achievement. *See* Ascription

Adjudication, 108–9. *See also* Dispute processes; Dispute-settlement agencies

Agnatic groups, 34–35, 221; fragmentation of, 34

Agnation, Tswana ideas concerning, 50–53. *See also* Agnatic groups

Anthropology of law, 3–21, 29, 240–42, 243–49; historical development of, 3–17; influence of legal theory upon, 5–11, 132–33, 176, 241–42, 243–49; theoretical traditions in, 5–17

Ascription, 37; relationship of, to achievement, 37–46

Bagakolodi, 26

Bailey, F., 13

Barkun, M., 20

Barotse, 3, 9, 10, 73. *See also* Lozi

Barth, F., 31, 32

Bloch, M., 29

Bogadi, 66, 67, 135–40, 141, 143, 145, 146, 149, 150, 154, 155, 157, 158, 159, 160, 161, 164, 177–78, 191, 194, 202, 203, 204, 205, 207, 209, 210,

211, 212, 214, 215; and affiliation of children, 159–61; consequences of presentation of, 139, 157–65; size of, 136; time of transfer of, 140

Bohannan, P., 8

Bonyatsi, 134

Bophuthatswana, 23, 24

Boswa, 76, 185–87, 203, 215, 222; devolution of, 185–87; significance of, 185–87

Bushong, 63

Career management, 64–68, 168–74

Casalis, J. E., 70

Colson, E., 13

Comaroff, J. L., 86

Constitutive order, the, 46–61; definition of, 68; the "house" in, 47–53; and the marriage system, 53–62

Court records, ix, x

Dilo tsa patlo, 135, 137, 150, 157, 158, 203

Dispute processes, chap. 4 passim; form of, 107–31; litigants' goals in, 110–12; logic of, 3, 216–42; normative change resulting from, 79–83,

289